A JUST FORGIVENESS

RESPONSIBLE HEALING

WITHOUT EXCUSING INJUSTICE

EVERETT L.
WORTHINGTON JR.

IVP Books

An imprint of InterVarsity Press
Downers Grove, Illinois

InterVarsity Press
P.O. Box 1400, Downers Grove, IL 60515-1426
World Wide Web: www.ivpress.com
E-mail: email@ivpress.com

InterVarsity Press® is the book-publishing division of InterVarsity Christian Fellowship/USA®, a movement of students and faculty active on campus at hundreds of universities, colleges and schools of nursing in the United States of America, and a member movement of the International Fellowship of Evangelical Students. For information about local and regional activities, write Public Relations Dept., InterVarsity Christian Fellowship/USA, 6400 Schroeder Rd., P.O. Box 7895, Madison, WI 53707-7895, or visit the IVCF website at <www.intervarsity.org>.

All Scripture quotations, unless otherwise indicated, are taken from the Holy Bible, New International Version®. NIV.® Copyright ©1973, 1978, 1984 by International Bible Society. Used by permission of Zondervan Publishing House. All rights reserved.

Figure 4.3 on page 94 is from Davis, D. E., Hook, J. N., & Worthington, E. L., Jr. (2008). "Relational spirituality and forgiveness: The roles of attachment to God, religious coping, and viewing the transgression as a desecration." Journal of Psychology and Christianity, *27, p. 301. Used by permission.*

Design: Cindy Kiple
Images: Katherine Lubar/Getty Images

ISBN 978-0-8308-3701-4

Printed in the United States of America ∞

Library of Congress Cataloging-in-Publication Data

Worthington, Everett L., 1946-
A just forgiveness: responsible healing without excusing injustice
/ Everett L. Worthington, Jr.
  p. cm.
Includes bibliographical references and index.
ISBN 978-0-8308-3701-4 (pbk.: alk. paper)
1. Forgiveness of sin. 2 Forgiveness—Religious
aspects—Christianity. 3. Christianity and justice. I. Title.
BT795.W67 2009
234'.5—dc22
       2009026588

P	19	18	17	16	15	14	13	12	11	10	9	8	7	6	5	4	3	2	1
Y	25	24	23	22	21	20	19	18	17	16	15	14	13	12	11	10	09			

Friend Charlotte and your family—
this is for you.

CONTENTS

INTRODUCTION

God redeems. Redemption is the beginning and end of forgiveness. This book is about forgiveness and the question, if we forgive, do we pursue justice? I examine forgiveness, justice and humility—which in many ways is the key to forgiveness—in individuals, families, communities such as churches, and the wider society.

Throughout life, we are wounded. My father was an alcoholic. My mother was murdered. My brother killed himself. My wife was injured in a car crash. My children have each had some tragic struggles. Each wound to myself or my loved ones hurts me. I carry these wounds into my family, my church, my work, my community and my society.

As a Christian, how am I supposed to look at these evils? How can I deal with them practically? My response cannot be governed by a simple how-to formula. If you are merely looking for simple answers to help you deal with injustice and suffering in your life, you probably will not be satisfied with this book. But if you want to explore the ways that justice, humility and forgiveness intertwine, then you'll find ideas and practical suggestions here. If you feel stuck when you think about injustice and suffering, this book can unstick your mind. If you feel mired in the same old emotional traps of anger, anxiety or depression, this book can get your feet moving again. If you feel trapped in the maze of family feuds, church conflicts, job jostlings or social struggles, this book can give you new direction.

I intend this book to be a thoughtful and thoroughly Christian exploration of justice, humility and forgiveness in the face of injustice and evil. Although I seek to be Christian in my approach, I believe—from many years as a teacher, researcher, counselor and writer who has addressed Christian and secular audiences equally often—that you can benefit from this book even if you disagree with my theology. I have attended Anglican, Baptist, Charismatic, Evangelical Free, Lutheran, Methodist, Presbyterian and Roman Catholic churches during my life. My theology is mostly Reformed and Augustinian, and philosophically I like much of Plato. But I also love Aristotle and the real-world theology connecting God and life through social acts and sacraments, which has been developed in Roman Catholic, Anglican and Wesleyan theology. Besides Jesus, my heroes in the faith include Peter and Paul, Augustine, Ignatius and Thomas Aquinas, Luther and Calvin, C. S. Lewis, Charles Habib Malik, Mother Teresa, and Malcolm Muggeridge. Thus I do not hold to a simple party line. I know that will bother some people, but I cherish the thoughtful reader's ability to evaluate and discern where my theology departs from his or hers.

If you have stuck with me this far, you are the thoughtful reader who can look at this book and courageously discern new ideas. You can then apply these ideas to create practical solutions to your life issues. Psychologist Kurt Lewin said, "There is nothing so practical as a good theory."[1] This is true in psychology when a theory is not airy-fairy speculation but is grounded in scientific observation. It is also true in theology when a theory is grounded primarily in Scripture and secondarily in church tradition and church life. In this book, I share a way of understanding our responses to injustice, suffering and evil that draws from both psychology and theology.

Evil happens. God has protected me and my loved ones, yet he certainly has not prevented injustice and evil from touching me. I have been richly blessed by God. Yet I cannot in my heart believe that God, at root, is primarily a dispenser of personal blessings or just a healer. What then is God's chief business with humans?

Jesus submitted himself to his Father, even unto death. Jesus endured pain, death and separation from God. All that suffering was not for his own benefit but for our benefit. After his resurrection, he appeared to his disciples. What was he left with? Wounds in his hands and side. Yet his wounds had been not so much healed as redeemed.

We experience wounds in virtually all ongoing close relationships. We live in imperfect societies that are torn asunder by wounds. Our churches split, and our houses of worship are desecrated. Our schools are marred by violence and conflict. Our civic organizations are characterized by strife and disappointment. Our ethnicity is devalued and attacked. Our gender is maligned. Our religion is devalued. Our nation is attacked. People try to hurt us, destroy our emotions, undermine our sense of self and sometimes kill our body. It is easy to focus on the injustices we face, the assaults to our honor. Our natural response is to counterattack. We want to get even, pay back, retaliate.

On one hand, society tells us to turn our feelings over to the justice system. On the other hand, the Bible tells us to turn our anxieties over to God (1 Pet 5:7). Jesus tells us to forgive, to love our enemies and to pray for those who persecute us (Mt 6:12, 14-15; 5:44). Does this mean that society and Christianity are inevitably opposed to each other? How can justice and mercy kiss (see Ps 85:10)? We are perplexed, shocked, enraged and sometimes embittered at the many ways justice seems to butt heads with mercy and especially with forgiveness.

- Rachel, a faithful Christian woman, is raped and beaten. She can't understand how a loving God could allow that to happen to her. She can't see how God would want, even demand, that she forgive.

- Abbie cannot forgive her husband of nineteen years who abandoned her and their three children to be with a lover half his age. Abbie did nothing to deserve this betrayal, yet she and her three children must live with the consequences. For forty-five minutes, she sat in my office and literally came undone, piece by piece. Her eye makeup ran down her face in jagged black streaks. Her nose streamed mucus onto her blouse.

A hair piece gradually slid from the top of her head to the side. Such was the force of her weeping. Finally, she grabbed the hairpiece and jerked, and her hair fell down in straggles. Unable to meet my eyes, she hesitantly said, "His lover was a man. He picked him up at a gay bar during an out-of-town trip. How can I ever tell our children? How can I live with the shame?"

- Chico and Margharita are locked in conflict, citing numerous injustices that the other has perpetrated. However, what bothers them most is that their two-year-old daughter is suffering because their angry arguments frighten her. They cannot forgive themselves. It isn't fair to their daughter for them to live in conflict, nor would it be fair to make her a child of divorce.

- Cynthia was disillusioned by her church. Its longtime pastor was accused of wrongdoing. Pressure mounted from some in the congregation until the pastor left. Everyone—whether they supported the pastor, opposed him or were uninvolved—was hurt. The church struggled to heal. How do people heal hurts that occur in a Christian church? Some people want to move on and not revisit the old issue. Others feel like the congregation must process the event because it still causes pain. How do the sides resolve those differences? How do they solve the problems that come from past hurts without breaking ties with old friends, abandoning brothers and sisters in Christ, or even driving people out of relationship with Jesus?

- Immaculée hid with seven people in a bathroom while almost a million people in Rwanda were hacked to death by machetes.[2] Many of these killings were done by people who claimed to be Christians. What about years of oppression in South Africa—often led by white Christians? How do people deal with societal transgressions? How do they respond when they are treated unjustly merely because of race, gender, tribe or nationality?

I was walking with a fellow Christian, Micah McCreary, in a high-crime area in Richmond. He is African American and grew up in a similar area in Detroit. We were approaching a group of teenage boys who looked like gang members. Micah pulled a pen from his pocket and clutched it hidden in his right hand.

"What are you doing?" I asked.

He kept walking. He stared straight ahead, not looking at them. "Never get near to a gangbanger without some kind of weapon," he said after we had passed them.

I grew up in a relatively tough part of Knoxville, Tennessee, myself, but that day I realized I did not understand the world Micah grew up in. I didn't understand the prejudices and racism he had faced or what it took to survive in that world.

These practical problems are not easily dismissed by glib assurances that mercy should triumph over justice or that justice and mercy ultimately kiss. We might trust God and believe God's Word, but we want to know how we are to respond.

If we are like Rachel—the woman who was raped, beaten and spitefully used—how do we forgive? If we forgive, do we pursue justice? If we cannot forgive, how strongly do we chase justice? What if the justice system turns its back? Do we take the law into our own hands like Dirty Harry?

What if we are like Abbie, the abandoned wife who had invested nineteen years into her marriage, suddenly left holding the bag after pouring our life and resources into a relationship? What would be fair in Abbie's case? Are we supposed to cheerfully press on without complaining? Without legal redress?

What if we are like Chico and Margharita, whose marital conflict is destroying their own welfare and that of their child? Should we dismiss self-condemnation as something we simply need to put aside so we can move on with life? Is the child merely a casualty of war? Should we put aside our own chance to have a fulfilled life to try to keep a child from pain?

What if we are a member of an oppressed minority or, like Immaculée, a member of a group whose neighbors were trying to kill them? What should we do to end oppression, prejudice and societal unfairness? While we are not all ethnic or cultural minorities, most of us have experienced some sort of prejudice. Perhaps we have been discriminated against for religious or socioeconomic differences, or someone has told us we are too short, too tall, too skinny, too fat, or not good-looking enough for a job. We can identify with discrimination, yet we do not know what practical steps we can take to end it.

Like Cynthia, most Christians have seen church congregations shatter. Church members can be unspeakably cruel to each other. Some churches, like the worldwide Anglican fellowship, might even fragment over emotionally charged doctrinal issues. We need to know how to respond.

Many harms seem almost unforgivable. Can we forgive the harms we suffer in relationships with family, friends and coworkers, in churches, work groups and society? And now "the $64,000 question": *Should* we forgive them?

We are all victims. We are all oppressors. We are all bystanders. We hurt those we love. We hurt those we don't value. We hurt those we don't know. And sometimes we stand by and watch others hurt the weak and helpless without lifting a finger or batting an eye.

Much has been written about the relationship between justice and forgiveness. Some say they are opposed to each other. If one gets justice in a court of law, is forgiveness more difficult? If one forgives, does that mean one can't seek justice? Or is a *just forgiveness* possible—forgiveness that works hand in hand with justice and neither gets overwhelmed by it nor overwhelms it? The psalmist said, "Mercy and truth are met together; righteousness and peace have kissed each other" (Ps 85:10 KJV). Can this happen in the twenty-first century?

I believe it can, for two reasons: First, we have a God who has created people who mirror the will to do justice and to love that already exists within the triune God. Second, God the Father redeemed us through Jesus' self-sacrificial love, which inspires humility within us. Out of humility, we can yield ourselves to God and be guided by God's Holy Spirit.

Yet knowing that God redeems does not mean that the kiss between righteousness and peace will be without bumped noses and mashed lips.

Sometimes the embrace occurs only after a painful bear hug or a strenuous wrestling match. As transgressions become more complex—from uncomplicated offenses by strangers to harm done by loved ones to wars or attempted genocide—conditions change. If we are to do our part to help righteousness and peace kiss in just forgiveness, we must understand justice and forgiveness separately as well as the humility needed to help them kiss. We must understand the challenges at each level of personal, social and societal complexity. Only then can we act within God's master plan to bring about a just forgiveness through humility.

In the first half of the book, I develop the tools we need to respond to transgressions with justice, forgiveness and humility. We will learn that we all calculate ever-changing injustice gaps when we are wronged. We are hard-wired to seek justice. Yet despite experiencing injustice, we don't always seek payback. We are also hard-wired to forgive.

What triggers the shift from justice motives to forgiveness motives? Both are natural. Both are virtues. The search for the triggers that trip these switches is a key to getting more control over our lives. Why do we forgive so magnanimously a major betrayal, and yet the next day when someone cuts us off in traffic, it drives us into a rage? A week later we are still ruminating about the incident. Finally, we decide to forgive, but resentment will not fade away.

We will learn that there are two different types of forgiveness. Each has different effects on our physical health, mental health, relationships and spiritual life.

We will also learn a model that explains why we sometimes pursue justice and sometimes forgive when we are hurt or offended. Sometimes we are humble, but other times we are arrogant. Sometimes we are empathic, but other times we harden our hearts. That model relates triggers, both within us and outside of us, to permanent structures in our environment and psychological experience and to the processes we then pursue.

In the second half of the book, we apply these ideas to groups. The issues become more complex as group dynamics come into play.

First, we look at forgiving in the family. It seems that those we love the most can hurt us the most. Second, we look at hurts inside the church. Sometimes the offense is wickedly deep. We will learn a model of relational spirituality that explains how church conflicts erupt and what we can do to ease or avoid them. Third, we look at the community—in the workplace and in the justice system. Workplace transgressions are different from—yet similar to—those in the family. Justice and forgiveness are both needed. In the justice system we ask, "Is there any room for forgiveness?" Fourth, we look at societal traumas. We will apply our knowledge of injustice gaps, our understanding of different types of justice and forgiveness, our model of triggers and structures, and our model of relational spirituality to understanding intrastate conflicts, mass killing, genocide and even international war. We will see how to avoid societal traumas and how to help people in other countries.

As we move from a Christian foundation to new working models to applications in social and societal situations, you will come to see how forgiveness and justice are united through humility. Then you can apply what you know to tough problems. We begin by exploring the tensions between justice and forgiveness, and we look at the many troubling questions those tensions raise.

PART 1

UNDERSTANDING

JUST FORGIVENESS

TENSIONS AND QUESTIONS

THE TENSIONS BETWEEN JUSTICE AND forgiveness raise profound and troubling questions. In some ways these questions pose the choice between love and power. An inscription found in the Libyan desert reads, "I, the Captain of a Legion of Rome, serving in the desert of Libya, have learnt and pondered this truth: 'There are in life but two things to be sought, Love and Power, and no one has both.'"[1] Yet with Christ there is both the crucifix and the empty cross. In humility perhaps some of the tensions between love and power, forgiveness and justice, can be answered.

I begin with three examples—one about my own recent failure in forgiving, a second within a family and a third about Holocaust survivor Simon Wiesenthal. In each story I raise questions. Then I start us on trying to untie these knotty questions, moving toward just forgiveness working in hearts, homes and homelands.

LOVE AND POWER, CRUCIFIX AND CROSS

God is loving, almighty, sovereign, good, merciful and just. God loves us enough to allow us to suffer, and then to redeem our suffering. God is giver and forgiver.

God also loves us enough to judge our acts. In modern society we think of judges as those who stand above life and pronounce judgments on wrongdoers. Yet the Hebrew concept of judgment was different.[2] Judgment came from a God who was a participant *with* his people, not from someone who stood above them. God is unique as a humble God. In sovereignty God humbly entered history, walking and talking with Adam and Eve. God judged their worst rebellion yet killed an animal to protect their lives. God covenanted with Abraham, walked with the children of Israel in the desert after their exodus from Egypt, gave the law to Moses, lived in the Holy of Holies in the temple, reigned with David and hung in there as the God of the exile and of the dispersion of Israel.

Then, in the centerpiece of history, God became a feeble man. Jesus was, as J. B. Phillips said, God-focused.[3] Jesus was born, lived and died in history. He was crucified for us feeble humans. He was resurrected as the first fruit of redemption, and he has prepared a place for us at the throne of God.

God has not changed in nature but continues in humility to interact with us in history through the Holy Spirit. We are empowered to live intimately because God lives inside us. Jesus has thus established the church as his body on earth. We have the awesome privilege to represent God on earth. Imagine God's humility in adopting humans!

Eventually God the Father will rise from his throne. Jesus will come again. History will culminate in the victorious story of Immanuel, God with us, the humble God—judging and showing mercy by humbly entering history and taking judgment for us.

It all begins with God. It all ends with God.

At the crossroads of history and our own lives, we contemplate the cross. On one hand, we see the crucifix. The figure of Jesus' broken body given in humble, self-emptying love stands before us. On the other hand, we see the empty cross. God's resurrection power is plain. Love and power. Crucifix and cross. Mercy and justice. Underlying all is humility. God is good. God walks in us and with us through human history, which screams of misery, snarls of evil, cries of dejection and quakes of terror. We all sometimes struggle with the paradoxes.

Can Forgiveness Get into Our Hearts?

I have felt God's love and care for more than six decades of this life. I know God. Yet I have questions. Why do I become offended so easily? How can rejections and betrayals, which in looking back are so slight, cause me such pain and wound me so deeply? I am a follower of Jesus and have God's Holy Spirit living within me. As Paul says, we are "more than conquerors" (Rom 8:37), yet I too often lose battles of self-control. Why do I act unjustly? Why am I not more loving, compassionate, sympathetic, empathic and forgiving? You might have experienced such dissatisfactions with your own self-control.

My defeats crop up in sneak attacks. Recently a group that I work with had an impassioned discussion. Someone has said that the battles in academe are so fierce because the stakes are so low, and this was one of those cases. As it turns out, this time I happened to be on the winning end of a close vote. So I was feeling good.

But as I walked out of the meeting shoulder to shoulder with a colleague on the other side of the vote, she couldn't resist getting in a payback jab. "Well, the old boys network rammed that through," she said.

To me, being subtly (or not so subtly) blamed for sexism came out of the blue. But what disturbed me was my reaction. I was hurt. I could feel my face freeze into a mask. You know the kind—intended to give away nothing, it actually gave away everything. I quickly disengaged.

Weeks later I still felt like cutting off relations with this coworker. How quickly little wars begin! How easily they are maintained!

Such experiences raise other questions. Can we avoid little wars? If so, how? Can we heal wounded egos? How? Can reconciliation occur if we hold ten thousand little grudges?

Can Forgiveness Get into Our Homes?

As a marital therapist, I have seen many toxic wars, wars between lovers who have shared each other's hearts and beds. Vulnerabilities discovered in love are exploited in hate. When betrayed, intimacy that had fired passion stokes engines that power battleships. Partners use their verbal cannons to assault each other. Without hope of victory, they seem to want only to drag the other into the depths with them.

Cheryl and Lawrence married at eighteen. They had children immediately. By the time these young parents were twenty-seven, their three children were in school. Then Lawrence lost his job. "I had too much time on my hands. I was needy," he admitted. So he gave in to lust with Melissa, whom he met at the gym. "It was a lot of secret phone calls and some enthusiastic but bad sex," he said. Soon he tired of the affair and broke it off. Melissa was wounded. She phoned Cheryl and "confessed" the affair. Cheryl was devastated—doubly so because Lawrence had not confessed first. And Cheryl was angry.

Cheryl and Lawrence went through six stormy months. After that, the gale-force waves that had rocked their marriage settled into periodic sloshing, battering waves that eroded the love they had once held. When they came to me for counseling five years later, they were adamant: "We want to save our marriage," they said. But it was soon clear that they only wanted some authority to declare the marriage dead and sign the death certificate. Oh, yes—and each wanted vindication.

"It's not my fault. He had the affair," Cheryl said. She implied the same in a hundred other ways.

"It's not my fault," countered Lawrence. "I admitted I was wrong."

"He only confessed *after* the slut told on him."

"She hasn't an ounce of forgiveness in her," Lawrence said to me.

"God will judge his sin," Cheryl said to me.

"God will judge her unforgiveness," countered Lawrence.

I had heard such arguments many times as a marriage counselor. Many couples have volleyed toxic insults back and forth.

Cheryl and Lawrence raised many other questions. Why did the affair and Cheryl's failure to forgive become the main focal points of their dissatisfaction? They had offended, hurt and devalued each other thousands of times over the years since the affair. Yet for both, that was the significant event. It was the volcano casting a shadow over all other events. Although the affair was long past in actual time, it was as real to Cheryl and Lawrence—perhaps even more real—than if it had occurred only yesterday.

Why could Cheryl and Lawrence not put the event behind them? Why could they not coexist in peace? Many other couples have weathered affairs. What kept Cheryl and Lawrence from doing so?

In fact, the affair was like a five-hundred-pound gorilla lounging on the sofa, somehow making other slights, wounds, indiscretions and offenses more potent. It even empowered seemingly harmless omissions. If Cheryl forgot that Lawrence had said their credit card balance was high and she purchased a pair of shoes, Lawrence took it as a punch to the stomach. It seemed clear to him that she was punishing him for the affair. If Lawrence said he would clean the family room but got delayed at work, Cheryl would say, "Your job is your mistress. You care nothing for me." How did history become the lens through which they viewed their entire marriage? Could counseling ever promote reconciliation with the big beast of the unforgiven affair in the room?

Both Cheryl and Lawrence were Christians. Their faith comforted them during the turmoil of their marital distress. Yet somehow it did not help them reconcile. Why not? Isn't our faith supposed to empower us for victorious Christian living? Why wasn't their faith helpful in this important aspect of their most intimate human relationship?

In my travels, I have seen some wonderful countries. Whether in South Africa, the Middle East, the countries of the European Union or throughout Asia, grudges and bitterness bubble to the surface with surprisingly little provocation. Closer to home, within the United States, I have seen prejudice and hate against Muslims, the French, Israeli Jews and virtually every ethnic group within the country. I have met people who hate Ted Kennedy or Pat Robertson, Howard Stern or Rush Limbaugh, although they know virtually nothing about them. Throughout the world, we seem to be grudge-holding people.

We cannot seem to live in peace. We all seem to believe ourselves to be the victims of injustice and prejudice. What kind of quirky economics can make it seem that, when resources are apportioned, *we* are the ones on the light side of the balance? And as in the case of Cheryl and Lawrence, how can a few historic injustices be so large, intimidating and omnipresent today that virtually every human transaction is seen through the lens of injustice?

In my personal experience, in the interactions of any couple, and in the economics of ethnicities or nations, one thing remains true: at every level the world revolves around each of us. Therefore injustices and grudges are everywhere.

These are troublesome questions at personal, social and societal levels. We know how we are to deal with these questions. Scripture has told us directly in Micah 6:8: "What does the LORD require of you? To act justly and to love mercy and to walk humbly with your God."

Micah's sage direction is true wisdom, but it raises "how" questions. *How* do we act justly? *How* do we love mercy? *How* do we walk humbly with our God? And *how* do the three work together to bring peace to individuals, relationships, ethnicities and countries? It would be comforting to believe that it would be enough to usher in world peace if each of us could be sincere Christians and treat others with love. But while these are great goals, the Bible suggests that a world of billions of sincere individual Christians is not a full answer. Scripture was given to communities, peoples and nations. Complexities arise in communities that exceed the sum of individual experiences. The way that justice, forgiveness and humility work together must be considered psychologically in individuals, but just as importantly, it must be seen in social and societal contexts. Personal, social and societal levels feed into each other.

CAN FORGIVENESS GET INTO OUR HOMELANDS?

Simon Wiesenthal was perhaps the most celebrated Nazi hunter produced by World War II. During the war he was in a concentration camp, and along with other Jews was forced to work in the nearby town. Jews died daily under the harsh labor conditions. Every morning the Nazis formed the Jews into a group and marched them through the town until each worker was positioned at his own work station. The townspeople watched silently. One day as the laborers marched through town, Wiesenthal saw a graveyard for German soldiers. Each tombstone was graced with a sunflower. As Jews were dying one after another, Wiesenthal wondered whether any of their graves would even be marked by tombstones, much less flowers.

One day Wiesenthal was summoned by a nurse in the hospital where he was forced to work. She led him to the room of a Nazi soldier on his deathbed. The Nazi was badly burned, his body entombed in bandages. His name was Karl. Karl asked Simon, "You're a Jew, aren't you?" Simon agreed. Karl said, "I'm going to die. But I want to tell you, a Jew, a story."

Karl made Wiesenthal listen as he described his part in a massacre of Jewish men, women and children. The Jews were herded into a building in the center of town, forced to carry cans of gasoline in with them. Then German soldiers surrounded the house and lobbed grenades through the windows. As they exploded, they ignited the gas cans inside. Soldiers shot the Jews who tried to escape from the inferno. Karl was particularly haunted by the memory of a young child with big, dark eyes who was held by his father. They jumped from a window. On the ground they were cut down in silence by the Nazi gunners.

When he had finished his horrific story, Karl asked Wiesenthal, "Will you, as a Jew, forgive me on behalf of the Jews for these murders that I have done?" Simon thought for a few minutes. Then, in silence, he walked out the door.

That night Karl died. After the war, Simon was still bothered by his response to the Nazi soldier. Had he done right by not granting forgiveness? By leaving in silence? Should he have forgiven Karl?

After the war Simon investigated Karl's identity. He visited Karl's mother, who held a high opinion of her son. Simon knew Karl to be an SS soldier who had confessed to gunning down men, women and children, yet his mother spoke of Karl's early years in the church. She spoke regretfully of Karl's attraction to the Hitler Youth. Simon was silent.

Three responses of silence characterize Wiesenthal's story. Bystanders were silent as the Jews were killed or worked to death. Simon was silent when Karl asked for forgiveness. Simon was silent when he could have told Karl's mother that he was a confessed murderer of men, women and children.

Years later Wiesenthal wrote of his experiences in a book called *The Sunflower*.[4] He invited intellectual leaders to read his story and to answer two questions: Had Wiesenthal done right by refusing to forgive? What would that person have done had it been him or her? Since its original publication, others have also responded to Wiesenthal's questions in new editions of *The Sunflower*.

Simon Wiesenthal's refusal to forgive raises numerous questions among the many respondents to his story. Think about your own answers. Should Simon have granted Karl forgiveness? Would *you* have granted Karl forgiveness?

Causes and consequences. Karl had a good upbringing from his parents, but peers led him down a road of prejudice, racism and hatred. Might extenuating circumstances absolve Karl from some responsibility for what he did? After all, life is not fair. Karl grew up in Germany in the 1930s. Had he grown up in the United States at that time, he would not have become a Nazi. Because he lived in Germany, he was unfairly placed in a peer group that pressured him toward joining the Hitler Youth.

Karl had grown up within the church. We aren't told why Karl abandoned his faith in favor of the Hitler Youth. Might toxic church politics, hypocrisy or repressive doctrine have allowed Karl to justify his abandonment of Christianity?

If Simon Wiesenthal had granted Karl forgiveness, what might have been the consequences? Would it have affected Karl's guilt before God or made a difference to other Jews? Would it have let Karl off the hook? Simon was merely a Jew in a concentration camp. He had no authority to forgive on behalf of those Jews who were murdered.

One must consider whether there would be social and societal consequences of such forgiveness, such pardon. Karl committed the public sin of murder. Perhaps that public sin calls for a public act of confession, which he carried out in confessing to Simon. Even Simon's telling of the story has societal consequences. If Simon had offered forgiveness in the name of the murdered victims, would that lessen societal inhibitions against murder? Do we have a social responsibility to hold people accountable for murder? Justice and forgiveness seem the most at odds when looked at from the societal level. Some people worry that forgiveness leads down a slippery slope toward forgetting. If we forgive perpetrators of Holocaust murders, they argue, we might as a society soon forget the Holocaust.

There might also have been personal consequences—both for Simon and for Karl—if forgiveness had been granted. If a person asks for forgiveness and is remorseful, contrite and apparently repentant, is it legitimate to refuse to grant forgiveness? Perhaps Simon was being selfish and hate-filled himself by refusing to forgive Karl.

There might have been spiritual consequences for Karl if Simon had forgiven him. On one hand it might have loosed Karl from his sin (Mt 16:19; 18:18). But on the other hand it might have prevented Karl from seeking forgiveness from God. Perhaps after Simon refused to grant his forgiveness on behalf of the Jews, Karl turned to God for forgiveness, repented and became a Christian. Or maybe Karl had already sought forgiveness from God and was finally trying to square things with a Jew.

We don't know what went on in Karl's heart and soul as he lay on his deathbed. Did his nearness to death make his confession less valuable? We cannot be sure of his motives because we cannot get inside his heart and mind. We might suspect that Karl was confessing due to fear or was trying to reduce his guilt and suffering in his last moments. Maybe he was not really repentant but merely wanted someone to take the burden of his guilt.

What about Karl's sense of duty and responsibility? Karl committed his crimes under pressure. He did not gleefully kill the Jews. Instead, he likely felt a sense of responsibility toward his peers who participated in the killing and his officers who ordered his participation. Karl might have felt he had no choice lest he himself be killed for disobeying orders. Surely he had a sense of responsibility and duty. Do these factors mitigate the evil of Karl's commission of murder?

As you can see, Simon Wiesenthal's story raises many troubling questions about the nature of forgiveness and justice, their limitations and their transformative effects. We can begin to unravel these tangles by shaking out the kinks in four knotty issues of justice: the injustice gap, the insistent belief that life is not fair, the big sinful event and the magical economics of payback. Then we will begin to consider humility. Finally, we will begin to examine forgiveness.

THE INJUSTICE GAP

The main point of *A Just Forgiveness* is that forgiveness and justice are not mortal enemies. They work together and affect each other in the ways that God deals with people and people deal with each other. If you have been offended at work, you can forgive without feeling you must be a doormat. In handling a conflict at church, you can be a force both for justice and forgiveness. In political wars—be they office offenses, family fracases, community conflicts or tribal tensions—you can apply what you learn from this book to be God's agent for love and truth.

Justice and forgiveness come together in the injustice gap.[5] The *injustice gap* is the ongoing tally we make, rationally or intuitively, that informs us how fair or unfair the outcomes surrounding a transgression are. The gap is the difference between my desired ideal solution (e.g., "I want him to crawl on his knees and beg me for forgiveness") and the current status as I now see it (see figure 1.1). For instance, if I see the offender as smug and self-righteous, the injustice gap will be wider than if I see the offender as broken and filled with remorse. We act based on our current injustice gap. Couples interact on the balance of justice as each partner perceives it, and their perceptions almost always differ. Groups also have a sense of how much injustice has occurred within a conflict. Different groups in society, and different people in the groups, perceive that injustice gap differently. The injustice gap drives people's motivation to respond with justice or forgiveness.

Both forgiveness and justice are complex. They cannot easily be reduced to simple definitions or prescriptions about whether and when peo-

"I want him to crawl and beg me for forgiveness."

"I no longer want him to crawl and beg me for forgiveness."

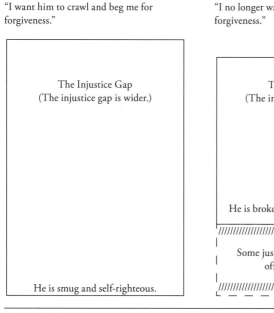

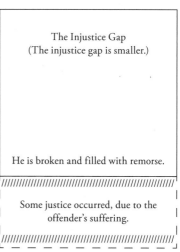

Figure 1.1. Two injustice gaps

ple forgive or seek justice. Rather there are different types and levels of both forgiveness and justice.

God is a just God who created people to bear the image of God. So we are sensitive to the size of our injustice gap. We also experience sin against us as unjust. Because people are fallen, we experience many injustices as others inflict injustice on us and as we self-centeredly interpret innocent acts as unfair because we don't get our way. We are all victims, and we feel that pain keenly. At the same time, we are all fallen. We exert and abuse our power and act as oppressors. We hurt those we love, those we don't value and even those we don't know. We seem to be keenly aware of the active injustice gaps in our life. We feel that life is unjust and that it is up to us to right those wrongs.

THE INSISTENT BELIEF THAT LIFE IS NOT FAIR

Life is not fair. Justice is not distributed equally. Divine forgiveness is available to all, but not all have equal chance to hear the gospel. It isn't fair that I grew up in the United States, where I have free access to the gospel, while many grow up where access is limited. God is just (i.e., we all deserve divine condemnation), but God is not always fair (i.e., some receive more mercy, grace, blessing and favor than do others).

Even though life is not fair, God is just and good. Jesus laid aside his divinity to become man. In his humility, Jesus fully empathizes with human struggles because he has experienced similar struggles, limitations and temptations. He is our advocate with the just and merciful Father. And he loves us. So justice and forgiveness intertwine like purple and scarlet threads to weave a tapestry. And the golden thread of humble love traces a beautiful, unifying highlight throughout, tying together justice and forgiveness.

THE BIG SINFUL EVENT

Not all transgressions are created equal. Some are what writer Malcolm Gladwell calls "tipping points."[6] They change our perspective. Transgressions that shift our perspective function as if they had changed the lenses in our glasses from rose-colored to dark shades. Remember Cheryl and Lawrence. Lawrence's affair changed everything. Cheryl couldn't take her dark glasses off. Instead of seeing the relationship as rosy and positive, she screened out those qualities. The size of her injustice gap was affected (see the first gap in figure 1.1). She felt that Lawrence's offense was even worse than she had originally thought, and she wanted more payback. She could see only the dark, negative events. That is the way the relationship will continue—dark—unless a positive transformation occurs.

Psychologists William Miller and Janet C'de Baca call such dramatic transformations "quantum changes."[7] They studied more than one hundred people who experienced quantum changes in order to find out what makes quantum changes tick.

Quantum changes can be positive or negative. Sometimes the changes are major emotional events, such as a religious conversion. Those dramatic changes drag other changes along behind them, like a comet's tail. Sometimes people seem to get stuck at a dead end. Failure and hopelessness can immobilize. Some events just turn people 180 degrees. For instance, Miller and C'de Baca describe one man who suddenly realized that he needed to quit drinking. He drove to school to pick up his child. While he was waiting, he convinced himself that he had time to go get just one beer. As he drove away from the school, he saw his child in the rearview mirror, but he did not stop. He got that beer. And that was the last one. He saw that alcohol had him by the throat. So he changed.

At other times God breaks in dramatically (see Rom 12:2-3). God knocked Paul blind and sideways (Acts 9:1-9). But God can also break in softly in an insistent whisper, like he did with Elijah, who found God not in gusts of wind or the tremors of an earthquake or the heat of a fire but in a still, small voice (1 Kings 19:11-13).

The big sinful event is a quantum change. Once an individual, a church, a community or a nation fixates on a big sinful event, it is like triggering an explosion; that event dominates the injustice gap. The event seems to be lit up while other ways of thinking are in the dark. Attempts at restitution flit like annoying gnats around eyes that are focused on grudge-holding or vengeance, and they are either batted away or ignored.

Unless they somehow get our attention. And that is the hope for dealing with the big sinful event. Some meaningful repair—perhaps a sincere, public apology and a costly attempt at relational repair—becomes a new trigger that changes the lighting.

The Magical Economics of Payback

When I misbehaved as a child, my dad took me to the bathroom. First he told me what I had done wrong. Then he told me he had to spank me. "This hurts me more than it does you," he always said. *But not in the same place,* I always thought.

At the root of the magical economics of payback is the truth that "this hurts me more than it hurts you." We feel our pain more than we feel the pain we cause others. When I sin, I cause God pain. I usually don't think much about the pain I cause God. Even when I am caught in my sin, I feel more that I have hurt myself than that I have hurt God. When someone hurts me, I complain and suffer. When I do the same thing to another person that was done to me, at most I feel guilty, and maybe I ease my trivial suffering with a quick prayer of confession and a bowl of ice cream or bite of chocolate.

The social problem occurs because the other person is having the same experience. Let's go through an example to illustrate. Suppose my adolescent son drinks alcohol. Let's say that objectively such an offense might cause me 5 units of pain (see figure 1.2). The police arrest him, which embarrasses and disappoints me, and I suddenly see the offense as a big sinful event. The hurt in my heart over this event now registers 10 units of pain. In my embarrassment and disappointment, coupled with my sincere desire to help my son learn obedience and develop good Christian character, I discipline him. I deprive him of privileges, and I require him to write an essay on the negative consequences of underage drinking on health, family and career.

Now my son is hurt. He feels the punishment is unfair. He thinks, *I am*

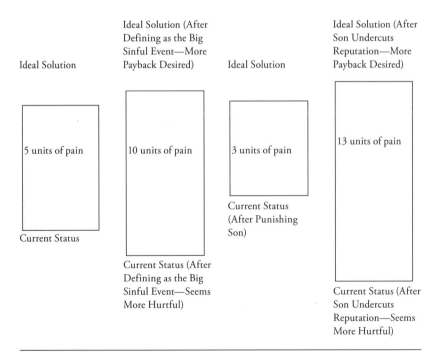

Figure 1.2. Changes in the injustice gap

already being punished by the court for my crime. This humiliation adds insult to injury. It is unfair.

When I imposed the punishment, I did so to reduce my own sense of the injustice my son inflicted on me. Though my "hurtometer" registered 10 units before the punishment, perhaps afterward it goes down to 3 units. I felt that I brought 7 units of justice into my injustice gap.

But my son feels that the punishment I considered equal to 7 units of hurt is more severe than that. He feels that it hurts him more than it hurts me. So his hurtometer that measures the injustice he feels toward me registers 10 units. He feels resentment and anger. *It's not fair,* he thinks. *I only did 5 units of hurt to Dad—and the court is punishing me for that. Now Dad is also punishing me 10 units.* Though I don't feel too badly after the punishment (hurt = 3), my son has a huge grudge (hurt = 10). So he may lash back—perhaps indirectly because he is still working off his loss of privileges. He speaks negatively of me to his teacher, claiming that I abuse him. That reduces his injustice gap from 10 to 5 units, and he continues to hold a 5-unit grudge.

But the 5-unit damage that he thinks he did to my self-esteem as a parent and to my reputation in the eyes of his teacher does not feel like a mere 5-unit injury to me; it feels more like 10 units. My son still has a grudge, and now so do I—a huge one. My hurtometer is no longer at 3 but now registers 13 units of pain (all of which is illustrated in figure 1.2).

This is the magical economics of payback. As both parties seek to bring their injustice gap back to zero after a hurtful event, they can do so only by increasing the other party's injustice gap. The economics of fair trade are simple: I sell a good or service that I think is worth X dollars, and a buyer pays X dollars for it. We are both satisfied. But in the magical economics of payback, both parties cannot be satisfied *at the same time.* At least one side always has an injustice gap. Repeated efforts to eliminate the injustice gap through payback only make the gaps larger.

HUMILITY AND JUSTICE IN THE GAP

How can the injustice gap, the insistent belief that life is not fair, the big sinful event and the magical economics of payback ever be reversed? These cycles are called positive feedback loops. They are anything but positive in their effects. They are called positive because each action increases the effect, like schoolboys who push each other harder and harder during a playground argument. So these feedback loops of growing hatred feed each other's hateful response. Both increase together. Hatred grows with each cycle.

To break the cycle, someone must step into the gap and absorb the pain and injustice. If, instead of giving tit for tat someone gives love, mercy and forgiveness, that is the only way to break the cycle of hatred. Moreover, that person usually must absorb the hatred not just once but repeatedly to make a difference.

Such self-sacrifice is almost impossible in our own fleshly strength. If we forgive and absorb the pain and injustice, the world says we are stupid. It says we have made ourselves a doormat that our enemy can wipe his or her feet on.

But this is exactly what Jesus did. His enemies unjustly harmed him. He humbly absorbed the injustice with love and mercy. The enemy's injustice required punishment from God. Jesus not only took the harm from the enemy, but he also took the enemy's punishment from God. That was the only thing that could end the cycle of sin, injustice, pain, payback and unforgiveness. Jesus did this in complete humility. As Paul says, Jesus "did not count equality with God something to be grasped, but made himself nothing, taking the very nature of a servant, being made in human likeness. . . . He humbled himself and became obedient to death—even death on a cross!" (Phil 2:6-8).

Jesus conquered sin and death by humbly absorbing suffering, pain and injustice. History has shown that raw power will not defeat injustice. At best, it subdues it for a while or pushes it underground, awaiting eternal eruption. At worst, those who pull down the mighty step into their shoes. Only love, mercy and forgiveness—in humility—can defeat injustice.

As Christians, we are the body of Christ. As the body of Christ, our hope of peace comes not in power but in love, mercy, forgiveness and humility.

Does this mean we should not combat injustice? Not at all. Jesus stood outside of Lazarus's tomb and wept over his friend's death (Jn 11:35). He lamented over Israel (Mt 23:37). He laid waste the moneychangers in the temple (Jn 2:14-22). Jesus will one day return to gather the faithful who will rule and reign with him (2 Tim 2:12).

We must seek to establish justice. We must seek procedural justice that ensures freedom and equal opportunity. We must tentatively advance our understanding of the cosmic justice we see taught in the Scriptures. I say "tentatively" because Christians understand the Scriptures differently, and we need enough humility to keep us from believing that we have a corner on truth. We must know in our hearts that we cannot, by our own strength or understanding, know God or live according to God's purposes. We must therefore yield to the Holy Spirit for such strength and understanding. We must know so deeply that God is God that we yearn to live according to Christ's ways and devote ourselves to knowing him with all our heart, mind and soul. We must abhor willful sin but in humility know that inevitably we will sin.

Thus it is only in humility that we can love, show mercy, forgive and work for justice. Humility is the root of all virtue. It is only in humility that we truly and sincerely acknowledge that there is only one God and that we are not God. Only in humility is there the possibility of personal, social and societal peace.

FORGIVENESS IN EVERY WILLING HEART, HOME AND HOMELAND

My life's mission is to do what I can to promote forgiveness in every willing heart, home and homeland. I believe this mission in some ways illustrates one mission of every Christian. There is a God-intended flow of love moving inevitably downhill. Like water, forgiveness flows from the higher to the lower (see figure 1.3). Forgiveness originates with God and flows freely to us. We receive it in our heart. From our heart, forgiveness flows into our home and to those with whom we interact daily, including others in the church. It then flows out into the homeland.

Figure 1.3. Forgiveness in every heart, home and homeland

This living water is not meant to be dammed up. We are not to hoard forgiveness in our hearts, homes, churches, communities, workplaces or nations. Rather, we are to let it flow. Any attempt to dam up the flow of forgiveness creates a dead sea in which life eventually cannot exist. If forgiveness isn't allowed to flow, it is like stopping the flow of our very lifeblood. Life will stop.

Yet completely unconstrained forgiveness is an ideal. We are to forgive like God forgives (Col 3:13), but we are only image bearers of God—bearers of the imago Dei—not God ourselves. God has strength, perfection and infinite resources. People cannot destroy God. Even on the cross, sin and death did not defeat God.

But we cannot forgive in our own strength. We are all too human, too limited, too fallible, and let's face it, too sinful. And the people we try to forgive—they too are all too sinful. We can't just let them off the hook.

We can't just absorb all the pain of their offenses because there are too many people who would take advantage of us again and again until we are depleted, defeated and destroyed.

Even worse, some people are simply takers. They seize whatever they can. They have rejected God and the work of the Holy Spirit, and they are sold out to Satan, sin and self. If we forgive without limit, won't evil triumph?

How can we forgive like God forgives in this imperfect world? It is one thing to forgive in our hearts and to absorb suffering. But it is entirely another to simply allow evil to exist, whether in our homes, churches, workplaces, communities or nation, or in the form of some evil tyrant or terrorist in the world. In such a world, how can we practice Christian forgiveness in our hearts, homes and homelands? And to keep the flow of forgiveness moving, how can we transmit it to other hearts, homes and homelands?

These are the tensions we grapple with daily. They will not yield to simplistic solutions. Forgiveness begins with the God who redeems. And it is only in humility that we can approach such a God.

HUMILITY

In 1994 Rwanda was torn apart by tribal violence that lasted one hundred days. The world looked on as Hutus hacked to death more than eight hundred thousand neighbors, friends and family members who happened to be Tutsi. Finally the Rwandan Patriotic Front, under the leadership of Paul Kagame, invaded Rwanda and ended the genocide.

I met Immaculée Ilibagiza in Nassau in 2008. She is a tall, beautiful woman, sweet of spirit, who loves Jesus deeply. In 1994 during the Rwandan genocide, she hid in a three-by-four-foot bathroom, first with five other women and later joined by two more.[1] The house of Hutu Pastor Murinzi was one of the few that had two bathrooms. He slid a wardrobe in front of the second bathroom door, barricading the women inside, where they hid for three months. During that time, crowds of killers repeatedly surrounded the house and several times searched it thoroughly. Immaculée wrote,

> I was deep in prayer when the killers came. . . . They were right there in the pastor's bedroom! They were rummaging through his belongings, ripping things from the wall, lifting up the bed, overturning chairs. . . . I covered my mouth with my hands, fearing that they would hear me breathing. They were only inches from my head . . . in front of the wardrobe. . . . The wardrobe banged against the door. I covered my ears and prayed: *God, please. You put the wardrobe there . . . now keep it*

there! Don't let them move it. Save us, Lord![2]

Inches from death, Immaculée humbly called on the Lord. God redeemed her from the lion's den, blinding the mob from discovering the bathroom that lay right behind the wardrobe. What a wonderful and sovereign Lord we have!

But while Immaculée hid in the bathroom, her brother Damascene was on the run. His story was revealed later by people who were involved with him.[3] Damascene was an athlete and a gifted student. He had a master's degree—something rare in Rwanda. Damascene's Hutu friend Bonn was hiding him. At first Damascene stretched out under the bed. Later he hid in a hole. Finally he tried to make a break for freedom, planning to escape in a boat piloted by a kindly fisherman. However, he arrived too late to catch the nightly voyage. The next day another "friend," Simoni, betrayed him. Under the guise of having Damascene's clothes washed before leaving on the boat that night, Simoni had Damascene strip to his underwear. Then a band of machete-wielding Hutus suddenly appeared and confronted Damascene. They dragged him into a public place and beat his near-naked body with the handles of their machetes.

"We have seen the bodies of the other cockroaches in your family," they said to Damascene. "But your beautiful sister Immaculée still lives. Where is she hiding? Tell us so we can have our pleasure with her."

Damascene said, "Even if I knew where she was hiding, I wouldn't tell you. You'll never find her. She is smarter than all of you."

"Is she smarter than you, with your master's degree? We caught you, and we'll catch her," said one.

Instead of begging for mercy, Damascene defied the mob. "What are you waiting for? Go ahead and kill me. Today is my day to be with God."

"You think you're so much smarter than us—just because you have a master's degree. Well, I always wanted to see what a master's degree looked like." The man swung his machete, splitting Damascene's skull. Then the mob hacked him apart.

Immaculée prayed, and Jesus answered her prayers. But Damascene's closeness to God did not prevent his death. Still, he stood his ground. Like Shadrach, Meshach and Abednego, he did not yield to the threat of death (see Dan 3:16-29). The three captive Jews said, "O Nebuchadnezzar, we do not need to defend ourselves before you in this matter. If we are thrown into the blazing furnace, the God we serve is able to save us from it, and he will rescue us from your hand, O king. But even if he does not, we want you to know, O king, that we will not serve your gods or worship the image of gold you have set up" (Dan 3:16-18).

God did not prevent the young men from being thrown into the fiery furnace, but he sent someone to walk through the furnace with them. He is Immanuel, God with us.

> Then King Nebuchadnezzar leaped to his feet in amazement and asked his advisers, "Weren't there three men that we tied up and threw into the fire?"
>
> They replied, "Certainly, O king."
>
> He said, "Look! I see four men walking around in the fire, unbound and unharmed, and the fourth looks like a son of the gods." (Dan 3:24-25)

God redeemed Shadrach, Meshach and Abednego, but not without letting them be bound and terrorized and thrown into a fiery furnace. But a fourth person walked with them in the fire, and they were unbound in his presence.

God is sovereign. God redeemed Immaculée as she prayed the rosary repeatedly. She battled Satan's temptation to hate those who hated her and wanted to gang-rape her and hack her apart. She listened to God's wooing her to forgive instead of to fear or to hate. Drawing on Jesus' words in Luke 23:34, she constantly asked God to forgive those killers who knew not what they were doing. Immaculée was an example of godly humility. She did not insist on any right to have justice—either during her period of hiding or afterward. God was with her in the three-by-four bathroom. Her rosary was her lifeline to God.

Yet Immaculée's brother was not granted safety from the hacking machetes. Instead, he went to be with God that day. And through Immaculée's telling of his story, his life has been redeemed on earth as it was in heaven. And people who have heard Immaculée's story have heard two faith-filled stories of humility.

According to C. S. Lewis, in the past God was on the throne of justice, and people in their fallen state stood accused.[4] In recent times we have enthroned ourselves and treated God as the accused. Yet God alone is sovereign, not us. And we need humility to admit it. If humility is a key to understanding the way that justice and fairness speak to mercy and forgiveness, then we ought to look more closely at what humility actually is.

WHAT WE LEARN FROM THE WISDOM OF AGES

First we can examine humility by drawing on the wisdom of bright thinkers. One of the brightest, Andrew Murray, said, "Self has nothing good in it except as a vessel which God must fill."[5] He also said, "Humility . . . is the displacement of self with the enthronement of God." Finally, "Humility is the blossom of which death to self is the perfect fruit."

It's all about a sovereign and loving God. When we understand in our deepest being that God is truly God, it is more difficult to be prideful. Yet Adam and Eve knew God. They walked and talked with their Creator in the Garden of Eden, but still they fell into sin. Since then, the story of humankind has been about redemption from that Fall. Each opportunity to act is in some ways a test of whether we are going to eat of the forbidden fruit or be the apple of God's eye.

Our choices, in essence, usually boil down to a test between love and power.[6] Which one will rule in our heart? As Fyodor Dostoyevsky put it, "Of some thoughts one stands perplexed—especially at the sight of men's sin—and wonders whether one should use force or humble love. Always decide to use humble love. If you resolve on that, once and for all, you may subdue the whole world."[7] It is empathy, compassion, sympathy and love for a fellow weak human that triggers a burst of humility. God's love apprehended triggers a chord in us—if we are attuned to it—that brings out humility.

Temptations to power usually come out of pride or hubris. The times we encounter human sinfulness against us, or against those we love, are the times that seem to most corrupt the image of God within us all. Those are the times when we are most tempted to power. We feel righteous. We feel right. We feel that we are defenders of the faith and that we must put down evil and lift up righteousness.

Sadly, however, most of the time this is not about God—it is all about us. We have been hurt and offended. We have been pulled down from our "rightful" throne. So we strike a blow for righteousness by lifting ourselves above the transgressor or pulling the transgressor down lower than we are. This is not about God's honor, regardless of how sincere we feel we are. It is, nine out of ten times, about defending our ego. Blows to the ego are most often the triggers that give rise to explosions of pride.

We avoid seeking our own glory and focus on God's glory by being preoccupied with blessing others. We often want to be humble, but the devil is in the details. We can't will our flesh to be dead, as Paul argues in Romans 7: "I do not understand what I do. For what I want to do I do not do, but what I hate I do. . . . For I have the desire to do what is good, but I cannot carry it out. . . . Who will rescue me from this body of death? Thanks be to God—through Jesus Christ our Lord!" (Rom 7:15, 18, 24-25).

But how does God redeem us from our inner sin nature that drives us to self-justification, self-protection and self-aggrandizement? James tells us: "Submit yourselves, then, to God. Resist the devil, and he will flee from you. Come near to God and he will come near to you. . . . Humble yourselves before the Lord, and he will lift you up" (Jas 4:7-8, 10). James also says, "Religion that God our Father accepts as pure and faultless is this: to look after orphans and widows in their distress and to keep oneself from being polluted by the world" (Jas 1:27). Paul says, "Do nothing out of selfish ambition or vain conceit, but in humility consider others better than yourselves. Each of you should look not only to your own interests, but also to the interests of others" (Phil 2:3-4). Former archbishop of Canterbury William Temple said, "Humility does not mean thinking less of yourself than of other people, nor does it mean having a low opinion of your own gifts. It means freedom from thinking about yourself at all." The counsel is consistent. We must let our focus on God trigger humility when we are hurt unjustly. When we become wrapped up in the tendrils of ego, we flex and flail and, in doing so, hurt others.

Humility requires some self-sacrifice. Thinking of others besides yourself—looking "not only to your own interests, but also to the interests of others" (Phil 2:4)—inevitably requires sacrifice. This is especially true in the face of an injustice. Protecting our own interests suggests that we get back what was lost, seek replacement of what was damaged or, if that isn't possible, at least make the guilty party suffer in return. Humility, though, thinks not only about ourselves but also about others. We do not become a doormat for the world. Rather, we sacrifice. But in doing so, we might also seek fair justice. We pursue just forgiveness, not merely forgiveness.

When we sacrifice, God can lift us up. God is sovereign and will pursue righteous plans. Sometimes those plans allow our humble and just forgiveness to elevate us. But even when we see no point to our suffering of injustice and unfairness, virtue may be working in us. Humility is building other virtues within us. As Andrew Murray said, "Humility is the only soil in which the virtues root."

WHAT WE LEARN FROM PSYCHOLOGY

Psychologists have only recently begun to study humility scientifically. Humility might not best be seen as an all-or-nothing character trait. Instead, humility might best be understood relationally. We can tell with some certainty whether someone known to us is humble. Relational humility means that we experience another person as humble in a particular relationship. We can say that a person is humble if four conditions are met:

1. We believe the person closely matches our ideal picture of a humble person.

2. We believe the person does not overestimate his or her position in relation to God and/or humanity.

3. We trust that, in our relationship, the person will treat us with dignity even if our needs, goals and priorities conflict with his or hers.

4. We believe the person would freely share himself or herself with someone who is needy.

The ideal picture of humility (the first condition above) includes being modest, self-sacrificing and altruistic. For a person to be humble, he or she must exhibit the positive "other-oriented" emotions: empathy, compassion, love and sympathy. The person must also be willing to share himself or herself with others and to submit to God, to goodness, to humanity and to the least of these. The humble person is attuned to God, humanity, virtue, the needy and, in his or her relationship with me, attuned to my needs.

What We Learn from the Christian Scriptures

The Christian Scriptures, beginning with the Fall, describe a legacy of human arrogance instead of humility before God. Adam and Eve disobeyed God (Gen 3). Human arrogance peaked in Genesis 6 with the flood. God decisively cleansed the earth, except for Noah and his family. After the covenant of the rainbow (Gen 9:1-17), God watched the nations arise through the families of the sons of Noah. Genesis 11 records another pivotal event in human arrogance—the building of the tower of Babel. Humans sought to "make a name for ourselves" (Gen 11:4). God confused their language to frustrate that arrogance. Perhaps now people would be more likely to depend on God rather than on themselves and their own tower building—but it was not to be.

The Old Covenant, or Old Testament, tells the story of Israel. Israel was separated from the surrounding cultures. Scripture reveals the fissures within the human soul, divisions within Israel and conflicts between Israel and its neighbors. Unity is shown to be impossible.

The New Covenant, or New Testament, Scriptures narrate the story of Jesus, God's Son. In an event unprecedented among religions, God humbly becomes a man and dwells with humans (see Phil 2:5-11). God's Holy Spirit now lives within humans. Jesus' body, the church, lives among humans. Paul admonishes Christians to have the same humble mind among each other that Jesus had as he dwelt intimately with humans and sought to partner with God in their redemption. It is only through the humility of God and human beings that the possibility of unity and redemption can ever occur.

At Pentecost the Holy Spirit came upon the crowd, and the miracle of speaking in tongues, as well as understanding them, occurred (Acts 2:1-12). God was answering human arrogance yet again. Only the Holy Spirit, not the human spirit, could repair the confusion of language that occurred at Babel. Unity was possible only through God's divine intervention, not through human interaction or initiative.

As we see the scriptural narrative unfurl, we are struck with the story of redemption. God has revealed his godly nature as a humble forgiver. We have been invited to respond to that nature by identifying with God and attuning ourselves to the divine character.

THE FORENSIC METAPHOR

God is both a just God and a loving God. We have all hurt God. Because he is sovereign, God has a perfect right, out of a sense of justice, to obliterate offenders. But that is not the picture of God we glean from the Scriptures. God is not pure, unadulterated justice. God is also merciful, as seen in a key passage in Exodus: "Then the LORD came down in the cloud and stood there with him and proclaimed his name, the LORD. And he passed in front of Moses, proclaiming, 'The LORD, the LORD, the compassionate and gracious God, slow to anger, abounding in love and faithfulness, maintaining love to thousands, and forgiving wickedness, rebellion and sin. Yet he does not leave the guilty unpunished; he punishes the children and their children for the sin of the fathers to the third and fourth generation'" (Ex 34:5-7). This passage is elaborated in many subsequent Old Testament passages, which increasingly omit the last part of verse 7 (see Ex 20:5-6; Num 14:17-18; Deut 24:16; Ps 86:5, 15; 103:8-10; 130:3-4;

145:8-9; Neh 9:17; Jer 31:34; Dan 9:9; Joel 2:13; Jon 4:2; Mic 7:18-19). God's mercy is further unfolded in the New Testament, which focuses on the work of Jesus. In that mercy, people receive forgiveness, and Jesus receives the punishment people deserve.

People offend and hurt God the Father through rejecting his love and through disobedience. Those rejections create a sense of injustice in God. The forensic metaphor says that humans cannot possibly do enough to pay for their sins. Thus, we all stand guilty and deserve God's condemnation. Paul says that all people are imperfect: "As it is written: 'There is no one righteous, not even one; there is no one who understands, no one who seeks God. All have turned away, they have together become worthless; there is no one who does good, not even one'" (Rom 3:10-12).

This explanation of divine forgiveness and divine justice shows us how justice and forgiveness can interact. We each have within us a *justice motive;* we also have a *mercy motive* (which relaxes the strict application of justice in response to feelings of love, compassion, sympathy and empathy) and a *grace motive* (which seeks to bless others in response to love, compassion, sympathy and empathy). Our justice, mercy or grace motives are triggered, becoming active in response to different circumstances. In the same way, God does not act the same in every circumstance.

God is characterized by both perfect love and perfect righteousness. People are at times neither loving nor righteous. They fall short of the glory of God and do not deserve to fellowship with the One who is completely and purely holy and loving. This failure of humans to be perfect, both by nature and by deed, is a fatal flaw that separates people from God. That separation is eternal. And it is not just the sins but also the sin nature of humans that cause the separation. God the Father's holiness demands separation.

Yet God is also loving. People were created for eternal relationship. In love, God the Father desires humans to be redeemed. But how can both aspects of God's character be manifest? Paul uses a metaphor to answer, arguing that human failure to be holy is *as if* each person has committed a crime—a capital offense demanding death (i.e., eternal separation). Jesus died for each human who accepts that act of grace. Jesus' death paid the price in full, giving life to the sinner and permitting eternal fellowship between the forgiven sinner and God the Father. Jesus is the *propitiation* for human sin. Sin is *expiated* (that is, sin is paid for). The full demands of justice were met when Jesus, who is fully God and therefore without sin, volunteered to die for us sinners. Jesus' death was an act of justice. But it was his humility that allowed justice.

In human society, justice fully pays for any crime that is committed. A convicted murderer may receive capital punishment. Yet that complete justice does not necessarily alleviate the suffering and pain felt by the victims of the crime. Similarly, Jesus' death fully paid for God's sense of justice. But Jesus' death did not fully remove the divine pain and suffering that human sin causes God the Father.

Let's say that a man's wife is murdered. The murderer is caught and sentenced to a life term in prison. Due to good behavior or a governor's act of clemency, the criminal is eventually released from prison. The murderer's debt to society is considered to have been paid. In the same way that a victim can forgive a spouse's murderer even after the criminal has been in jail for thirty years and paid for the crime, God the Father can forgive the sinner even after Jesus has purchased the sinner's life with his own undeserved death. God's forgiveness is not about justice. It is about erasing godly emotional suffering through an act of love, compassion, sympathy or empathy for the guilty criminal.

DIVINE FORGIVENESS AND
INTERPERSONAL FORGIVENESS

At a basic level, there are two different kinds of forgiveness: divine forgiveness and interpersonal forgiveness. Divine forgiveness is God's forgiveness of humans. It is a human's simultaneous experience of God's justice, mercy and grace motives. Interpersonal forgiveness is forgiveness between and among people.

In some ways divine forgiveness is similar to interpersonal forgiveness. At least it is clear that the two concepts are linked together. First, God has a purpose in forgiving, and that purpose intertwines divine forgiveness with divine justice. God's purpose is to unfold a divine story of redemption. Humans, too, have a purpose in forgiving, and it also intertwines forgiveness with justice. It is not involved with an eternal plan, but it can help restore a relationship. Second, God makes a provision—Jesus' becoming the propitiation for sin and expiating it—that simultaneously accomplishes justice and shows mercy. Similarly, in interpersonal forgiveness, it is often easier for people to forgive when some justice has been experienced. Third, God makes a demand for the offender's repentance that is coupled with forgiveness of the offender. Among people, too, repentance of the offender can help us forgive (though in biblical forgiveness, repentance of the offender is not required for interpersonal forgiveness). Fourth, when we sin against God, God's forgiveness wipes out God's barrier to relationship. Interpersonal forgiveness also opens the door to reconciliation (but neither party is required to follow through on reconciliation). Fifth, in both cases, forgiveness may be experienced "internally" by the one who was wronged and extended (i.e., offered "externally") to the offending party, but forgiveness may be either accepted or rejected.

We also need to understand the differences between divine and interpersonal forgiveness. First, God is able to know people fully. Yet people cannot fully know God, each other or even themselves. Interpersonal forgiveness thus requires humility. We cannot be completely sure, regardless of how certain we *feel,* that hurts or injustices are completely one-sided. Second, within the Scriptures, interpersonal forgiveness is unconditional, whereas divine forgiveness is conditional. Divine forgiveness is based on divine truth, justice, mercy and love, which are granted from an omniscient, merciful and just God. Because God knows people's hearts, God can condition divine forgiveness on a person's repentance. But humans are called to forgive unconditionally, for several reasons. Humans are commanded to forgive unilaterally because we are finite (i.e., we cannot know the hearts, minds or intentions of the transgressors). Humans are morally corrupt and thus are moral equals, in no position to judge each other. God is ultimately the judge, so humans are not to judge.

In examining forgiveness, we must consider Jesus' teaching about divine forgiveness and about the way divine forgiveness relates to interpersonal forgiveness. Jesus teaches about forgiveness and about his unity with God. He says, "I and the Father are one" (Jn 10:30). He forgives sins, and the people respond, "Who can forgive sins but God alone?" (Lk 5:21). Jesus does not refute the truth evident in their question.

Jesus teaches that people can expect to be forgiven by God to the extent that they forgive others (Mt 6:12, 14-15). He gives us this command in a Scripture passage that embodies humility. People are expected to reflect both the heart and the righteousness of God. God is a merciful and gracious forgiver of sins against God. People, therefore, are to be similarly oriented in mind and heart. They are to forgive others. They cannot expect God's mercy and grace if they do not reflect God's heart by forgiving others. We cannot expect forgiveness from God if we do not forgive humans who harm us.

Jesus treats this as a doable task. Jesus wants us, in humility, to change our behavioral intention toward the person who sins against us. We are to decide not to seek revenge and not to avoid the person (as long as it is safe to be in a relationship with him or her). We are to decide to release the person from any social debt incurred *against us*. (On the other hand, there may still be social consequences to which the person may be held accountable.)

Jesus does not require us to experience emotional peace. Jesus does require us to decide, in humility, to act in forgiveness and love. We see God not as a cold, unfeeling judge who towers over a condemned prisoner; rather, God came down in humility from the judgment bench to live with people, experience their frailty and connect empathically with them. He is in intimate relationship with us because he humbly entered that relationship, bringing mercy and forgiveness through Jesus' loving relationship with each of us. Humility is at the root of finding a modern-day way for justice and forgiveness to interact with each other. Humility is how forgiveness and love meet. Humility is the platform on which righteousness and mercy kiss (see Ps 85:10).

Jesus' own humility is crucial in bringing together justice and mercy. Forgiveness is, of course, commanded by Jesus. We will receive a blessing for forgiving: God will not refuse to forgive our own sins. We can, therefore, decide to forgive others. Sometimes that decision must be an act of our will.

Scripture appeals to us to forgive because God forgives us first (Eph 4:32; Col 3:13). Thus, our gratitude in response to God's grace and mercy can empower our emotional forgiveness.

In addition, we can forgive *because we are blessed* when we forgive. First, if I carry around condemnation, I make myself bitter and emotionally distraught. By setting myself afire with resentment and hatred, perhaps I am hoping to choke the offender on the smoke. Sometimes the person toward whom I am bitter might not even know that I hold such resentment. It makes little sense to hate. Avoiding bitter feelings is one blessing of forgiveness. Second, by eliminating negative feelings, I can experience benefits to my mental, physical, relational and spiritual health.[8] Forgiving because one is interested in one's own health produces real forgiveness. But, as we might suspect, such forgiveness is not as deep or long lasting as when forgiveness is based on altruism or agape love, which is entered into through humility.

Altruistic forgiving can produce deeper forgiveness, but it is more difficult. It takes longer. There are several scripturally derived motives for forgiving. We can forgive because we

- are motivated by love (Col 3:13-14);

- are grateful for having been forgiven by God (Eph 4:32);

- desire to remain in a loving, forgiven relationship with God the Father (Mt 6:12, 14-15);

- want to receive a blessing (1 Pet 3:8-13);

- are to reflect God's image to others (Eph 5:1); and

- acknowledge that God is the ultimate judge (Rom 12:19).

All of these motives play a part. If we really, humbly understand who we are and how inadequate we are to accomplish our own agendas, we gain humility. If we see God as sovereign, we gain humility. If we believe and are grateful for the gracious work of redemption Jesus accomplished on the cross and the kindness of God the Father in granting complete emotional forgiveness, we gain humility.

Yet humility is difficult to experience. Pride seems so much more central to our experience when we are wronged. We place ourselves on the throne—but we turn out to be ugly idols. We crown ourselves with rhinestone crowns. We see ourselves as American idols who sing our own praises, though off-key. Our songs of self-praise are at least one tone too high.

In our hearts, we may want to be more humble. But how?

LEARNING TO LIVE HUMBLY

Nix narcissism. Narcissism focuses on self. It gives us an inflated sense of self. Let's not, like Narcissus, fall in love with our own reflection.

Eliminate entitlement. Entitled people believe that they are superior to others and deserve special treatment. They are preoccupied with requiring others to treat them fairly. They are caped crusaders for righting injustices against themselves. They whine about people who take advantage of them. They blame others for misunderstandings. They are easily offended and often feel unappreciated. Others owe them. "Sure, I'll forgive," they might say, "when the offender pays me every cent he owes—with interest." Even then, they feel entitled to the offender's gratitude. Don't let entitlement gain title to your life.

Puncture pride. The writer of Proverbs reminds us, "Pride goes before destruction, a haughty spirit before a fall" (Prov 16:18). Benjamin Franklin once noted, "Pride that dines on vanity sups on contempt." Pride leads us to look down on others.

Equalize egoism with empathy. We naturally focus on ourselves. Country singer Toby Keith's song titled "I Wanna Talk About Me" sums it up. Yet, paradoxically, that song gets something right. The singer names all the ways that he focuses on his romantic friend. Then he says that *sometimes* he wants to talk about himself. First, we should have empathy.

Then, once in a while, we can think of ourselves. But we need to keep a balance.

Prevent poor self-esteem. Poor self-esteem can make people want to serve others and to do it modestly to avoid attention. When we feel like a worm, we wiggle to avoid being stepped on. Poor self-esteem, however, is not the same as humility. Poor self-esteem focuses on the self. Instead, we should aim at honest self-confidence. Oswald Chambers said, "Self-confidence is either petty pride in our own narrowness or the realization of our duty and privilege as God's children."[9] Self-confidence walks a knife-edge; it cuts through the human heart just like good and evil.

Leap from the limelight. Modesty avoids attention. And modesty is often a good thing that oils the social and societal wheels. But modesty isn't the same as humility. Sometimes the two do go together. But modesty can also fail to be a pure behavior. It can arise from shame, low self-confidence, parental scolding to be modest or group pressure. Most of us think modesty is more attractive than pride, so we might even adopt an aw-shucks false modesty. The finger that points to God to give credit can focus attention away from the other three fingers—hidden by the thumb—that point back at us.

God is greater than the self. Humble people often feel that they are responding to God's calling to vocation or to service. We should seek to be humble. In his letter to the Philippians, Paul tells us, "Your attitude should be the same as that of Christ Jesus: . . . taking the very nature of a servant . . . he humbled himself and became obedient to death—even death on a cross!" (Phil 2:5, 7-8).

There is an inherent paradox in striving to be humble. We cannot fully reach humility by striving for it. There is, in a fundamental way, no dividing line between the arrogant and the humble. We cannot achieve humility alone. Good and evil indeed pass through the heart of each person. Our efforts to be humble are undermined by our own heart.

Chasing after humility is like trying to catch air in our hands. When we grasp it, it swooshes away. But when we rest with our hands open toward the heavens, air comes to rest in our hands. To experience humility, then, is not to grasp or to strive toward it, but to rest as we seek to bless others. When we are moved from within to bless others, a humble spirit can descend upon us like air resting in an open hand.

In a little book called *Humility: The Quiet Virtue,* I closed with these words:

> Humility is a Pegasus that serves others. It is bridled with grace and modesty. It rises to the heavens bearing others to a higher life. It is others who recognize and appreciate the love, power, and accomplishments of the Pegasus, humility, not the winged horse itself. For humility is the quiet virtue.[10]

Humility within the godhead is the key to divine forgiveness. Humility within our own human hearts is the key to interpersonal forgiveness in situations where an injustice has occurred. Now let's look at justice.

JUSTICE

JUSTICE IS A CRUCIAL ELEMENT IN OUR psyche, in relationships with other individuals, and in societal relationships, but justice alone cannot bring peace.

In John Grisham's first novel, *A Time to Kill*, two Mississippi rednecks motivated by racial hatred (Billy Ray and Willard Cobb) rape and beat ten-year-old Tonya Lee and then throw her body from a bridge.[1] When Tonya's father, Carl Lee Hailey Jr., hears about it, he takes up his shotgun and hides in the courthouse where the accused will be arraigned. The next morning, in front of hundreds of witnesses, Carl Lee shoots the two men as they are marched into court, wounding Deputy Looney in the process.

The novel explores the question, Is there a time to kill? Was Carl Lee justified in shooting the two rapists who sought to kill his daughter?

Lawyer Jake Brigance takes Carl Lee's case. The jury consists of voters in the county—twelve white people. The ethnic tensions mount throughout the book. Can Carl Lee get a fair trial with a white jury in this Mississippi town? The case draws national attention. Political and social organizations (like the KKK and African American rights advocacy groups) seek to use the trial for their own political purposes. Pressure is brought to bear on Jake, his family and his friends.

During the trial, Deputy Looney is called to the stand to testify. He unambiguously identifies Carl Lee as the one who shot the two men. The prosecuting attorney has him limp around to draw sympathy from the jury. Then Jake is called to cross-examine him.

> "Now, Deputy Looney, Carl Lee Hailey shot you in the leg."
> "Yes, sir, he did."
> "Do you think it was intentional?"
> "Oh, no, sir. It was an accident."
> "Do you want to see him punished for shooting you?"
> "No, sir. I have no ill will toward the man. He did what I would have done. . . . Those boys raped his little girl. I gotta little girl. Somebody rapes her and he's a dead dog. . . . We oughta give him a trophy. . . . He's a hero! Turn him loose!"[2]

The battle lines were clear. Carl was clearly guilty of shooting the men who had raped, injured, and tried to murder his daughter. He had shot to kill with full knowledge of what he was doing. But was it the capital crime of homicide? Or is there a time to kill?

By the end of the trial, the jury seems hopelessly deadlocked—about evenly divided. It looks like a hung jury, but the jurors decide it would be morally wrong to send the case to retrial in the future if there was any chance of a decision. *Spoiler alert: In the following paragraph, I reveal the book's conclusion. If you do not already know what happens, you might want to skip that paragraph.*

In the book (in contrast to the movie, in which Jake delivers a persuasive monologue), juror Wanda Womack helps break the deadlock. Her intervention is simple. She asks the members of the jury to shut their eyes and imagine the crime in detail—with all of the ethnicities reversed. "What if the rape had been of a ten-year-old white girl by two blacks? What if she were thrown off of a bridge and left for dead? What if that white girl's father had shot the rapists? Would you," Wanda asks the all-white jury, "convict him? Write your answer on a blank piece of paper."

Twelve votes said "free him." So the jury freed Carl Lee.

A Time to Kill is all about justice, and it rips apart the fabric that covers up the ugly parts, revealing justice as a complex and messy subject. Carl Lee was driven by revenge. As we contemplate the crimes of the two men against the helpless young girl, we are drawn empathically into Carl Lee's mind. We have to admit that there is something deep within us that wants to see those two rapists brought to justice. Carl Lee killed the two men in plain view of hundreds of witnesses. Their mother was aggrieved. Their friends were deprived of friendship. The men lost their lives. Doesn't that crime deserve justice as well?

The facts of the case are open and shut. The law was broken. The revenge motive was clear. The killing was hot-blooded but premeditated. The legal system is set up to remove emotion from such decisions. Our justice system aims to prevent revenge killings and blood feuds. The state, not the girl's father, puts alleged criminals on trial. When Carl Lee committed his revenge killing, it went against the law that keeps our society civil and prevents personal vendettas as retribution for harms.

But personal justice collides with legal criminal justice in A Time to Kill. Through empathy, we readers are drawn into siding with Carl Lee. Even within the fictional narrative, it is through trying to draw empathy from the jurors that Deputy Looney is allowed to limp around the courtroom, pointing out people's positions during Carl Lee's shooting spree. In the end, it is through vivid, emotional empathy that the jury is convinced to decide as it did. On both sides, the battle for justice was fought on the battleground of empathy.

In A Time to Kill, Grisham creates a moral dilemma. The rape was wrong. So was Carl Lee's murder of the two rapists. Two wrongs don't make a right. But Grisham, by using the key experience of empathy, argues that sentencing Carl Lee to death would be a third wrong. And three wrongs also do not make a right.

We all have individual justice motives; I believe we are hard-wired for justice. Yet I believe we are also hard-wired for empathy. How we act—to bring forth justice or mercy—depends on the strength of the justice motive versus the grace motive and, most importantly, on which motive is triggered.

TYPES OF TRANSGRESSIONS

There are not stark boundaries between types of transgressions, only shades of gray. But there seem to be differences between transgressions that are acts of offense or harm versus transgressions that are failures to meet needs. It is generally easy to see an overt offense. When a parent sexually abuses a child, that act of harm leaves a profound wound. But when a parent fails to give a child love, care, approval or acceptance, the child and others may not notice, even though that, too, can leave a deep wound. It is only later as an adult that the person might realize what was missing.

Even more difficult, people are defensive. We tend to blame others for our own shortcomings. This came about first with Eve blaming the serpent, and Adam blaming both Eve and God. Defensive blaming is not any less sinful, because it is part of fallen human nature. We know our tendency to point fingers and try to avoid taking responsibility for our own sinful acts. So if an adult comes to believe that a parent did not give him the love, support, care, intimacy or guidance he thinks he deserved, the conclusion may be tinged with self-doubt. *Are my parents really guilty of insufficient love? Am I just making excuses to protect a guilty conscience? How much did childhood neglect really contribute to my current behavior? How much healing could I have experienced since childhood if I had only listened to God or to other wise advisers?*

In many relationships we experience hurts. Our coworkers may stab us in the back. But don't they also sometimes fail to support us? Our own children may get in trouble or reject our love. But don't they also fail to be grateful for the sacrifices we make for them? Whenever we are hurt or offended, usually the offensive act is just half of the story.

In each case, specific acts of transgression are usually easier to identify than are deficits. We are wired to notice what is there more than what isn't there. Once we notice, however, we can then begin the hard work of trying to cooperate with God, who can redeem the hurt.

TYPES OF JUSTICE

There are several distinct types of justice. These include distributive justice, retributive justice, restorative justice and procedural justice. Of course, there is also revenge—or, as we like to think of it when we feel vengeful, just getting even. *Distributive justice* attempts to distribute resources either equally or equitably (even if what is equitable is not strictly equal). *Retributive justice* seeks to mete out punishment that will equalize suffering between wrongdoer and victim or will be fair payment for the crime. *Restorative justice* seeks to find equitable and just solutions for social wrongs by involving victims in determining how to provide satisfaction for wrongdoing without removing the wrongdoer from the community. *Procedural justice* attempts to specify fair processes for dealing with matters of conflict or potential conflict. Each type of justice is concerned with responsibility of all parties, accountability and fairness. In each type of justice, an essential ingredient is restoration of equality after an act has resulted in an inequity.

Developmental psychologists have proposed two theories of morality that describe moral development. Lawrence Kohlberg touts a logical, rational justice.[3] Carol Gilligan describes relational justice, which she claims is more descriptive of women than men.[4] Cultural psychologists have shown how some cultures, such as U.S. culture, are oriented more toward individual values, rational reasoning, self-control and making decisions— very Kohlberg-like. Other cultures, such as Japanese culture, are oriented toward communal values.

Among men and women and in individualistic and collectivistic societies, both rational and relational justice can be found. This should not be surprising. God is both logical and relational, and all people bear that image.

JUSTICE AT THE INDIVIDUAL LEVEL

The justice motive. Melvin Lerner identified a justice motive deeply rooted within human beings.[5] Whenever a person experiences a hurt or offense, one of the first responses is to seek to right the wrong that was done. This justice motive is a primitive urge. It is especially strong in in-groups. For example, animals such as chimpanzees share food, and alpha males tend to punish chimps who try to take more than their share.[6] But the limits of distributive justice seem to extend only as far as the boundaries of the in-group, or (in animals) the troops in which they live. Animals do not seem concerned with distributive justice across species. They don't even seem to care about other troops in the same species. The same tendency occurs in humans. We do not seem to care much for those who are not members of groups to which we belong. Distributive justice, then, seems to depend on whether one sees a person or subgroup as part of one's in-group.

Christianity has within its Scriptures a justification for making stark distinctions between in-groups and out-groups. The Jews were God's chosen. Other groups were not chosen. Christians are given special rules for dealing with other Christians, and those rules are different from the rules for dealing with nonbelievers.

But at the same time, Jesus changed everything. All people—not just Jews—can be blessed by Jesus. Paul urges Christians to break down the dividing walls of hostility between groups (Eph 2:11-22). John reveals that anyone can receive Christ's blessing (Rev 3:20). James urges Christians to treat all people equally (Jas 2:1-4). And Jesus taught that our neighbor does not necessarily share our religion (Lk 10:25-37).

A thoughtful person might conclude that the differences between in-groups and out-groups are keys to peace between groups. Thus, if we are interested in world peace, we might strive to see commonalities across boundaries. Seeing how much we are alike, others might extend the in-group boundaries outward and thus be less likely to engage in competition, hostility and violence across groups. Regardless of how we look at it, we seem to be able to draw boundaries so there is always an out-group, which feeds future conflict.

The "just world" belief. Early in their lives people develop a sense of a just world—perhaps around the age of three.[7] People think that the world ought to be fair, and they become upset when it isn't. Thoughtful people come to realize that the world is not fair. But unfairness of any kind still activates our justice motive. The degree to which it is turned on is determined by whether I experience an injustice, someone close to me does, or whether I inflict an injustice.

Because I feel injustices to myself more keenly than I feel injustices to anyone else, my justice motive is jet-propelled to resolve personal injustices against me. I usually ignore injustices that others experience, unless I can empathize. Then I *might* help them. In those cases my justice motive isn't jet-propelled, only car-engine-propelled. But to my shame, recognizing, admitting and trying to resolve injustices that I might inflict on someone else are powered merely by roller skates with sticky wheels.

When people's assumption of a just world is violated by an injustice, they activate their justice motive to reestablish a sense of justice. Moral anger and outrage provide the fuel when the justice motive really gets cranked up.

Differing perceptions of transgressions. Our justice motive is turned on when we observe that a transgression has occurred. A transgression is a violation of physical, psychological or moral boundaries. One doesn't even have to be harmed for one to perceive that an offense has occurred. Consider a criminal situation. In some states, a person who attempts a crime can receive the same sentence as a person who actually commits the same crime. Legal systems have taken various avenues to deal with attempted murder or attempted robbery. For example, if a person contemplates murder or robbery, no state requires that the person be put in jail. However, in some states, if a person takes a substantial step toward committing the crime—such as buying a deadly poison or casing a bank—the person is considered legally guilty of the crime. This is called a subjectivist stance. In other states, a person has to actually commit the crime to be judged guilty for it. This mirrors the "no harm, no foul" rule of some sports. This is considered an objectivist stance.

In still other states, the law is a compromise between the pure subjectivist and pure objectivist stances. Here the person has to be considered in "dangerous proximity" of committing the crime to be judged guilty. "Dangerous proximity" means being so near to committing the crime that the crime is virtually impossible to avoid. If a robber in possession of burglary tools hides outside of a house waiting for the family to go out one night, the robber is in dangerous proximity of committing burglary.

Apart from official legal systems, in different states people usually have private ideas about guilt and punishment for crimes. Princeton psychologist John Darley has studied how people respond as they judge closeness to committing a crime.[8] For example, if a potential offender merely decides he is going to commit murder, how responsible for murder is he judged to be? On average, the respondents said he is 15 percent responsible. If he takes a substantial step toward committing the crime, he was judged 25 percent responsible. If he is found in dangerous proximity to committing the murder, he was judged, on average, 60 percent responsible. If he carries out the murder, not surprisingly he was judged 100 percent responsible.

Let's look at another example. Bill was caught by his wife, Lisa, while he was looking at pornographic pictures on the Web. "Yeah, I know it's wrong," said Bill. "Lisa and I have discussed it. But I just don't think it's the big deal that she does. After all, I wasn't unfaithful. I wasn't even near to being unfaithful." Bill is taking an objectivist stance and defining unfaithfulness strictly. He is reasoning objectively that only real sexual contact with another woman makes him guilty of infidelity. Lisa might be profoundly upset because she is taking a subjectivist position. To her, Bill's act of looking at pornography and perhaps imagining sex with another woman is an act of unfaithfulness. At the minimum, it puts him in dangerous proximity to infidelity. Not surprisingly, Lisa and Bill will argue about the act.

The role of memory. Justice cannot seem to bring lasting peace because people's memories differ. People see transgressions in the light of their memories, and memories generalize. Sometimes memories of old wounds flood the mind, sometimes not. Situations differ. Some triggers fire up lots of fears. If one situation triggers a painful memory, the emotional impact of the wrongdoing is multiplied. Even worse, we start to attach a cluster of painful memories to a person. Then if that person ever transgresses again, we remember. We soon conclude, *She can't be trusted.*

Similarly, we generalize about other people. If a member of a group or family offends us, we might feel negatively toward the entire group or family. We may conclude that all Christians are not thoughtful or all Jews are insensitive or all Muslims are fanatical. We sow the seeds of prejudice.

The injustice gap. As we recall from chapter one, the response to each transgression depends on the size of the injustice gap. The bigger the injustice gap, the stronger the justice motive. The bigger the gap, the more angry, bitter and resentful we feel. If the gap persists, it can lead to lurking, vengeful motivation that seeks an object to project the guilt onto and direct the anger toward.

Many offenses create separate injustice gaps. Thus the offenses can be treated as somewhat independent of each other. But the fact is, if an offender repeatedly offends, the same offense is perceived differently the second or the tenth time. With each offense, we conclude that the offender is more incorrigible. So resolving subsequent offenses requires more restitution, apology and repentance to make amends. Thus these separate offenses are not fully independent of each other. In fact, history and memory play a big role in the perception of each new offense.

People may narrow the injustice gap and thus reduce unforgiveness in many ways. These include *social acts* such as exacting revenge or pursuing retributive justice. By seeing the offender suffer, people achieve retribution. But social acts that restore relationships through restorative justice—like seeking restitution and pursuing socially just conditions—can also narrow the injustice gap.[9] Unforgiveness can be reduced by *spiritual acts* such as turning judgment over to God for divine punishment of the offender, trusting that God is in control or praying for the offender. Unforgiveness may also be reduced through *psychological acts* such as unconsciously denying one's unforgiveness; projecting unforgiveness onto another person; cognitively reframing a transgression in a way that excuses, justifies or denies the injustice; forbearing or accepting the transgression; or forgiving.[10] These coping responses are not necessarily independent. For example: a criminal steals a man's car. The man holds a grudge. Eventually he might reduce unforgiveness by accepting that bad stuff happens. When the criminal is convicted and sentenced to jail, the victim might reduce his unforgiveness further because he has seen justice done. Later he might completely forgive the car thief.

Both offender and victim can affect the size of the injustice gap. If the offender apologizes sincerely for an offense, that restores some personal justice. If the victim were to exact revenge on the offender, then the victim will also reduce his or her own injustice gap. (From a social point of view, however, we can see that the victim's retaliation will increase the offender's injustice gap, thus making the cycle of violence and offense more likely to continue.)

Not every harm or slight, especially a small one, remains in our minds as an injustice gap. Negative feelings do not remain forever attached to small hurts. Thus we can close our injustice gap. For small hurts, we usually simply forget. If a person jostles me in the street, I usually forget about it within a few steps. It isn't important, so I don't keep remembering it. If there were no consequences from the accidental collision—such as coffee spilled on my new shirt or a bruised muscle—then my short-term memory won't even turn the incident over to long-term memory.

Problems arise when we experience a large injustice. The injustice gap yawns and spews out the venom of unforgiving emotions and vengeful motivations. We feel righteously indignant. *How could the offender be so callous, so unfeeling, so insensitive, so wrong?* We believe deep in our soul that justice is necessary. We might see ourselves as God's appointed tool to administer justice. Or we might hope that the person will be punished by a valid authority such as the courts or a workplace supervisor.

It is hard to completely close the injustice gap. The basic difficulty is that my offender and I perceive things differently. This is true even if we experience exactly the same thing (which isn't true when one is the offender and the other is the victim). For example, Susan and LaShonda are subjected to an electric shock of 15 volts. Using a 10-point scale, Susan describes the shock as inflicting 1 unit of pain. LaShonda describes it as inflicting 3 units of pain using the same scale. But it isn't that LaShonda is a wimp. The next day, after playing an exceptionally strenuous rugby match and nursing several injuries, LaShonda rates the same 15-volt shock as 0 units of pain. Different life circumstances can affect our experiences of injustice and its pain in the same way.

In interpersonal interactions, I usually experience pain to myself as more painful than I estimate it to be for others. Recall the magical economics of payback from chapter one. By retaliating strongly for an injustice, one can close one's own injustice gap only by further widening the other person's injustice gap. People might decide that they don't want to feud any longer and that they are just going to live with their injustice gaps. But living with unforgiveness, resentment and unforgiving motives—even if people are committed not to act on those motives—is still stressful.

JUSTICE AND PUNISHMENT

We have within our brains and bodies a natural response to transgressions. Injustice turns on our justice motive. In fact, our brains love for us to get even.

Ernst Fehr and Klaus Schmidt described a study in which participants who had felt that they had been betrayed were given a chance to either fuss at the betrayer or force the betrayer to give up some money, say ten dollars.[11] The rub was that participants had to give up ten dollars of their own to force the betrayer to give up ten dollars. The brain activity of respondents was observed in MRI units as the study was conducted. For those who insulted their betrayer, only the usual pathways associated with anger were activated. But for those who chose to punish their betrayer, even at equal cost to themselves, their pleasure pathways became active. Their brains registered the same kind reward from payback as people do from eating chocolate.

Fehr and Simon Gächter conducted another study.[12] Groups of four players played a game for a fixed number of rounds. In some groups one of the members could punish a "free rider," someone who was taking advantage of cooperating group members. For the groups that were allowed to punish free riders by exacting a little revenge now and then, all players got progressively richer throughout the game. Thus vengeance helped the group. But for the groups that could not punish free riders, the game resulted in players who took advantage of others round after round.

Psychologist Michael McCullough, taking an evolutionary perspective, showed that revenge might have been adaptive throughout history because it can do four things: (1) it can balance a moral ledger (as in the free rider problem above); (2) it can teach a transgressor a lesson (also seen in the illustration above); (3) it can feel good (i.e., stimulate the pleasure pathways in the brain); (4) it can raise the self-esteem of the punisher (i.e., the punisher feels good about exacting justice).[13]

What do we hope to accomplish by punishing someone? We can again look at the criminal justice system to discern why people might punish others who they think are wrongdoers. Darley suggests that historically there are five reasons why people believe criminal offenders should be punished: (1) just deserts, (2) rehabilitation, (3) individual deterrence, (4) deterrence of people in general and (5) incapacitation.[14] Philosopher Immanuel Kant believed people held a deep sense of morals. He thought that the punishment ought to fit the crime as much as possible; the criminal should get just deserts. Rehabilitation is a second excellent theoretical reason for incarcerating one who has been convicted of a crime. However, the dynamics of prisons make rehabilitation an unlikely occurrence. In fact, prisoners are more likely to learn more about high-level crime from other prisoners. The major champion of the third and fourth reasons for incarcerating criminals, an individual or group deterrence motivation, was Jeremy Bentham. Bentham argued that punishment could deter an individual from doing wrong. Furthermore, when others see criminals being punished, they might be less likely to do wrong so as to avoid punishment. Finally, incapacitation is a legitimate motive to incarcerate an offender. The punishment deprives the person of the liberty to commit the same crime again. However, incapacitation only works if the offender's prison experience does not motivate or teach him or her to commit more crimes when finally released, or if the person is incarcerated until death.

Darley, along with Kevin Carlsmith and Paul Robinson, examined the relative strengths of people's motives for criminal punishment.[15] They concluded that, in the United States, people usually recommend criminal sentences to give criminals their just desserts rather than for rehabilitation, incapacitation or deterrence (of the individual or of others). Punishment is about fairness, payback and balancing the books.

JUSTICE AT THE SOCIAL AND SOCIETAL LEVELS

As we have seen, justice is built into humans, but justice alone almost never brings peace to an individual. That is doubly true at the social and societal levels.

Justice occurs because of societal structures and processes, but it also occurs informally between pairs of people in relationship. I call this *social-level justice* or merely *social justice*. If two people have equal injustice gaps, we might think they have peace between them. This is not necessarily the case. Both may hold a grudge.

This is not to say that partners cannot overlook differences and behave civilly or even lovingly toward each other. Or even that partners cannot talk with each other and formulate a joint narrative that essentially agrees that life must continue dispite their grudges. But it does show that the idea that social justice involves merely balancing degrees of wrongdoing is too simplistic. Social-level justice is dependent on the situation and on the perception of each person in the situation.

This is complicated even further because memories are involved. Of course individuals have memories. But relationships and groups also have memories. They pass those along to each other and to the next generation.

Societal-level justice is much more complex than social-level justice. *Societal justice* involves people who observe interactions between pairs, people who remember past wounds involving in-groups and out-groups, and people who remember interactions between institutions and individuals or institutions and groups. The difficulties in determining societal justice are magnified greatly in comparison to a pair of people trying to work out a fair solution to a conflict. Each member of society maintains his or her own injustice gap. Each holds his or her own perception of the injustice gap. But each also lives in a web of dyadic relationships and group dynamics.

Societal justice is complex not merely because it involves more people whose perspectives need to be accounted for; societal justice is also complex because people in groups are independent agents who often seek to take justice into their own hands. They may strap a bomb to themselves and blow up other people in the name of a cause or in an attempt to correct an injustice. They might seek to assassinate a leader. In any peace negotiation, the sides must be aware of the "hothead factor." This is a recognition that individuals in each group may do extreme acts. If the entire group is held responsible for an act of its most extreme member, then peace negotiations and agreement will inevitably be sidetracked. A lone terrorist can hold the entire peace process hostage through one act of terrorism or vengeance.

Why is it so difficult to arrive at social and societal justice?

The role of memory. Researchers who study memory tell us how impossible it is to remember details accurately. Generally we store merely the *essence* of a memory. Then we re-create a logical story to thread together the pieces that we remember. What we remember depends greatly on what we pay attention to. Roy Baumeister and his colleagues performed a study in which people observed a conversation between an offender and a victim.[16] As people observed, they imagined themselves to be either the victim, the offender or an impartial observer. People made the same number of memory errors regardless of the perspective they adopted while observing the conversation. But their errors were self-serving. That is, victims remembered how much they suffered, but offenders did not. Offenders remembered saying they were sorry, but victims didn't remember that. Impartial observers remembered some of each and forgot some.

Human memory is limited. People remember the same events differently and yet are absolutely certain they are remembering correctly. This is just as true for groups as for individuals. Groups focus on events relevant to their own survival and don't pay enough attention to the suffering of others. Or if they do pay attention, they don't see the suffering of the other side as very important.

The bad outweighs the good. If I am texting as I cross the street and nearly get blasted by a car, I will remember that near-death experience. It is crucial for survival. My body is wired to make me remember. But if I get a hug from a friend for texting her, I might or might not ever think about it again. If I forget, I might miss out on one of the many rewards of a good friendship, but I won't die. So my body and brain are not poised to remember good events in the same way that they are wired to remember bad events. Roy Baumeister surveyed hundreds of experiments that all tell the same story: the bad is stronger than the good.[17] It takes about five or six good events to equal the emotional impact of one bad event. And the math can be even worse. Remember the big sinful event from chapter one. If a bad event has poisoned one's whole way of looking at a relationship, then it might take as many as fifteen to twenty-five good events for every negative one—sustained over time—to turn back the tide.[18]

Differing perceptions of causes. Inquiring minds, so they say, want to know. And when unjust things happen, we all want to know why. At root of that natural desire is the belief that if I only knew why, I could change things. But that doesn't always turn out to be the case. According to Edward Jones and Richard Nisbett, actors and observers in a given situation differ in explaining the causes of events.[19] We live within our own skin looking out. As actors, we construct explanations of what happens on the basis of what we see and hear. If you get angry with a friend, you see and hear his or her behavior and words. *So*, you think, *why did I get angry? It was obviously because of what he or she did and said.* You can see how difficult it is to arrive at social justice when we naturally see the other person as to blame, even if we are the wrongdoers.

When we observe others doing wrong, we usually search for personality explanations for their behavior. Suppose we observe Ruth, a coworker, abusing Kiesha, another colleague, who passively absorbs the abuse. It would not be good for our survival to assume that this was merely a one-off happening with no lasting meaning. We want to use our observations to inform us how to act around Ruth (the bully) and Kiesha (the wimp). As social creatures, we are created to learn from the experience of others. So we attribute causes of social and societal wrongs to internal unchanging personalities and plan our interactions accordingly. When a person or group has been unjust, we naturally assume that they are, by nature, unjust. If injustice is seen to be at the center of an individual's personality or a group's identity, it is no wonder that overcoming the effects of societal injustices is so difficult.

Our own pain outweighs others' pain. Social justice is difficult, as we have already pointed out, because we live inside our own skin, with its sensors for physical and emotional pain. We naturally develop a sense that injustices we experience are far more severe than the injustices we inflict.

Injustices trigger other associations and memories. If my coworker Ruth-the-bully turns her venomous tongue on me, I might let it slide, like water off a duck's back. But injustices in my other relationships might sneak into the current situation. If I have a history of being abused or if I have recently gone through a heated conflict with my adolescent daughter, I might squash Ruth. Injustices also have a way of escaping the narrow boundaries of the moment of their occurrence and rushing in from the past. I suddenly recall that time last year when Ruth was so vicious. *I won't let that happen again,* I think.

Some events are like trip wires in a minefield where the mines are wired together. One wrong step can set off a chain of explosions that might have been lying dormant for years. These triggers and associated permanent structures (like memories and associations) will turn out to play a major role in determining how we respond to injustice, as we'll see in chapter five and beyond.

Social justice and societal justice are so difficult that we wonder how they might ever be accomplished. Our memories keep us prejudiced against justice. Memories are twisted by self-serving biases. We remember the bad much more than the good. We remember what we see—others' provocative acts—and not what we do, and we treat others as if their wrongdoing is part of their never-changing personalities or group characteristics. Memories for our own pain are grooved more deeply than any pain we inflict. We have an entire network of memories of similar injustices that might be triggered by the current injustice.

One additional quality of memory makes social and societal justice difficult. We want a consistent picture of events, so we often revisit our memories. As we replay our memories like late-night reruns on television, we actually change them. We keep working with the memories to find meaning in them. This is helpful when it comes to relieving grief. We want to find some meaning in important losses, and if meaning wasn't there before, our memory inserts it, sometimes years later. You may have heard someone you know trot out a new understanding of a painful event, one you've never heard before, even though you have heard twenty-five retellings of the story. You know that your friend is not lying. But the new understanding of the story has made her "remember" things she never remembered before.

Let's recap what we know about justice. God is just and loving and has built that sense of justice and love into creation. Humans are flawed and fallen. We cannot manifest justice and love perfectly, but we still are called by God to be responsible and to try to bring about God-informed justice as we discern it.

Justice is experienced by each of us individually. We each have a strong justice motive, but as fallen creatures, we contaminate our pursuit of justice. We want to be fair and establish fair relationships. The dark side of our justice motive, however, is that we are strongly motivated to punish people who do wrong. This often means that we seek revenge. We try to take justice out of God's hands and exact it ourselves. So we struggle with whether we can yield to God, trusting in divine justice. Our hearts can be at the center of a tug-of-war. Our justice motive pulls against our mercy motive. We might not feel personal peace about whether we are to pursue justice or forgiveness.

Conflict also pervades societal justice. In societies, police and military entities enforce justice. When a country has a weak or corrupt police force or army, the likelihood is higher that people will take the law into their own hands. Vengeance, honor crimes and bloodlust killings increase. Militias proliferate. When crimes and civil disputes occur, the courts decide justice. The judicial system is constructed around dispassionate justice. That is, justice decisions about guilt and punishment are, we hope, made without relying on emotion. Judges are called "triers of fact," not "triers of feeling." Despite this grand concept, the justice system is not without emotion. Attorneys work hard to get judge and jury to think either that an injustice has been done and requires punishment or that an innocent person has been unjustly accused and must be protected from unfair punishment. One of an attorney's chief tools is the ability to get the judge and jury to feel empathy for his or her client. Feelings are used equally by both sides, as is dictated by procedural justice. But still, an attorney's skills play a big part in how well he or she can promote empathy for his or her client. The emotion of empathy is enlisted to work alongside of justice.

Sin clouds the waters of pure justice. As Christians, what often concerns us about our justice motives is our inconsistency. We know that God desires us to act justly and that vengeance not ours to enact. We are also troubled when we find that our justice motive is bent toward exacting vengeance. Most acts are complexly motivated. Maintaining our honor, holding onto our dignity and keeping our self-respect are all worthy objectives aimed at self-protection. But sometimes baser motives get mixed in, and we merely want to hurt someone who hurt us or someone we care about. At those times we may sense that we have morally failed by not trusting the God who is there.

We should not expect peace from pursuing justice—no matter how elegantly conceived. Justice alone is inadequate to solve the problems of individuals, couples or societies. In Grisham's book *A Time to Kill,* when the justice issue was resolved, peace reigned. But I thought the ending in the movie version was more true to life than the book's conclusion. In the movie, when the jury's verdict was announced, violence erupted. Justice brought peace to Carl Lee, but it did not bring peace between the ethnically polarized groups of that society.

Our individual injustice gap is associated with negative emotions, self-protective motivations and unconscious evil desires. Try as we may, we can almost never close the injustice gap ourselves by correcting injustices. If we eliminate our own feelings of injustice, we create or widen an injustice gap in other people. Some may retaliate. Some may dislike the solution and protest violently. Justice isn't enough, by itself, to bring peace. How do we deal with this impossibility of bringing about peace and happiness through justice?

FORGIVENESS

IN *THE SUNFLOWER,* WHICH I SUMMARIZED in chapter one, Simon Wiesenthal invites us to imagine what our response to Karl, the Nazi soldier, might be. What if you as a Christian were called in front of a dying soldier of a different religion, a member of an army committed to the genocide of Christians? Imagine that you have seen your brother, sister, mother, father or children killed by soldiers like this one. The soldier looks you in the eye, tells you he has killed your people and asks that you grant forgiveness to him. What would you do?

Personally I would be anxious about my courage. Could I even say what I really believed in the face of this pressure? I don't know. I am glad that I have never been placed in such a crucible to feel such heat and pressure.

Wiesenthal's experience raises some exceptionally difficult questions about forgiveness and justice. First, what exactly is forgiveness?[1] Second, how is it related to justice? Third, what role does humility play in relating forgiveness and justice?

WHAT IS FORGIVENESS?

Forgiveness has been confused with several closely related ideas, but most experts now distinguish forgiveness from these alternatives. Let's first look at what forgiveness is *not.*

Forgiveness is *not* reconciling. Karl might well have been hoping for reconciliation. That is, he might have been hoping that Simon would accept him with a restored sense of trust. He might have hoped that his sincere, emotional deathbed confession would persuade Simon that Karl was trustworthy. Similarly, forgiveness is *not* exonerating, that is, finding that a person who was thought to be guilty is in fact innocent. Forgiveness is likewise *not* justifying, or excusing one's behavior. If Simon felt that Karl really had not done anything wrong by slaughtering innocent people—that it is just a part of war—then Simon would say Karl's act was justified. It would not need to be forgiven because it was justified. If Simon believed Karl was coerced at gunpoint to kill innocent people, Simon might say that such an excuse makes the act more understandable. Finally, forgiveness is *not* condoning, or saying, "What you did is okay." It is not saying, "Your act isn't important" or "You didn't really hurt me" or "I'll let you off the hook this time."

Instead, forgiveness holds the offender responsible for wrongdoing.

Karl did not ask Simon to say, "I don't hold this against you. You are going to meet God, and he will punish you." That would not be forgiving; that would be saying, "God will exact divine justice. I don't need to hold a grudge or get even myself. God will do the dirty work."

Karl did not ask Simon to forbear. Karl did not say, "Please expend effort to suppress your negative feelings towards me." That would not be forgiving but forbearing.

Karl did not ask Simon to forgive him personally, one-to-one. He did not say, "I'd like a report on your private inner experience. Can you decide to forgive me personally? Can you change your emotions and motivations toward me?"

Karl *did* ask Simon to say to him that he was forgiven on behalf of those affected. Because he asked Simon to say something about others' condemnation, he was dealing with the societal context of forgiveness.

Decisional and emotional forgiveness. An individual's experience of forgiveness involves two different types of forgiveness: decisional and emotional. *Decisional forgiveness* is controlling our behavioral intentions.

Emotional forgiveness is experiencing emotional replacement of negative, unforgiving emotions with positive, other-oriented emotions. Emotional forgiveness is often slower to materialize and less under our control. It activates mercy and grace motives, which thus replace revenge, avoidance and grudge-holding motives. How much emotional replacement is enough? Is emotional forgiveness complete when all negative emotion has been eliminated so that the victim feels neutral toward the offender? Or should the victim continue to feed in positive, other-oriented emotions until a net positive emotional state is felt toward the offender?

The outcome of emotional forgiveness depends on who the offender is and the victim's goal toward the offender. For instance, if the offender is a stranger or a person with whom one would not seek a continuing close relationship—like Karl—the desired outcome is usually neutrality. We just want to get rid of negative feelings and motives. We wouldn't want to hang out with Karl.

In contrast, if the offender is a loved one, we would not feel content to say, "Well, at least I don't hate you." We would want to eliminate negative emotions and motives, but we'd want to go beyond neutral feelings to achieve some positive emotion toward the loved one. Emotional forgiveness replaces negative emotions. It stops at neutrality in forgiving strangers, and it proceeds further in forgiving a loved one.

Forgiveness changes things. It is like the pressing the restart button or Ctrl-Alt-Delete on a computer. It unsticks relationships that were frozen into recrimination and reboots the social computer.

Decisional and emotional forgiveness are two different types of forgiveness, not two related processes or two halves of a single process. We may make a decision to forgive and never feel emotional peace about it. Take for example a drunken truck driver who crosses the median and hits a car head-on. The driver of the car is paralyzed. She decides to forgive the truck driver, and she holds onto her decision for the rest of her life. Yet as she struggles with her disabilities and the subsequent problems deriving from them, she might feel resentment, bitterness, anger and perhaps even hate for years after the crash. She made a decision to forgive, but she does not have emotional peace. I have seen Christians (and others) condemn such people because they could not experience emotional peace. True, the victim would feel happier if she could also experience emotional forgiveness, but that does not make her decisional forgiveness invalid.

Experiencing decisional or emotional forgiveness is different from *saying*, "I forgive." Both decisional and emotional forgiveness occur within a person's skin. But the ease or difficulty of deciding to forgive or of experiencing emotional forgiveness depends on the social context of the events. When two people talk about transgressions between them—perhaps apologizing, maybe offering restitution—those interactions can determine whether or how quickly or slowly an individual will forgive. The two-person social context affects forgiveness but is not itself forgiveness.

Suppose Karl had said to Simon, "I see that I have made you feel unsafe by killing those people. I also see that I have hurt you by hurting those other Jews because you are a Jew. Can you forgive me for hurting you?" That would have provided a social context for Karl's request that Simon forgive him. Simon might have said to him, "I forgive you"—though in reality he did not. That statement would not have been forgiveness and should not be confused with it. Forgiveness happens (or doesn't happen) inside the forgiver's skin. An announcement of forgiveness might be completely sincere, but it just as well might be a lie, self-deception or an attempt to avoid any further discussion.

When others are involved—witnessing what happens, being told about the transgressions or being part of a group involved with them—it describes the societal context. Karl's request for forgiveness was in the societal realm. When he asked Simon to forgive him on behalf of the Jews, we don't know exactly what he was asking for, but most of the possibilities were societal. He might have been asking, "Will you speak forgiveness as a proxy for others?" Of course, Simon had no legitimate position—such as elected leader for all Jews everywhere—to speak on behalf of those Jews. He had no official position as a spokesperson for the murdered people. Thus, Simon could not legitimately speak for others.

Perhaps Karl meant, "Will you speak forgiveness on behalf of God?"

That question might stand on a bit firmer ground. Simon might have evaluated Scripture and concluded he could speak forgiveness on behalf of God. (As Christians, we may have been given some authority by God to declare forgiveness on his behalf. For example, in John 20:22-23, Jesus appears to his disciples after his resurrection. He says, "Receive the Holy Spirit. If you forgive anyone his sins, they are forgiven; if you do not forgive them, they are not forgiven." Of course, theological disagreements exist about who may legitimately forgive sins or declare God's forgiveness of sins, and also about what happens spiritually when this occurs.)

Maybe Karl meant, "Will you say that you forgive me so I will feel more peace?" Or maybe he meant, "I have made peace with God, but I need some person to agree before I can feel at total peace." We simply do not know enough to understand exactly what Karl was asking Simon for. We can guess that he was not really concerned about whether Simon forgave as an individual. Rather, Karl was probably asking for reassurance that God and perhaps Jews *could* forgive him. Of course, Simon's answer (and ours) would depend not only on how we understood forgiveness personally, but also on how we see it operating at social and societal levels.

Decisional and emotional forgiveness in Scripture. What if Karl were to ask us to forgive him? Would we? Should we? God is clear in Scripture. We must decide to forgive. When Jesus teaches his disciples to pray, he links forgiving those who have offended us to our being forgiven by God (Mt 6:12, 14-15). Jesus prayed, "Forgive us our sins, as we have forgiven those who sin against us" (Mt 6:12 NLT). I believe Jesus is talking about decisional forgiveness, not emotional forgiveness. Later Peter asks Jesus, "How many times shall I forgive my brother when he sins against me? Up to seven times?" (Mt 18:21). Jesus answers, "Not seven times, but seventy-seven times [or seventy times seven]" (Mt 18:22). Most theologians interpret this to mean that we must forgive every time, regardless of the number. But let's be literal. Can we emotionally forgive a person (literally) 490 times, or even 77 times? Sadly, most of us operate by the rule "Burn me once, your fault; burn me twice, my fault." For most of us, it would be almost impossible to emotionally forgive someone who harms us

77 times—and even then it would have to be someone we care deeply about, such as a spouse, parent or child. With decisional forgiveness, the story is different. Even though it would be really hard, we could decide to forgive even someone who hurts us continually.

Emotional forgiveness is found in Scripture as well. Remember Jesus' parable of the lost son (Lk 15:11-32). The father shows the same kind of emotional forgiveness that characterizes God. We see the heart of the father in action. The younger son wounds the father deeply by saying, in essence, "I can't wait until you die. Give me my share of my inheritance now!" What an insult! Then the son squanders his inheritance on sinful living. He returns to the father hoping to work for him. Instead, the father grants decisional forgiveness. He cancels the debt that came from the son's insult. The father doesn't want work from his son because the debt is gone. The father wants father-son love. But the father also experiences emotional forgiveness. He has no resentment, bitterness, hostility, hatred, anger or fear—no unforgiveness toward the son. He replaced those emotions with agape love for his son, based on empathy, sympathy and compassion.

Our heavenly Father wants us to have this same forgiving heart. He wants us to forbear, to experience and grant decisional forgiveness quickly and to replace negative emotions with the positive emotions of love, empathy, sympathy and compassion for the person who harmed us. God *requires* decisional forgiveness of us; God *desires* emotional forgiveness.

When it comes to expressing forgiveness, however, we enter the social and societal realms. Expressing forgiveness has consequences. It can let people avoid responsibilities and create even more unjust relationships. Not expressing forgiveness also has consequences, which are no less potentially damaging to relationships and society. Unexpressed forgiveness can persuade an offender that saying "I'm sorry" or repenting doesn't matter. It can lead the offender to try to protect himself or herself against payback. Thus it might trigger preemptive attacks or emotional cutoff.

Expressing or not expressing forgiveness is a matter of how that expression fits with another social and societal concept—justice. Thus we must make wise decisions about what is or isn't just forgiveness. Reason can carry us part of the way. Social instinct can help. Empathy is very important. But spiritual discernment is essential.

How Are Forgiveness and Justice Related?

Forgiveness and justice are connected through the injustice gap. When people are wounded, they feel an injustice gap (refer to chapter one and figure 1.1). The injustice gap is experienced internally, but it is influenced by the social and societal context in which the transgression occurred and how people respond to it. But the size of my injustice gap depends on how much or how little personal justice I feel relative to the amount I want. If the person asks me for forgiveness, expresses sincere contrition, cries, wails and begs me to let them clean my toilets, then each of those actions increases the justice I feel, making it closer to what I desire. Thus, it narrows my injustice gap. (The toilet cleaning might actually push felt justice near to the top.) That means justice is intimately connected to forgiveness.

Forgiveness and justice are connected by personal emotions and motives. When I perceive some justice to have occurred, it makes me feel more righteous, more fulfilled. It makes me happier. My sense of desired justice is to some degree vindicated. As we saw in the previous chapter, justice—even if it is vengeful—activates reward pathways in the brain. Justice can also activate personal motives that make us want to forgive and not just pay back the offender.

Forgiving has benefits for physical health, mental health, relational and spiritual health.[2] Decisional forgiveness has minimal health effects. Most of the health benefits come through reducing our stress responses when we emotionally forgive. Mostly we reduce our risk for cardiovascular problems—strokes, heart attacks and arterial disease—and immune system problems. There are also mental health effects of forgiving. Loren Toussaint and Jon Webb have shown that these result mostly from reducing *rumination,* which is obsessing about grudges.[3] Rumination has been associated with many mental health disorders—depression, fear and anxiety, anger disorders, obsessive-compulsive disorders, and posttraumatic stress disorders. By granting decisional forgiveness and experiencing emotional forgiveness, we slow down if not stop rumination. Relational benefits can also be derived from forgiving. People who are forgiven usually do not continue to be defensively hostile. People who forgive are more open to improving their relationship. But it is expressing our forgiveness truthfully and sincerely that benefits relationships. Both decisional and emotional forgiveness will strengthen us to keep acting as forgiving people.

For Christians, the biggest benefits of forgiving are spiritual. Not only did God direct us to forgive, through the prayer and the follow-up teaching Jesus gave his disciples (Mt 6:12, 14-15), but forgiveness is simply good for our spirit. Forgiveness is difficult for anyone—Christian or not. If we do it, it is like strengthening our muscles. When we push against weights, we grow stronger physically. When we forgive wrongdoing, we grow stronger spiritually. Christians derive extra benefit. Because forgiveness is difficult, we turn to God. That helps us know and depend on him even more. Giving in to hate, bitterness and revenge is easier than forgiving. It is like eating cheesecake and sitting passively in front of the television. We may enjoy it, but it makes us flabby.

In many ways God makes it easier for Christians to forgive. He gives us scriptural words emphasizing that forgiveness is his word to us. Jesus in his humanity gave us the ultimate example of the human-divine, going to the cross that we may be forgiven. God gives us a community of like-minded believers to encourage us to forgive. And not least, he gives us his Holy Spirit, who lives within us. So we have inside help at forgiving.

Thus we see that we are motivated both by justice and forgiveness. If we take the easy route and satisfy our justice motive through revenge, we damage our spirits. But if we take the hard road and choose to forgive, we open our spirit to God's nutrients.

WHAT ROLE DOES HUMILITY PLAY?

It is easier to transcend the injustice gap and make a decision to forgive when we understand God's heart. That moves us to humility. At the human level, it is easier to forgive if we are not wrapped up in our own ego or in defending ourselves. It is also easier to forgive when we have the humility to see that we, too, may have offended. We are partly responsible. Finally, if we are humble, we are more likely to swallow our pride and express sincere forgiveness when we experience it internally.

God's heart of love revealed from the origin of humanity. God's heart of love has been evident from the beginning. When Adam and Eve sinned (Gen 3:6-7), they hurt God. God responded in love and mercy when he sacrificed an animal to clothe their nakedness (Gen 3:21). But God was also just (Gen 3:14-19). He pronounced the fulfillment of his law—Adam and Eve would be separated from the intimate fellowship of the Garden (Gen 3:23), and they would die (Gen 2:17; 3:22). From the beginning, both justice and mercy flowed from the Lord.

God's heart of love revealed throughout the Hebrew Scriptures. The Hebrew Scriptures have many notable examples of interpersonal forgiveness. Joseph forgave his brothers. David forgave Saul and others. Hosea forgave Gomer. But most attention is given to God's forgiveness of the people of Israel. In Exodus 34:6-7, which I quoted in chapter two, we find a passage that emphasizes God's love and mercy. This passage and variations of it are cited throughout the Hebrew Scriptures. As time passed and the day of Jesus' birth approached, God's mercy was emphasized more than justice.

God's heart of love revealed through the birth, life, death and resurrection of Jesus. When Jesus set aside his divinity and later gave up his life (Phil 2:5-8), he illustrated the unselfish, humble love at the center of Christianity. Jesus showed that God, motivated by love, initiates salvation for humans. Based on this divine initiation of love, Jesus advocated a radical personal and communal moral system, which transforms social relations—at least as Christianity has understood them.

God is the source of forgiveness. Within the Godhead, God the Father is characterized by justice and mercy. In Romans 11:22 Paul says, "Consider therefore the kindness and sternness of God: sternness to those who fell, but kindness to you, provided that you continue in his kindness. Otherwise, you also will be cut off." Transgressions violate trust and cause pain and anger. Throughout history, people have offended and hurt God the Father countless times. God's injustice gap—the gap between reconciliation with humans and all the pain inflicted by all of humanity—is huge. We are justly condemned to an eternity out of fellowship with the Godhead (Rom 3:23).

When Jesus died for humans as the propitiation for our sins, he paid the debt, satisfied the demands of the law and took our sins on him so we would be healed (Rom 3:24-25; Eph 5:2; Col 2:13-14; Heb 7:26-27; 10:12; 1 Jn 2:2). Jesus' death satisfied God's justice. By analogy, a murderer who dies through capital punishment fulfills the demands of the law. Justice is served. Yet the surviving family members of the murder victim are still in pain. Justice narrows the injustice gap but rarely closes it. Forgiveness can heal the pain within the injustice gap that justice alone did not reduce.

We don't know how this actually works with God. Scripture doesn't use scientific terms like "injustice gap." But it seems that the same might be true of God the Father. The just demands of the law were taken care of by Jesus' sacrificial, propitiatory death. God counted it as our righteousness (Rom 3:26; 5:9). Justice was served. It is reasonable to imagine that God was still in pain. But God the Father, through mercy, compassion and love (Jn 3:16) replaced holy anger with divine love. That was God the Father's emotional forgiveness. It came through and acted conjointly with Jesus' death. We are blessed (Rom 8:31-32). We have received the comfort of being forgiven, and we are thus motivated to give that comfort to others (2 Cor 1:3-7).

The Holy Spirit empowers us for mission and service. The Spirit gives gifts to those who become Christians (Rom 12:6; 1 Cor 12:4; 14:1; Eph 4:7; 1 Pet 4:10). The Holy Spirit promotes fellowship. He calls people into an adopted family and unites them into one body (1 Cor 12:27; Eph 4:4-6, 16; Col 1:18; 2:19).

Understanding and truly knowing God's heart can help us have the humility to forgive our family, our Christian brothers and sisters, our neighbors and even our enemies. While we were God's enemies, he forgave us (Rom 5:10). Can we have the humility to forgive like that?

Let's think about Simon Wiesenthal's difficulty in forgiving Karl and his challenge to Christians to consider whether we could forgive someone who had slaughtered our fellow Christians. Not long ago I had this conversation with a pastor whom I'll call Pastor Descantes. As we discussed Wiesenthal's dilemma, Pastor Descantes said, "We are admonished in Colossians 3:13 to forgive as God forgives."

"Yes," I said. "Let's look up the passage."

We read from verses 12 to 14, where Paul says, "Therefore, as God's chosen people, holy and dearly loved, clothe yourselves with compassion, kindness, humility, gentleness and patience. Bear with each other and forgive whatever grievances you may have against one another. Forgive as the Lord forgave you. And over all these virtues put on love, which binds them all together in perfect unity."

After reading it, I said, "From the context, Paul is not saying we should copy some process of divine forgiveness. Paul is talking about forgiving freely and in love."

"I think you are straying from the plain written word," he said. "This passage teaches that we don't have to forgive Karl. First, Paul was writing to Christians about forgiving other Christians. Karl wasn't a Christian. Second, even if it did apply, God forgives us when we repent. Karl may have said he was sorry, but he did not show repentance before God. I don't want to relax God's standards of requiring repentance. So we shouldn't have to forgive Karl."

I responded, "Are we only to forgive fellow Christians?" I pointed out that God through Jesus forgave each of us while we were yet sinners (Rom 5:6). And we have examples of Jesus forgiving people (e.g., Mt 9:2; Mk 2:5; Lk 5:20) and praying to God to forgive those who were crucifying him even when they were not believers (Lk 23:34).

Pastor Descantes was doubtful. "I'm not saying that we are not to forgive non-Christians. I'm saying that in Colossians God is telling Christians how to forgive other Christians."

"Are we only to forgive the truly repentant?" I asked.

"Yes," Pastor Descantes quickly jumped in. "Karl may not have been truly repentant—just scared or covering his bases. In no place in Simon's story does Karl confess to God or vow to renew his faith. He isn't repentant. He's only sorry. That isn't enough. If God won't forgive, I shouldn't have to."

"We don't know whether God forgave Karl," I said. "First, God is sovereign. He is a being not bound by time, like we frail creatures are. So even *before* people are repentant, God works in their heart to ready them for repentance, to bring people to them who will invite them to salvation, and to shepherd their salvation and their repentance for specific wrongdoing. We humans can do virtually none of these. If we wait for a person to be fully repentant for wrongdoing, we might simply not see the repentance, not recognize it even if we see it or not be privy to the person's heart."

"I'll grant you that," said Pastor Descantes. "We cannot know with certainty. But we must discern based on the person's behaviors."

"I disagree," I said. "Yes, we must make some discernments, but I believe we are called to forgive even if we discern that we should not trust a person. God is infinite and all-knowing. We are not. Thus Scripture makes it easy for us. It advocates unilateral forgiveness for all who wrong us. God does not want to put us in the role of being a judge of whether a person is truly repentant or not."

"Yes, we do disagree. I think we must discern a repentant heart before we forgive," said Pastor Descantes.

"Let me draw on the argument made by a friend of mine. David Stoop, a Christian marital and family therapist, teaches that God requires us to forgive.[4] We're held accountable if we don't forgive [Mt 6:12, 14-15; Lk 6:37-38]. If repentance of the offender were required before we could forgive, then *we* would not have our sins forgiven by God if the offender refused to repent. An angry offender could hold us hostage from God's blessing of forgiveness by refusing to repent of his or her wrongdoing. Forgiveness is based on humility. Humans cannot know the motives of the transgressor's heart. So the victim should be merciful and humble, willing to grant forgiveness without requiring repentance."

I continued, "In Luke 17:3-4, Jesus said, 'If your brother sins, rebuke him, and if he repents, forgive him. If he sins against you seven times in a day, and seven times comes back to you and says, "I repent," forgive him.'

This verse does not argue for required repentance. It simply doesn't say what to do if the offender doesn't repent. Based on the weight of New Testament Scriptures and the witness of Jesus' life, I say this: We must forgive anyway. Jesus did not mention an offender's repenting when he told Peter to forgive seventy-seven times [Mt 18:22]."

"But Luke 17 says, 'If he repents, forgive him,'" Pastor Descantes countered. "You tell me not to presume to know the offender's heart, and I agree with you there. Yet you seem to be presuming to know God's mind. The message of Scripture is that God forgives those who come to him humbly. Karl is not doing that—or doesn't seem to be."

"Yes, I agree. I don't know whether Karl is penitent. But I think the message of Scripture to us humans is to forgive regardless."

"That is another place we differ," said the pastor. "I think the plain words of Scripture are clear—'If he repents, forgive him.' You are reading something into Scripture that isn't there. We are to forgive like God forgives. God requires repentance. So should we."

Our conversation was pointed but was conducted with mutual respect. I'll leave it to you, the reader, to discern what God says to you about this.

Forgiving from the heart. We see decisional forgiveness in Jesus' parable of the unforgiving servant (Mt 18:23-35). A servant who owed a debt to the king received forgiveness based on mercy from the king. Afterward this servant was unwilling to grant decisional forgiveness to another servant who owed him a debt. The king responded to the servant's lack of mercy and agape love with severe punishment. He did not change his mind. He did not rescind his forgiveness. The abuse of the servant's debtor was a new affront to the king. Forgiveness happens within a context. Because the unforgiving servant had been forgiven so much, he should have granted decisional forgiveness quickly. Instead, he flew in the king's face. He showed that he could not make a decision to forgive—even the pittance owed him, even when he had been forgiven much. So he was punished severely because his new transgression was an affront to the king and effectively refused the king's mercy.

We are then told, "This is how my heavenly Father will treat each of you unless you forgive your brother *from your heart*" (italics mine). Note that in the context of the Bible, forgiving "from your heart" does not mean emotional forgiveness. Rather, it is closer to a heartfelt decision to forgive. The king was not upset because the unforgiving servant showed anger toward his debtor. We might even imagine that if the servant had released the debtor from his debt despite his anger, the king would have been satisfied. The king was upset because the unforgiving servant was not willing to change his behavior and release the debtor from his debt. It is the social and societal act, which reflects a lack of decisional forgiveness, that upset the king.

God wants us to have this same forgiving heart: to forbear hurts; to grant decisional forgiveness quickly, not grudgingly; and to replace negative emotions with the positive emotions of love, empathy, sympathy and compassion for the person who harmed us. God requires decisional forgiveness of us. God desires us to experience emotional forgiveness. Both are seen in Scripture.

Dealing with unforgiveness. All Christians are admonished to grant decisional forgiveness (Mt 6:12), but what if they cannot experience emotional forgiveness? If we can't dampen our hurt or anger completely, are we doomed to misery? No. People use many strategies to cope with negative emotions. Many of those strategies are consistent with Scripture. Only a few—such as revenge (Lev 19:18; Deut 32:35; Rom 12:19)—are explicitly forbidden.

We might simply accept the event and move on with our lives. Or we might turn judgment over to God and disavow our right to judge (Gen 18:25; Mt 7:1). Or we might convince ourselves that the transgression wasn't as harmful as we had thought. For example, instead of holding a grudge against his brothers, Joseph said, "You intended to harm me, but God intended it for good to accomplish what is now being done, the saving of many lives" (Gen 50:20). Learning that a person's actions, which we had assumed were wrong, were in fact just and fair can also reduce unforgiveness, just as learning of mitigating circumstances behind a wrongdoer's actions can help us forgive. Or we might just forget with the passage of time.

Forbearance is the inhibition of initial revenge and avoidance motivations. When we forbear, we consciously try to squelch unforgiveness or not to act in anger or vengeance. Forbearance is scriptural. It is not the same as forgiveness. It involves squelching anger (Ps 4:4; Eph 4:26). Paul contrasts forgiving and forbearing within the same passage (in Col 3:13 RSV; Eph 4:1-3). Forbearance takes its toll. It is hard work to control negative emotions and behavior. It can use up our energy. Forbearance also usually leaves resentment smoldering beneath the surface, ready to burst into flames if the person hurts us again.

We might also seek justice to reduce the injustice gap. Forgiveness and justice sometimes seem to clash, but they can also work together. Justice is certainly consistent with Scripture: "It is unthinkable that God would do wrong, that the Almighty would pervert justice" (Job 34:12). Further, Scripture says, "This is what the LORD says: 'Maintain justice and do what is right, for my salvation is close at hand and my righteousness will soon be revealed. Blessed is the man who does this'" (Is 56:1-2). The prophet Amos says, "Let justice roll on like a river, righteousness like a never-failing stream!" (Amos 5:24). Other passages abound (Deut 16:20; Is 56:1; Mt 7:1-5).

So we might reduce our feelings of unforgiveness by seeing justice enacted by the courts. For example, if we see that a court has convicted and punished a criminal offender, then justice reduces the injustice gap. Emotional unforgiveness can subside. If a person observes ironic natural consequences or believes that God has punished an offender (e.g., Acts 5:1-11), then observing natural or divine justice also reduces the injustice gap. In each case, unforgiveness is reduced even though emotional forgiveness does not occur.

Personal justice can also reduce unforgiveness. I'm not talking about personal revenge but what the transgressor can do to make things right. When one person transgresses against another, the transgressor essentially says, "I'm superior to you. I can wound you and get away with it." If a transgressor tries to balance the emotional books through confessing, repenting, expressing regret, apologizing sincerely, offering restitution or punitive damages, or making amends, then the victim perceives more personal justice. Unforgiveness is reduced. We are more likely to forgive.

PRACTICING FORGIVENESS EVEN WHEN IT'S HARD

Whether or not people experience emotional forgiveness and peace is affected by many things, as I illustrate in figure 4.1. How easy it is to forgive depends on the size of the injustice gap. If we can narrow the injustice gap, we can lessen negative unforgiving emotions. As negative emotions subside, they are more easily neutralized by positive, other-oriented emotions. Emotional forgiveness is more likely.

The crux of figure 4.1 is that group motives may move us either to decide to forgive or to forbear, and personal motives may move us to emotionally forgive as well. Forbearance and decisional forgiveness affect each other (see the bidirectional arrow) because they suppress negative emotions and behaviors, respectively. Either or both can lead to emotional forgiveness, which can result in personal peace. It is possible that forbearance can lead to acceptance and (through acceptance) also to personal peace, but forbearance could result in rumination, which will not lead to personal peace. In short, there are several pathways to personal peace, and experiencing emotional forgiveness is one of the most certain.

Christians accept the importance of forgiveness and practice it. Forgiveness is at the center of Christianity. God, out of mercy and lovingkindness, forgives through Jesus' death on the cross. When people respond in gratitude to having been forgiven by God, part of their natural response is to forgive those who have harmed them. Almost all people can forgive family and friends who hurt them—especially when it is in their own best interests to do so. But following Jesus' instruction, example and commands—out of gratitude for what God has done for us—we Christians are to forgive even our enemies. That idea challenges us, and it absolutely befuddles the non-Christian world.

Christians respond out of a changed spirit and thus experience changed emotions and motivations. Love is the Christian's response to God's love. Jesus boiled down the essence of the law into two summary

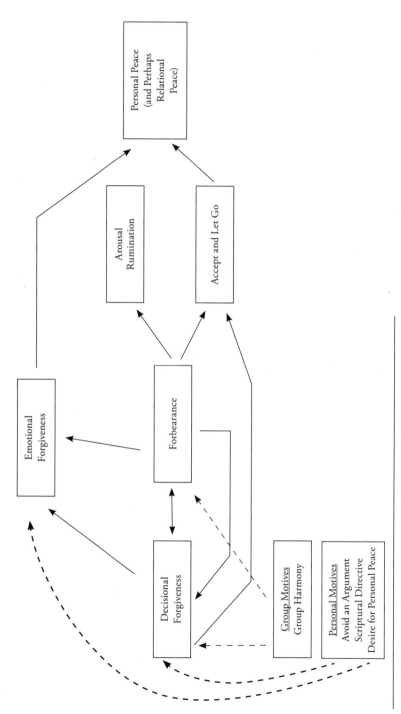

Figure 4.1. Decisional forgiveness, emotional forgiveness, forbearance and peace

commandments: "'Love the Lord your God with all your heart and with all your soul and with all your mind.' This is the first and greatest commandment. And the second is like it: 'Love your neighbor as yourself.' All the Law and the Prophets hang on these two commandments" (Mt 22:37-40; see also Mk 12:28-34). Christianity also emphasizes humility (Phil 2:1-11). Peter counted humility as a cardinal virtue, saying, "Finally, all of you, . . . be compassionate and humble. Do not repay evil with evil or insult with insult, but with blessing, because to this you were called so that you may inherit a blessing" (1 Pet 3:8-9). God is forgiving (Ex 34:6-7). He is merciful. In response, we are also to be forgiving.

Why doesn't our experience match our theology of triumphant forgiveness? Christians have experienced God's mercy and grace. God freely gave Jesus to die for us (Rom 5:1; Col 2:13-14). Having received such gifts from God, Christians should be ever merciful and quick to forgive. We *should* be, but too often we are not. Our experience is more in line with Peter's when he whined to Jesus, "Lord, how many times shall I forgive my brother when he sins against me?" (Mt 18:21). Our inability to live up to our high calling to be forgiving people can motivate us to react in several ways. We might fool ourselves into believing that forgiveness isn't important. We might quickly say that we forgive but never really release grudges. We might work to forgive, but do so in the flesh, so we can say, "Look what I have done!" Or we might work sincerely and diligently to forgive because we want to be transformed by the renewal of our minds (Rom 12:2). Clearly, we *should* cultivate the final response. Yet how do we rely totally on Jesus and still work conscientiously to forgive?

Our effort and striving alone are not sufficient. A movie titled *The Mission* captured well the essence of forgiveness. Rodrigo Mendoza (played by Robert de Niro) was a slave trader in South America. When he got in a fight with his brother and killed him with a knife, Rodrigo finally repented of his sins. Father Gabriel, head of the mission serving the Indian tribe from whom Rodrigo had been taking slaves for years, offered him a journey in penance. As part of this journey, Rodrigo dragged a bag of heavy Spanish armor to the top of the waterfall near where the Indian tribe lived. The Indians spotted Rodrigo as he collapsed to his knees under the weight of his burden and the depressive knowledge that all his suffering was not enough to cover his guilt. So he awaited his deserved death at the hands of the Indians. The chief motioned, and a warrior rushed toward Rodrigo with a knife. He jerked back Rodrigo's head—and then slashed the rope tied to the bag of armor, kicking Rodrigo's burden over the cliff, where it was covered by the clear, fresh water below. Rodrigo collapsed in the joy of freedom. He could not work his own forgiveness. He could never repair the injustices he had done. Someone else had to grant him forgiveness. Forgiveness cannot be grasped by hands clenched in effort but only by an on-your-knees, openhanded attitude receptive to mercy, grace and love. Forgiveness burst upon Rodrigo as a surprise. In the end, forgiveness is a gift of mercy, grace and love. There is a place for both justice and human effort, but striving can take us only so far.

We cooperate with the Lord. We have a part, and so does God. Our part is to try to understand forgiveness, discern when we need to practice it and admit the limitations of our own self-effort. In our own power, we are incapable of truly forgiving in a spiritually meaningful way. Through Jesus' work applied to us, though, God can do remarkable things. He can work forgiveness through us. Two verses capture this dilemma: "I [Jesus] am the vine; you are the branches. If a man remains in me and I in him, he will bear much fruit; apart from me you can do nothing" (Jn 15:5). Yet, "I can do everything through him who gives me strength" (Phil 4:13).

We put off unforgiveness and put on forgiveness. Christians do not forgive because it is easy—it isn't. Christians forgive because it is right and because we are responding to God's love and forgiveness of us. Christians believe that with the fall of humanity, things became abnormal. Humans can no longer let nature take its course. Instead, we battle the principle of sin. When we are transgressed against, we must fight unforgiveness. We cannot give in to our natural inclination toward emotions of resentment, bitterness and hatred, and motivations of avoidance and revenge. Evolutionary accounts of forgiveness and revenge argue that both are adaptive to survival. What is adaptive, however, is not necessarily good. "Might makes right" is adaptive, yet it is not right in God's sight.

We put off this old, sinful nature by fighting against it (Rom 6:1-4, 12-14; Gal 5:19-21; Col 3:5-11). We likewise must forbear, forgive and seek justice. By doing so, we put on a new, redeemed nature (Rom 6:5-11, 17-19; Gal 5:22-26; Col 3:12-17). This battle is not winnable by independent human effort (Rom 7:14-24). We can only win by cooperating with God (Rom 7:25–8:11; Eph 2:8-10; Phil 2:12-13).

Chris Carrier was abducted at ten years old.[5] His abductor took him to a remote location in Florida, where he repeatedly stabbed him with an ice pick in the chest and abdomen. When Chris's cries finally got to the man, he told Chris he would take him home. He lied. Instead, he shot Chris in the head. Chris woke up hours later with a headache and without the eye destroyed by the bullet. He made his way from the swamp to a road, where a Good Samaritan eventually stopped and took him to the hospital.

Years later Chris was working as a youth pastor. A police officer came to Chris and told him, "The man we think abducted you is dying. We have no evidence to bring him to justice, but it isn't right that he should die without being confronted for his crime against you. Will you come and see him?"

When Chris walked into the dying man's room, he recognized him. Chris's Christian values outweighed his natural sense of vengeance. Chris helped care for this man during his final weeks of life. There is no greater love a human can have than this.

FORGIVENESS IN CONTEXT

Forgiveness does not happen in a vacuum. It happens in the midst of conversation, accusation, distraction, interaction and inaction. The social and societal contexts can make or break forgiveness. Let's look at those contexts as illustrated in figure 4.2, where I have summarized them, taking into account everything in this chapter (and more). On the left side of the figure, the levels of forgiveness are indicated: divine forgiveness, individual forgiveness (decisional and emotional) and relational forgiveness (so-

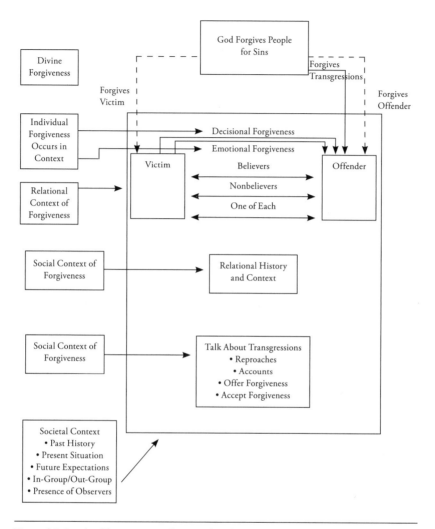

Figure 4.2. Levels of forgiveness and its social and societal contexts

cial and societal). On the right side of the figure, we see the interactions around forgiveness. God is the supreme forgiver of both victim and offender. At the interpersonal level, the victim might or might not decisionally and emotionally forgive the offender, depending on social and societal contexts. The contexts might trigger attention to internal and external structures and processes and bring about forgiveness. Or triggers might direct attention away from forgiveness.

Forgiveness occurs within our skin, but it always occurs in some relational context. We must not confuse the context with forgiveness. But we cannot ignore the context if we are to understand forgiveness and if we are to forgive.

My friends and professional colleagues Steve Sandage and Mike McCullough worked with me to build a model of relational spirituality and forgiveness (see figure 4.3), based on theology that LeRon Shults and Steve Sandage developed in their book *Transforming Spirituality*.[6] I have begun to study this model scientifically with my colleagues Donnie Davis and Joshua Hook.[7] In figure 4.3, each of the parts is labeled with letters: *V* for victim, *O* for offender, *T* for transgression, *S* for the Sacred. This also allows me to discuss the importance of the relationships between each part: *OS, VS, TS, VO, VT* and *OT.*

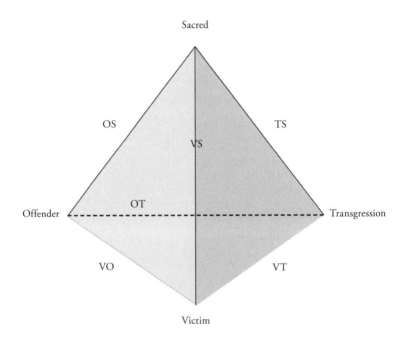

Figure 4.3. Spiritual appraisals of relationship in the model of relational spirituality and forgiveness

Let's use the model to consider a particular offense. Let's say that I treated one of my daughters, Becca, unfairly because she got in trouble at school. Becca's teacher phoned, saying Becca had talked back to her and had been generally disruptive in class. I didn't listen to Becca's side of the story, though as it turned out, she had reacted strongly to some medication that made her hyperactive. Instead I jumped to the conclusion that the teacher (a responsible adult authority, I assumed) was correct and that my daughter was wrong. So I punished Becca. I restricted her free time for a week and required her to write a long essay about why she should obey her teacher.

Note that perspective is all-important here. From Becca's perspective, she was the victim of unfair punishment. She felt victimized. But from my perspective, I felt that Becca had betrayed my trust and that I was the victim. We both must deal with these different perceptions at the same time. For simplicity, I'll discuss only my own experience, in which I am the victim (V) and Becca is the offender (O).

However, at the interpersonal level, my daughter is not just an offender and I am not just an innocent victim who unselfishly sacrifices to raise a Christian daughter (and this is the thanks I get—betrayal of my basic values!). We are each individuals, but we are not isolated. We share beliefs and values, histories and memories. We have a relationship, and the nature of the relationship conditions how we act. In this case our relationship (VO) is loving. But that love shows up in many ways. Sometimes it is pure, but sometimes my love is mixed with fear or embarrassment, as in this example, and I make mistakes. Imagine how things might have gone if our relationship were characterized primarily by judgment, anger and mistrust instead of love. I might have grounded her for life or taken away her library card and burned it in a public ceremony.

Added into the mix is the transgression (T). In Becca's first five years of school, she has never been in trouble. So her transgression is a one-off event.

What would have happened if my relationship to the transgression (VT) was loaded with emotional baggage from my own past? Suppose that in elementary school I had a buddy who hit me—as I remember it, he had a biker jacket and a "Born to Kill" tattoo—knocking out one of my teeth. Yet the teacher had a boys-will-be-boys attitude, so she didn't punish him. I have stewed about this injustice for years. In this case my reaction to Becca's alleged misbehavior might be quite harsh. Psychologically (and unconsciously) I would be retaliating for an injustice I experienced forty years ago.

Becca also has a relationship to the transgression (OT). For her, it was random. She didn't even understand her own misbehavior. It was the medication that made her hyper.

As a Christian, I hold God to be Sacred (S), and thus, I have a personal relationship with God (represented as VS, the relationship between the victim and the Sacred). My relationship with God is complex, similar to any relationship between humans. At times I feel closeness and intimacy, and at times distance and alienation. At times justice comes to the fore, and at times mercy is important. The nature of my current relationship with God will probably strongly influence my reaction to Becca. If I am distant and angry with God or feel that God has wronged me, I might punish Becca harshly because my sense of injustice flows over into my relationship with her. If I feel close to God, I might be merciful toward Becca.

The relationship between the transgression and the Sacred (TS) is also important. If I see Becca's rebellion as a spiritual problem, it will have added significance for me as a Christian. I will want to deal decisively with the problem, lest Becca grow up without respect for authority, which I might see as a spiritual danger for her. But if I see Becca's troublemaking as a normal rite of passage, I might not even feel that I must punish her.

I have saved until last the victim's perception of the offender's relationship with the Sacred (OS). This relationship is extremely important later in the book, when we look at forgiveness in social and societal settings. It is not so crucial within the family because there people usually share common relationships with God. When they do differ, however, forgiving can be difficult. The OS relationship is especially important when we see the offender as not having the same faith we do. This can be true even in the church. I have seen pitched battles between people in the same congregation over what is or isn't scripturally consistent behavior. Church members and lifetime friends can characterize the opposition as not having a right relationship with God. I have heard people say, "You are a heretic," because the other person believes in women elders, supports the war in Iraq or does not support an amendment to the Constitution to reverse *Roe v. Wade*. If we turn people into "enemies," then we feel okay about not treating them as brothers and sisters.

OS is not the actual relationship that the offender has with God; another person cannot know that. OS is the victim's perception of the offender's relationship with God, and especially how that relationship compares to the victim's own.

Back to our example. I perceive Becca as having a child's version of my relationship with God (OS). So if I think she betrayed me, it really hurts me. The closer the similarity in spiritual relationship that I perceive between the offender and me, the more I feel betrayed and hurt by her transgression. However, because I perceive Becca's relationship to God as similar to my own, I will also forgive her more quickly than I might forgive someone totally alien to God.

Let's use the same model to look at Simon Wiesenthal's situation. Simon (V) was a Jew (VS). As far as Simon can tell, Karl (O) was a fallen Christian (OS). Certainly Karl was in a very different place spiritually than Simon (the perception of the offender's relationship to the Sacred is very different). The OS relationship screams at Simon, "Don't forgive!"

Karl confessed to killing other Jews. As Jews would understand it, this is the ultimate sin. Karl is trying to completely kill God's people, Israel (TS, Simon's understanding of the relationship of the transgression and the Sacred). The TS relationship lines up with the SO.

Simon might have had enormous empathy and compassion for Karl (VO). After all, Karl was suffering terminal burns. Even on his deathbed, he was troubled about the murders he had committed. He felt guilt, contrition, shame and suffering for his transgressions (OT). But despite Simon's likely empathy and compassion for Karl, Simon's spiritual considerations (i.e., VS, OS and TS) apparently dominated. Decisional forgiveness was not triggered in Simon. Even if Simon could forgive Karl internally, he certainly did not believe he should express that forgiveness. He felt little emotional forgiveness. Instead, he felt spiritual separation from Karl and his transgressions. Simon walked away from penitent Karl in silence.

Let's stop and summarize. Forgiveness is something that we base on God's forgiveness of humans. We forgive freely yet also pursue justice. We can only keep forgiveness and justice in balance in the humility of understanding who we are in Christ.

We pursue a humble and just forgiveness in relational contexts—social and societal. If we keep these distinctions between experiences of forgiveness and the context in which they occur clear, we will think and act more consistently when we are trying to experience healing from a transgression and perhaps trying to reconcile with an offender.

5

DEALING WITH WRONGDOERS

FORGIVENESS IS INTIMATELY INTERTWINED with justice. Divine, personal, social and societal levels of justice provide contexts within which we forgive. It is through humility that we can reconcile forgiveness and justice. A just forgiveness requires us to take wrongdoers seriously.

Let's say Pastor Ted is unfaithful with Mildred, the church secretary with whom he works daily. His service as pastor has been stellar for twenty years. What should the congregation do? Are twenty years of faithful, dedicated Christian service negated by an hour of indiscretion? Is that justice? Should the congregation simply forgive and forget? Should they fire Pastor Ted so he can move to a new location and start a new pastorate? Would that fly in the face of guidelines for church discipline? The congregation might be shirking its responsibility to restore the pastor to good graces. From Pastor Ted's perspective, whatever happens will probably seem too harsh. It will be hard for him to forgive those who punish him.

Of course, different members of the congregation have different relationships with Pastor Ted and different expectations of him. The couple Pastor Ted was counseling about their troubled marriage will be devastated. The head of the worship committee, who had lunch with Pastor Ted each Tuesday to plan the service, will be shocked. Mildred, who grew up in the church and lived in the community for thirty-eight years, feels like her life has been ruined. She believes Pastor Ted seduced and manipulated her into having sex. She cannot forgive him. Pastor Ted thinks the sexual encounter "just happened" because they spent too much time together without anyone else around. What about Pastor Ted's wife, Suzanne? Should she forgive? Under what circumstances? Must Pastor Ted make some reparations to Suzanne before reconciliation between them can be achieved?

Pastor Ted is remorseful. He can't seem to kick constant self-recriminations. To whom can he confess? Is this just between him and God?

In this chapter we examine how people can deal with wrongdoers in ways that lead to healing. Sometimes wrongdoers are intimates, sometimes they are almost strangers. At still other times, people need to figure out how to deal with their own wrongdoing. Guilt and remorse might be interfering with healing and also might be barriers preventing the one who was harmed from forgiving. The central question is this: Can people reconcile? To answer that question and learn how to follow through to healing acts, we need to consider how people talk about transgressions and how we deal with our own sin.

Thus far I have described the tension between justice and forgiveness (both decisional and emotional). We've said that humility helps to resolve the tension. But seeing God as sovereign can be difficult. If we do, though, we get a sense that we are not the center of the universe. That helps us consider how we can seek justice and yet also forgive. We have drives for both justice and forgiveness. While the two can come into conflict, usually they do not have to. Humility helps us seek justice without placing ourselves in a position of a godlike judge of the person who offends or hurts us. Humility helps us understand that we can pursue justice until we are satisfied, but if we become satisfied, rarely will the other person be satisfied. Two people's injustice gaps cannot both be closed at the same time by justice alone (see chapter three).

Forgiveness helps us transcend the injustice gap (see chapters two and four). It takes away the unrelenting pressure that the injustice exerts on us. Deciding to forgive is what God requires of us. Experiencing the personal peace of emotional forgiveness is what God desires for us.

Because our forgiveness, which is internal, depends on divine, relational, social and societal contexts (refer to figure 4.2), we want to restore social and societal balance if we can. Restoring a just community after wrongdoing requires that the parties do three things: First, they must develop or activate a sense of humility before God. Second, they must act in love to restore as much justice as possible. Third, they must decide to forgive and experience emotional forgiveness. Doing these three things allows people in conflict to reach peace, to pursue the resolution of past injustices that have not been adequately dealt with and to set up structures that prevent future problems. It is this third aspect we now examine—how to forgive.

THE FIVE STEPS TO REACH FORGIVENESS

During the last twenty years I have developed a five-step method that people worldwide have used to forgive faster and more deeply than they could before.[1] My many collaborators and I have found it to be effective when applied in groups, by counselors with individuals or couples and even with individuals who use a workbook or read about it. Both Christians and nonbelievers have used it effectively, as we have shown in several controlled psychological studies.[2]

People learn five steps to REACH forgiveness. You can learn the steps quickly, but to forgive, you must apply them repeatedly and often. You must not let your memory of a transgression trigger only old pain and perhaps resentment and rumination; you must let your memory of the transgression trigger your memory of the five steps. And—this is the hard part—you must apply the method until you REACH forgiveness. Then, tomorrow or next week, if painful memories occur again, trigger the five steps to REACH forgiveness again.

The five steps are not magical. In fact, they are merely a mold into which God pours forgiveness. Once the God-initiated forgiveness solidifies, you can throw away the mold. It is hard to build a sandcastle at the beach without a mold, even though I have wet sand. I can do it, but it's hard. Similarly, I can forgive without the five steps to REACH forgiveness. But it is easier if I use them.

The five steps to REACH forgiveness are rooted in replacing negative emotions associated with anger, fear and unforgiveness with positive emotions associated with empathy (and perhaps sympathy, love, compassion or even romantic love). First, remember that decisional forgiveness requires a decision to forgive. So it is helpful to decide to forgive and sincerely follow through, even though emotional peace will take more time than merely making a decision. Even if someone has not firmly decided to forgive, however, he or she can still learn emotional forgiveness using the five steps. Experiencing some relief of negative emotions can free people to make the decision to forgive.

Here is an exercise that helps people grant decisional forgiveness. If you are struggling with a hurt you cannot let go of, try this yourself. Stand up and extend your arms out in front of you. Cup your hands together, as if you were holding a bird captive in them. Imagine that this is the memory of the harm and all of the attached bad feelings. Because you don't want those feelings to attack you, hold them tightly and keep your tightly closed hands as far from you as possible. As you hold your arms outstretched for as long as you can, you feel the weight of those negative feelings dragging you down. You feel the heaviness they create in your arms and shoulders. The grudge you feel is a weight that pulls you down. It can even put you at risk for ill health. As you continue to hold your arms outstretched with your hands cupped together, imagine the grudge struggling for release, like a captive bird. When you are ready, open your hands, let the grudge go and drop your arms to your sides. Make a decision to forgive, and imagine the grudge flying off, circling the room and escaping outside. Tell yourself that you want to forgive, that you do not want to act bitterly or angrily toward the person who hurt you. You want to start over, to break the old patterns of behavior in which you have been trapped and to give the person the benefit of the doubt. God gave you a new heart and a clean slate when you became a new creation (2 Cor 5:17). Similarly, you want to give the person who hurt you a clean heart and a clean slate.

Now you are ready to begin the hard work of emotional forgiveness. You will follow five steps to REACH forgiveness. Walk with me through the five steps.

R—Recall the hurt. When we are hurt, we often try to protect ourselves by denying our hurt. To heal, we must recall the hurt as objectively as we can. Don't rail against the person who hurt you. Don't expend fruitless effort in finger-wagging. Don't waste time wishing for an apology that will never be offered. Don't dwell on your victimization. Instead, admit that a wrong was done to you. Then try to do something really difficult— try to see the situation from the other person's point of view.

E—Empathize. Empathy is seeing things from another person's point of view. It puts a human face on suffering. To forgive, try to feel the transgressor's feelings. Even though it is difficult, try to identify with the pressures that made the person hurt you. How would he or she explain the harmful acts? Empathy is only one of the emotions you can use to reduce a grudge. You can also sympathize with, feel compassion for, experience agape love toward or kindle romantic love for the transgressor. Each of these can help you replace the unforgiveness. You might not want to see things from the point of view of the one who harmed you, but if you can, over time it will bring you the peace of emotional forgiveness.

To feel empathy, try an "empty chair" dialogue. Pretend the person who hurt you is sitting in an empty chair next to you. Tell the person of your hurt, of the consequences, of the pain you experienced. Then move to the empty chair and imagine yourself as the offender. Tell your side of the story. As the offender, you probably did not intend to do harm. What were you thinking, feeling or trying to accomplish that ended up being offensive and hurtful? After pouring your heart out as the offender, change back to your original chair and respond. Keep the conversation going until there is little left to say. If empathy is walking in another person's shoes for a mile, it is also sitting in another person's chair for a few minutes.

A—Altruistic gift of forgiveness. Have you ever harmed or offended a friend, parent or partner who later forgave you? Think about your guilt. Then consider how you felt when you were forgiven. As you remember how you felt when you were forgiven—free, light or unburdened—you might be more willing to give a selfless gift of forgiveness to the one who hurt you.

C—Commit publicly to forgive in a way that can be observed. If you make your forgiveness public, you are less likely to doubt it later. You don't need a crowd of observers. You can be the only observer if you wish. Write it down in a letter: *Today I forgive [name of your offender].* Make yourself a certificate of forgiveness. Or involve other observers: Tell a friend, partner or counselor that you have forgiven the person who hurt you.

H—Hold on to forgiveness. When you doubt whether you have forgiven the offender, there are many ways to stop forgiveness from slipping away. One of those is to read the letter or certificate you wrote during the commitment stage.

PUTTING THE MODEL TO REACH FORGIVENESS INTO PRACTICE

Knowing that you must take five giant steps to forgive is not the same as knowing how to take those steps. You will forgive best if you identify specific people you want to forgive. Think back through your life. You can probably remember at least ten old grudges that you haven't thought about for a while, but when you do, you still get upset. Then practice trying to forgive each person. Apply the five steps to REACH forgiveness to one person at a time. Pray for the people. Imagine showering them with blessings. Imagine naming each person's good qualities without allowing yourself to indulge in criticism or judgment. Identify ways you could show love to each person.

Transgressions can occur in almost any setting, but some settings seem to invite transgressions. Consider your past or present romantic relationships. They put egos on the line. Is there a romantic partner you want to forgive? Consider your family of origin or other families that you have been in as you grew up. People in your workplace can offend—often repeating offenses over a period of years. The church, too, is not free of offenses. Society is full of offenses with roots in ethnic, class and cultural differences. Note some specific transgressions. Remember, forgiveness occurs one transgression at a time.

Now that you have considered several areas in which you might harbor unforgiveness, recall several specific incidents that you want to try to forgive. For each incident, ask yourself these questions:

How serious is the transgression? Small transgressions annoy us. Large ones can turn our world upside down. Put off trying to forgive those that upset your world until you have gained confidence with smaller hurts.

How raw is the wound? Don't choose wounds to forgive where the blood is oozing or the bleeding is still fresh.

Is the person you want to forgive absent from or present in your life? In an ongoing relationship, the offending person will react to what you do. He or she can deliberately or accidentally hurt you again, which can compound unforgiveness.

Try to think of at least two people whom you can practice forgiving. If you can think of four or more, even better. You will have the most success if you think of a specific incident in each case. Now try to forgive each of those hurts. Remember, you can't forgive in the abstract. Forgiveness occurs when you work through *specific events with specific people*. For each incident, you may find it most helpful to write a short account of the offense. Some anger and hurt may resurface as you write. Then work on forgiving. Try to decide to forgive by standing and releasing the grudge from your outstretched hands, as I described earlier. Then move deliberately through the five steps to REACH forgiveness. (Test your memory. Can you recall what each of the letters in REACH stands for? If not, look back and review. How did you do?) Think through the five steps to REACH forgiveness with each remembered hurt in turn.

RECONCILIATION

We are hard-wired for both justice and forgiveness.[3] In any relationship and in any particular situation within the relationship, it is the circumstances that determine which aspect of our being dominates. Even the most God-loving, gentle person can be provoked to angry retaliation by someone who acts obnoxiously enough for long enough if there is no prospect of escape. Even the biggest, baddest bully can be softened if something evokes a tender memory of a loved one or turns on his or her generosity or altruism gene by acting vulnerable.

What are the conditions that tend to turn on a forgiving spirit instead of an avenging spirit? McCullough identifies three conditions, which humans may even share with other nonhuman primates.[4] First, people want to forgive if they believe the offender is no longer dangerous and is unlikely to inflict more harm. Second, they want to forgive more often if the relationship is valued. Third, they want to forgive more often if they conclude that the offender is worthy of their care.

Let's take a look at chimpanzees (yes, they're a long stretch from humans). Within a normal chimpanzee troop, many conflicts occur. There are squabbles over hierarchy. Usually a chimpanzee troop has a well-defined pecking order. Frans du Waal, director of Emory University's Yerkes Primate Center, describes a time when the top spot in that particular troop was up for grabs.[5] Yaroen, the longtime alpha male, had become too old to defend his top position against the aggressive and nasty Luit. So Yaroen made an alliance with Nikkie, who was number three in the pecking order. Yaroen traded some sexual access to the females for Nikkie's help. Together Yaroen and Nikkie kept Luit in line.

When Yaroen and Nikkie had a falling out, though, Luit dominated. He was an unpopular alpha male—a mean tyrant and bully. His dominance lasted a few weeks until Yaroen and Nikkie patched up their differences. The night the alliance was repaired was fatal for Luit. Yaroen and Nikkie attacked him in his sleep, castrated him and chased him through the compound until he bled to death. Yaroen and Nikkie were willing to reconcile because they were valuable to each other.

Primates have clear reconciliation rituals. When two chimps have a conflict, the lower status chimp will usually initiate reconciliation. A pant-grunt says, "Okay, you win. You are bigger and stronger than I am. Can we be friends again?" The higher status chimp usually responds by allowing itself to be groomed. The pant-grunt display of submission not only signals that safety can be expected, it also promises the grooming. Grooming lowers the higher status male's blood pressure. The lower status male thus becomes more worthy of the higher status male's care.

Humans also have unique signals that can calm conflict and stimulate reconciliation. Forgiveness, if it occurs, happens in interpersonal contexts (recall figure 4.2). Forgiveness depends on (1) a person's beliefs, values and other mental structures (such as memories, goals, expectations, etc.); (2) well-practiced, often automatic processes of thought or action; and (3) situational triggers that can activate the person's beliefs, values, mental structures, and habitual thought and action processes. Thus there are structures in people's minds and physical and psychological environments. A dynamic, ever changing process keeps shifting people's attention.

Let's look at an example. Sue has hurt the feelings of her sister, Aleta. Sue says she is sorry. Aleta recalls her mother, who always said she was sorry but continued to abuse Aleta. So Aleta says, "Yeah, right." Sue feels rejected but perseveres, saying, "How can I make it up to you?" The interactions flow back and forth. Some interactions trigger thoughts, feelings and actions that push Sue and Aleta closer. Others drive yet another wedge between them.

I have identified four steps in reconciliation: decide, discuss, detoxify and devote. I explain each thoroughly in my book *Forgiving and Reconciling,*[6] and we'll go into more detail in chapter six. Here is a capsule summary.

Decide. Decisions are needed to move down the path toward reconciliation. We must decide whether, how and when to reconcile. Reconciliation is something God desires but does not explicitly require.

Reconciliation is voluntary. Not even God will reconcile with everyone. He will not reconcile with Satan or his followers. God does not make our reconciliation with any person sacred. Thus we do not have to reconcile. Generally God wants people to reconcile, especially with other believers. However, the Israelites were directed not to reconcile with various nonbelievers or worshipers of false gods. It might not be safe, prudent or possible to reconcile with others. For example, if a person has sworn to kill me, God doesn't generally want me to attempt reconciliation. Under rare circumstances we may be directed by God toward such reconciliation, but generally speaking we are not directed to pursue unsafe reconciliations. In other cases, reconciliation might be safe, but it could lead us into compromising alliances or coalitions. When Hitler and the Nazis occupied France in World War II, some of the French collaborated with the German occupying troops, which compromised their integrity. In some cases, it simply is impossible to reconcile. If a person who harmed us has moved away, lost touch or died, reconciliation is not possible. Note also that successful reconciliation might still mean that we each go our separate ways.

Once we decide that we want to reconcile, we must make additional decisions. To what degree do we want to discuss the reconciliation head-on versus just act as if we have put the matter behind us and hope the other person does the same? Also, we must decide when we want to start moving toward reconciliation. Initiating a discussion when our partner is stressed and frazzled might doom it to failure from the outset. Waiting a week may mean things have gotten out of hand. We need discernment to make the best decision possible.

Discuss. Situational triggers can motivate people toward forgiving, grudge holding or vengeance. These triggers alert us to structures that occupy our attention. For instance, suppose I work for a corporation whose corporate values specify that "We strive to treat each other with dignity." This slogan is posted above the door where employees enter work. If I have a serious falling out with my coworker Beth, my efforts at reconciliation depend on the structures and processes that capture my attention. I could be affected profoundly by the sign posted at the entrance to the building. It might make me want to live up to its noble aspiration.

However, other triggers alert us to different structures—some that compete with and others that reinforce the desire to reconcile. Perhaps Beth cops an attitude. Every sight or sound of her is a provocation to anger. Mental triggers—like remembering a workplace feud in my past—could fire me up. Spiritual triggers—like praying for her in my morning devotional time—might help.

One set of crucial processes includes the way we discuss the transgressions. If I ask Beth for an explanation of her wrong behavior, I can do so with grace or harshness. "How could you be so cruel?" is a nonstarter. It will close off possible reconciliation from the outset. Or I might say, "Usually you are so diplomatic. I was really surprised at how angry you seemed. Can you help me understand?" The second approach is more likely to lead to a productive talk. It doesn't blame, and it even asks for help. These are called reproaches, and they can be harsh or graceful.

When we reproach someone we believe has harmed us, the person will usually give an *account*. Beth could say, "To heck with you!" That would be a *denial* or refusal. It doesn't admit wrongdoing and abruptly shuts off further talk. She could say, "I said those hurtful things to our boss because you insulted me in the board meeting yesterday." This is a *justification*. It blames or says, "I had a great reason for doing or saying what I did." An *excuse* gives mitigating reasons for behaving wrongfully: "Yes, I said hurtful things, but it was because I had a migraine." The best account for leading to reconciliation is a *concession* or confession. It admits wrongdoing, shows regret, apologizes and offers restitution. It thus takes justice seriously by offering restitution, and it exemplifies humility in admitting wrongdoing, showing regret and apologizing. It is a humble, just concession. It also asks, "Can you forgive me?"

When one person asks for forgiveness, the other might say no; not now; maybe; yes, but later; or yes, now. "No" closes doors. "Not now" says, "I hurt too much and don't want to consider it now. I might in the future." "Maybe" says, "I'll think about it and decide later." "Yes, but later" says, "I definitely will forgive, but it will take time." "Yes, now" says, "I forgive you." However, this is usually decisional forgiveness, and negative emotions might persist for a long while. The potential forgiver has many choices. These include holding out for strict, tit-for-tat justice. But the choices can also include a humble just forgiveness, which matches the humble just concession of the offender.

The offender can then accept whatever forgiveness is offered, realizing that he or she is not entitled to any forgiveness, regardless of how contrite he or she has been. However, some offenders experience so much self-condemnation they are inconsolable.

Detoxify. Relationships that have harbored unforgiveness often need to have the relational poison neutralized. This usually requires rebuilding habits around positive interaction. It also may mean that former adversaries try hard not to provoke each other. Finally, former adversaries need to have an attitude of latitude toward small relational failures and an attitude of gratitude that appreciates the other person's efforts to make the relationship better.

Devote. Eliminating negative interactions from a reconciled relationship is essential. However, for the relationship to flourish, new positive interactions must be instituted. Most marriage experts say that in happy marriages at least five times as many positive interactions are needed over the negative interactions. But in marriages that are recovering from problems, between fifteen and twenty-five times as many positives are needed.[7] Recall how a big sinful event can be a tipping point or quantum change that darkens partners' views of the relationship (see chapter one). To change that view, lots of focused work is needed to build devotion. This same principle exists at every level. It is just as hard to restore a positive workplace or community as to turn around a troubled marriage.

Reconciliation may not end with living "happily ever after" together. Look at Jacob and Esau. There were alliances and betrayals as Jacob and his mother conspired to trick a blessing from Isaac (Gen 27). Jacob fled from Esau's anger, wrath and potential revenge. Esau's honor had been impugned and his birthright stolen.

Jacob experienced the natural consequences of his treachery—he himself was tricked (Gen 29). Eventually, though, Jacob turned and moved back toward Esau so that reconciliation could occur. As he did, he had to confront himself and wrestle with God, and he was broken in the experience (Gen 32).

To reconcile, Jacob had to show Esau he was now penitent and safe (Gen 32–33). He showed penitence, regret and contrition, made restitution, and sought restoration. Jacob and Esau were reconciled. Yet they did not live together afterwards. They went their own ways (Gen 33:16-17).

The endpoint of reconciliation may not be close communion. Sometimes, even among God's chosen people, reconciliation means singing two melodies in counterpoint instead of barbershop quartet harmony.

SELF-FORGIVENESS

Reconciling with a wrongdoer can be challenging. This is especially true when we ourselves are the wrongdoer and are battling self-condemnation.

Self-forgiveness might sound easy to those who have never struggled with self-condemnation. All you have to do is just let go of the self-blame, they might think. But consider this. A few years ago I read Pumla Gobodo-Madikizela's book about her interviews with Eugene de Kock, the chief architect of police suppression of the anti-apartheid movement in South Africa.[8] He earned the name Prime Evil. As I read of the horrid murders, torture, beatings and suffering that de Kock inflicted on his fellow citizens, I had a pure fantasy. I asked myself what I would think if de Kock had said, "I've considered all the torture and murders I've committed, and I have decided to forgive myself." It seemed to me that such glib self-forgiveness would not be enough. It would let de Kock off the hook. It would offend my sense of justice. Glib self-forgiveness would not be just self-forgiveness.

Why is it so hard to forgive ourselves? Dealing with self-condemnation can be harder than dealing with condemnation from the one we have wronged, and self-forgiveness can be harder than forgiving someone else. There are many reasons why it is difficult. First, when people try to forgive themselves, they play two roles at the same time—wrongdoer and forgiver. That requires mental gymnastics. Second, self-condemnation often seems incessant. When we condemn ourselves, our mental accusations are inescapable. We live with our thoughts every waking hour. Third, we have insider information. We know the many times that we have erred or disappointed ourselves. We can see how unrepentant we really are. Regardless of how close our relationship may be with someone else, we do not see all of that person's failures, and he or she can't see all of ours. But we can see our own. Fourth, we usually have harmed others. Perhaps they and even those who observed the wrongdoing join our condemnation. Fifth, we often have a sense that we have also sinned against God, nature or humanity, which adds to our guilt and shame. Sixth, people often pressure themselves to forgive themselves. Some people believe that they must forgive themselves before they can be mentally healthy. That pressure to forgive the self adds weight to self-condemnation. Ironically, people condemn themselves for not forgiving themselves. Seventh, when we have been wronged by another, we might feel that the burden is on the wrongdoer, not us, to make the first move toward reconciliation. But when we fail ourselves, there is no other. We feel the burden alone. Eighth, many people hold themselves to higher standards of behavior than they hold others. This might include perfectionists and those who are anxious and plagued with guilt. It might include people who were shamed as children. It might include normal folks who hold high expectations.

If those reasons don't make self-forgiveness difficult enough, here's the really hard part: self-forgiveness is only the tip of the iceberg. Suppose a man loses his temper and strikes his six-year-old child. The father may forgive himself but still be wracked with negative feelings. Why? By striking his child, he changed his entire conception of himself. Before he struck his child, he was not the type of father who would strike his child. Now he is. His understanding of who he is, is fundamentally altered. It takes time, effort and discomfort to change our self-concept.

Do we even need to forgive ourselves? When we are forgiven by God, do we need self-forgiveness? We do not need it for salvation. Jesus' death was sufficient for the legal expiation of our sin. But we might need self-forgiveness because our emotions are stirred up. If we commit a crime but the governor pardons us, we are free from the law. But we might still feel guilt and shame. Consider Karla Faye Tucker, a participant in a brutal murder. Later she became a Christian, and Jesus forgave her. She may have felt forgiven by God, but the state did not forgive her. Not everyone in the victim's family forgave her. So despite knowing that God had forgiven her,

Karla had many reasons to feel guilty and ashamed and had full knowledge that the murder she committed had lasting consequences. We may know that Jesus died for our sins, but sins still have social consequences. We need to make them right with others.

We are fallen creatures. We may not be capable of bringing about justice in human society for our sins. We may not be able to make things right. We *should* feel some guilt to inhibit a repetition of our misdeeds. Most people are not liberated when a well-meaning fellow Christian says, "Jesus paid the price. Your guilt is illegitimate." That in fact makes them feel guilty and may shame them for feeling guilty, and it forgets that their acts had real ongoing social consequences.

Peter said, "Cast all your anxiety [burdens, guilt] on [Jesus] because he cares for you" (1 Pet 5:7) and Jesus said, "My yoke is easy and my burden is light" (Mt 11:29). Indeed, Jesus does lighten our burdens. Yet divine forgiveness does not leave us without social guilt. Even when we have assurance of our acceptability to God, we should still determine whether we can actually do something productive to make things right for those we have harmed. If there is something we can do, we should do it. If not, we must accept it.

Often we feel guilty and ashamed, but we don't know what for. We feel ashamed, unworthy and bad. We cannot identify any specific act for which we need forgiveness. We feel like we need forgiveness for being imperfect, for being a failure or for taking up air that someone else could better use. Often guilt and shame arise from having developed an insecure attachment or from some trauma in childhood we think we caused. Sometimes it is because our parents treated us as if we were never good enough to deserve their love. Self-condemnation, then, has many causes, but they boil down to actually doing bad things or seeing ourselves as unable to live up to our self-imposed standards or expectations.

Where can we find help for forgiving ourselves? If self-forgiveness is so difficult, where do we look for help? Christians look first to Scripture. In Scripture we find many examples of self-condemnation. Recall David. David had an affair with Bathsheba and then had Uriah, her husband, killed. God sent Nathan to confront David. In the passage in 2 Samuel, we find that David's first response was contrition: "Then David said to Nathan, 'I have sinned against the LORD.' Nathan replied, 'The LORD has taken away your sin'" (2 Sam 12:13). In Psalm 51, however, we read a beautiful and poignant lament to God from David: "Have mercy on me, O God, according to your unfailing love; according to your great compassion, blot out my transgressions. . . . For I know my transgressions, and my sin is always before me. . . . Create in me a pure heart, O God, and renew a steadfast spirit within me. Do not cast me from your presence or take your Holy Spirit from me" (Ps 51:1, 3, 10-11). Although David immediately confessed to God, and Nathan assured him of forgiveness, David still struggled with the sin that was always before him. Neither his feelings nor his guilt disappeared upon God's divine forgiveness.

Although we find many examples of self-condemnation in Scripture, we find zero examples of self-forgiveness. We cannot simply declare ourselves forgiven, as in my imagined anecdote about Eugene de Kock.

Social perspective. First, let's make a distinction. Remember Eugene de Kock. He did evil. He harmed, tortured and killed people, leaving loved ones aggrieved and bereft. Now imagine a woman who is depressed because she feels she has disappointed God—she has not been humble enough, she has judged others, she has hated her enemies, she hasn't prayed enough and she isn't perfect enough. I don't know anyone who would think that the social effects of this woman's failings are in the same ballpark as de Kock's crimes.

Divine perspective. De Kock's crimes have far more social consequences than those of the self-condemning woman. However, from God's viewpoint, the woman is just as guilty and in need of God's divine forgiveness as de Kock. Sin is sin, and humans cannot free themselves of the stain of its guilt, regardless of how contrite, penitent or hard-working they are. If you had to swim from Israel to Virginia—across the Mediterranean and the Atlantic—but I only had to swim from England to Virginia, there would be miles of difference in how far we each must swim. But we would both drown. We cannot by our own effort relieve our guilt before God.

Similarly, there are miles of moral differences between de Kock and the self-condemning woman. But neither can forgive himself or herself before God and be free of sin. Only through Jesus' death and God's love and mercy can divine forgiveness happen. Through Jesus' act of self-sacrifice, he closed the injustice gap before God. God forgave us on Jesus' behalf.

Nevertheless, I might still condemn myself. Suppose I commit armed robbery and am sentenced to prison. But suppose an innocent man agrees to take my punishment. Because of that, the governor pardons me. Legally I am free. But emotionally I still might condemn myself—and rightly so. I did something heinous. I stole. I terrorized. I made people suffer. And now, to save me and satisfy justice, another innocent person will suffer. I feel rightful self-condemnation.

Self-condemnation does not mean that I denigrate the work done by the governor, by the one who took my punishment or by others who worked on my behalf. It also does not mean I do not appreciate what the governor did. But I am still self-condemning. Easing my emotional self-condemnation, then, is not as simple as accepting God's love, mercy and legal pardon and never looking back, thank you very much. My act had social, spiritual and psychological effects, and I (and others) might suffer from them. As you can see, I am separating my legal status as forgiven by the governor from my emotional self-unforgiveness. Emotional self-forgiveness involves more and might be complicated further by cultural context.

Is self-forgiveness particular to individualistic cultures? The preoccupation some people have with self-forgiveness might depend on whether they live in an individualistic, guilt-based culture. In an individualistic culture, people are preoccupied with the self. Whereas they may care about other people, their main consideration is usually how oneself is affected by one's acts. Failures are often occasions of self-condemnation. Undoubtedly, however, people in collectivistic cultures who strive to maintain honor and avoid bringing shame to their groups also experience self-condemnation. In fact, they might feel even more self-condemnation due to group pressure than would an individual in an individualistic culture. Similarly, without the easing of group or family condemnation, they might be perpetually trapped in self-condemnation. Self-forgiveness might be something they cannot possibly understand, at least until they are freed from group shame by others in their society. Only then can they seek to forgive the self.

How does one deal with self-condemnation and forgive oneself on a personal level? Because a self-condemning person usually really has transgressed against someone, the person must first accept and admit that. In some cases, self-condemning people are down on themselves not so much for what they have done as for who they are or for failure to meet unrealistically high standards of performance. In those cases, people must reassess the reality of their expectations and standards.

Deal with God. As Christians, we believe that we have sinned against God. As David said, "[Lord], against you, you only, have I sinned" (Ps 51:4). We therefore must first make things right with God. That might mean we partake of the sacrament of reconciliation, confess publicly or simply pray. We cannot by ourselves make things right with God—no matter how much blood, sweat and tears we exude trying to earn forgiveness. Jesus already has made things right. But by acting obediently to God's Word, we agree with God, in humility, that we cannot clean ourselves from the stain and stench of sin.

But we have a part. Psalm 51 also says, "The sacrifices of God are a broken spirit; a broken and contrite heart, O God, you will not despise" (Ps 51:17). We must accept mercy from God, which is given through grace.

Evaluate our standards and expectations for our behavior. If we feel we have done wrong or if we condemn ourselves for our imperfections, we must evaluate our standards. Are they tougher than we would impose on others? Are we, like the Pharisees of Jesus' day, requiring more strict behavior than even God does (Mt 23:13-32)?

Change unrealistic standards and expectations. Often it takes years of psychotherapy to change expectations. It can involve analyzing the truth of my self-judgments in light of God's Word, re-exploring old traumas and wounds, healing of memories and perhaps forming good adult attachment bonds that can compensate for poor early attachment.

Deal with those we harmed. Next, if we determine that we have really harmed others, we must try to make things right with them, to the extent it is possible. We must resist the sinful human urge to let ourselves off the hook. Making amends for real wrongdoing is a responsible step. It is mandated in Scripture (Mt 5:23-24; Ex 22:3; Lev 6:5).

Scientific research on forgiveness has also shown that repentance is hard to do. Repentance is physiologically arousing. Charlotte Witvliet and her colleagues investigated the physiological responses of wrongdoers. She had people think about a time when they sinned against someone, and she observed their physiological responses.[9] Their responses were much stronger if they did not feel forgiven than if they did feel forgiven.[10]

The more we adjust the balance of justice by repairing damage or making reparations for harm, the more we reduce the injustice gap and make it easier to forgive ourselves. Then we might be ready to deal with the harm that we have done to ourselves through the transgression.

Grant decisional forgiveness to ourselves. We can make a decision to forgive ourselves. At some point we must accept that we can never do all that is necessary to completely close the injustice gap. We may have to stop trying to make it up to a harmed party who is inconsolable. But decisional self-forgiveness is undertaken only after one has done everything that one reasonably can do to make amends.

Seek to experience positive, merciful emotions toward ourselves. Deciding to forgive ourselves does not mean that emotional forgiveness will quickly follow. We need transformed emotions, not just a committed decision, for emotional self-forgiveness. We should seek to empathize, sympathize, feel compassion for and even love ourselves. (Loving ourselves is not the same as feeling we are good, wonderful and perfect. Instead, it is seeing ourselves as fallen and flawed but nevertheless valuable to God.)

We are also to pray for our enemies, for those who persecute us. In self-condemnation, that means praying for ourselves. Perhaps we can eventually experience emotional self-forgiveness in this way—eroding our self-condemnation with empathy, sympathy, compassion and realistic love for ourselves as precious but fallen creatures.

Accept ourselves as flawed in a way we didn't want to admit. As we saw, however, merely forgiving oneself for an act does not necessarily change our negative self-concept. We need to integrate the new information into the revised self-concept. We must rethink the boundaries of the self. Eventually we must repair damage to the self.

Psychotherapists have developed many ways to help people change their self-concept, self-image and self-esteem. Most are long-term treatments. Thus if we believe that we can work for just a few hours to eliminate all negative feelings about ourselves that arise from self-condemnation, we will be disappointed.

Resolve to live virtuously. Finally, we should resolve to live virtuously. This requires living with the knowledge of our imperfections but pleading that God will not let them get the upper hand.

Give ourselves space to fail. When we fail—and we will fail—Jesus Christ will come down to our level and lift us up. He will say to me and to you, as he did to Peter, "Do you love me?" (Jn 21:17).

We'll say, "Lord, you know I do."

He'll say, "Feed my sheep."

Peter later says—and he should know—"The God of all grace, who called you to his eternal glory in Christ, after you have suffered a little while, will himself restore you and make you strong, firm and steadfast. To him be the power for ever and ever. Amen" (1 Pet 5:10-11).

DRAWING IT ALL TOGETHER
FOR SOCIAL APPLICATION

In the second part of the book (chapters six through nine), we consider four applications of our understanding of forgiveness: in families, in the church, in the communities and in the world. We have seen that the principle for a just forgiveness—allowing justice and forgiveness to blend—occurs through humility. As we apply Micah 6:8, we find that humility will draw together the threads of justice and forgiveness into an empathic guide for action.

Eyes, arms, knees and wings. Let's compare humble just forgiveness to a magnificent heavenly winged creature, created to glorify God. Eyes represent injustice. When we get a tiny speck in our eye, it is all we can see. It makes us cry. It frustrates us. It becomes our primary experience, never out of our minds, until we remove that speck.

Arms are for balance. Lady Justice, the icon of justice, ironically has her eyes blindfolded (to show that justice is blind to favoritism), but in our analogy we see that we need to treat the wounds of injustice or they will not heal. Lady Justice carries a sword in one hand. She must protect against people who would unfairly perpetrate injustice for their own ends. In the other hand, she carries a scale. Scales balance injustice and justice. They are to bring a sense of fairness into play. The scales are also aimed at staying in balance. If we wield only the sword, justice will be lopsided.

Humility is represented by our knees. We cannot wield justice effectively from on high, pretending we are gods. We must yield to the God in heaven. This is the true basis of the justice system in the West. In the Magna Carta of the thirteenth century, King John was forced to kneel to a sense of law from God rather than to exercise his version of law. In the West, we say *lex rex* ("law is king"), not *rex lex* ("the king is law"). From our knees, we are in the perfect posture to discern what really should be just and unjust—the posture of humility. It is God who knows, and we can only seek to discern.

Forgiveness is represented by wings. Wings do not prevent us from experiencing injustice and pain and suffering. But with wings we are lifted from the slough of pain to soar above injustice.

However, we need a guide for action that can help us know precisely how to respond to different challenges requiring just forgiveness. In general, most of our responses are a product of structures, triggers and mental processes. I have only hinted at these up until now, but here I develop them into a model (see figure 5.1).

Structures. Our acts come out of structures in our lives. Structures are things that are relatively permanent. We have mental and psychological structures. These involve memories, values, beliefs, expectations, attitudes,

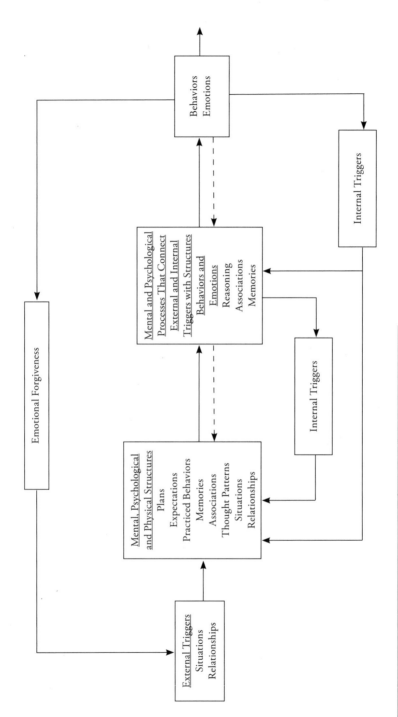

Figure 5.1. Structures, triggers and mental processes

dispositions and personality. These structures have arisen from our genetic makeup, our experiences and the ways our bodies operate (including our brain).

Some mental structures are more permanent and more accessible than others. For example, our personality is at the bedrock of our identity. But even personality changes as we move from relationship to relationship. For example, I act differently at work, at home, at church and during a heated tennis match.

Other internal structures are less fixed than personality. For example, core values are tenaciously held, though occasionally some event will shake one's core values. Attitudes are not quite as strongly adhered to as values. Most beliefs are less strongly held, followed by opinions and preferences. Memories seem permanent, but research shows they are more malleable than we usually think. Mental skills and abilities also are generally permanent mental structures. Note that our relationships can have a big effect on what we value, believe and think.

Not all structures are psychological or mental. When I walk into a church building, I act differently than I did on the street in front of the building. When I walk into a university lecture hall for class, no one has to tell me to sit down, stop chatting, listen and take notes. The structures associated with a university classroom trigger classroom behaviors. My relationships also are structures. I relate much differently to my wife than I do to my children, my tennis buddies or friends from church. Each person's presence guides me to think and talk in predictable ways when I am with him or her.

We also have a relationship with the triune God, which is like other structures in our lives. It can be important and often influence our thoughts, feelings or behavior. Or it can be a structure with which we rarely connect. Finding God depends on seeking God. If we direct our thought processes, motives and emotions toward finding God, we will trigger thoughts and emotional processes that help us see God's continual presence more often.

Not all of our psychological, mental, physical and relational structures are consistent with each other. Thus our behavior tends to be directed by (a) the most naturally salient structures, which come into our awareness most often and most easily, and (b) structures that are activated by frequently encountered cues. So we must consider the triggers that activate attention to structures (see figure 5.1).

Triggers. Triggers likewise can be internal or external. If we begin thinking along a well-worn mental pathway, the chances are that we will continue down the mental rut. One thought, one image, one association triggers the next. Emotions and moods can be powerful internal cues that trigger psychological experiences. Powerful negative emotions evoke memories and associations from times when we were in a similar mood. Internal processes can trigger other internal processes.

Triggers can also be external. Seeing a certain friend activates a high-five or knuckle-knock. Waking up at 5 a.m. to the smell of fresh coffee and sitting in the chair where we have morning devotions can trigger intimacy with God. A question by a friend can trigger memories of traumatic childhood events. Any happening that is associated with a memory, image or experience can trigger it.

Our behavior depends on which structures are triggered. The relatively enduring structures in our lives sometimes seem consistent to us. But actually many of them are surprisingly inconsistent. We learned different behaviors in different situations. We may think of ourselves as pretty consistent, but when we examine the cold hard facts, we aren't consistent at all. For example, I am typically social, lighthearted and reverent when I'm at church. That is the way I was brought up. In the Navy I could be a rah-rah leader. On the soccer field I was intense yet incompetent. In the classroom sometimes I'm a comedian, sometimes a pedantic, pontificating professor. So today I have a lot of internally inconsistent skill sets. Yet I see no contradiction. Each situation triggers a radically different, and inconsistent, skill set.

Mental processes. Psychologists call this a person-situation interaction. What it boils down to is this: Triggers from my past and my present cause different parts of my beliefs, values, skills and behaviors to be manifest. I experience *mental processes* (see figure 5.1). Those associations, recollections of memories, and reasoning patterns take me down familiar paths of experience and (importantly) *make me absolutely oblivious (in the moment) to other experiences.* I then act and emote using particular *behavioral processes,* thinking they are the most normal thoughts, behaviors and emotions in the world. In the unlikely event that I were to think about it at all, I might think, *How could I act differently?*

Most Christians have a knowledge and skill set that favors forgiveness. But we also have an inherent need for justice, especially punitive justice, when we are wronged. We know how to be humble, and as Christians we practice humility as much as we can. But some things just trigger arrogance in us. Perhaps a rival is making an in-your-face point that you disagree with, but he or she misquotes a Scripture. It's hard not to smirk. We hate ourselves afterward when things like this happen, but somehow we can't stop the arrogance.

We find ourselves in a lot of different social situations. Those situations trigger different thoughts, behaviors and emotions. When we are with family, family-related structures and processes are most likely to be triggered. In the church, workplace, community or world, other processes are highlighted. It is no wonder we surprise ourselves with our inconsistencies. We want to be consistently Christian. But how do we make Jesus our number one priority—not just as an affirmation of our faith, but as structures, triggers and processes that govern our moment-by-moment lives?

That application of our understanding of justice, forgiveness and humility is our focus in the second part of the book. We will attempt to analyze how forgiveness, justice and humility interact in each situation, providing practical guidelines for governing our actions in those situations when transgressions occur.

We want to live the life God requires of us. Here is the way Eugene Peterson puts it in *The Message:*

But he's already made it plain how to live, what to do,
    what God is looking for in men and women.

It's quite simple: Do what is fair and just to your neighbor,
        be compassionate and loyal in your love,
And don't take yourself too seriously—
        take God seriously. (Mic 6:8)

Our mental processes take us down promising and unpromising roads. But in addition to taking every thought captive for Christ (2 Cor 10:5), it is the structures we build into our lives—like our emotional bond to God—and the Christ-related triggers that turn on behavioral and mental processes that we must consider.

All of this sounds very theoretical. Let's apply these ideas in examining humble just forgiveness in the family, church, community, society and world.

PART 2

LIVING OUT JUST

FORGIVENESS

JUST FORGIVENESS
IN THE FAMILY

THE FAMILY IS THE PRIMARY LIFE laboratory where forgiveness is necessary. We grow up there, and our blood relations make for strong emotional bonds. We all would like to have warm family relationships. We know, though, that living together for many hours a week, many (if not most) weeks each year and many years over the course of our lives, relationships get strained. How do we ease those strains? How do we deal with the times when we hurt our primary partner? The likelihood of divorce is high, even for Christian couples.[1] We don't want to be a statistic.

The glue that holds a family together starts in our own relationships with our parents or parental caregivers. From birth we form a strong emotional attachment to our primary caregiver, usually our mother. For many people, that emotional attachment is secure. A secure attachment gives us a strong basis for exploring the world. We have a source of connection to return to when the challenges of the world tax our coping skills.

But sometimes our attachment relationship is not secure. Insecure attachments often are expressed as anxious or avoidant relationships. Anxiously attached people are fearful and hypervigilant about rejection. Avoidantly attached people are loosely connected and don't form strong emotional bonds. They tend to withdraw when challenged. We see, then, that we form a general stance toward relationships because of the experiences we have in our early years within the family. This is an important warning for parents to attend to child rearing.

A secure or insecure attachment relationship with the mother and father can affect a person's feelings of attachment with God.[2] Because we learn emotional behavior in the family, we often conclude on the basis of our interactions in the family that we might not be able to trust God either.

We can repair our adult attachment relationships even if our attachment from early childhood was insecure.[3] This is clear from research on children who have been raised in very stressed, deprived and impoverished childhoods. These children develop the capacity for good relationships even with disastrous family-of-origin relationships. Usually they report that at least one relationship with an adult—a sports coach, a teacher, a youth leader—was warm and accepting.

In marriage, partners can help heal each other. For example, my family-of-origin relationships were poor. My mother was supportive but had unipolar depression, which periodically required hospitalization and often affected her moods. My father was away three out of four days working on the railroad. When he was home, especially as I reached middle-school age, he was often drunk. When he was drunk, he was mean. Now that I am a psychologist, if I were to look at someone with my family-of-origin and socioeconomic status, I would not be optimistic about how he might turn out. But God was the wildcard in the deck, in mercy dealing me Kirby, who became my wife. She was warm and accepting. Having a reparative relationship with her helped me to develop a more secure relational attachment style. Thus romantic partners can be healing agents for each other. The really good news is that even if we have an insecure attachment to God, God does not have an insecure attachment to us. Furthermore, God diligently seeks us. When Jesus wants to repair our attachment style, he can do it!

As we look at justice, forgiveness and humility within the family, we will start with the couple. We will consider how to make just responses during reconciliation between couples, and that will serve as a backdrop to the remainder of the chapter. Then we will see how both parents and children feel transgressions in the family, and how forgiveness might come to the aid of both parents and children in smoothing out the wrinkles in the emotional bond. Finally, we will examine an increasingly common situation in the family—the strains that go along with aging adults.

JUST FORGIVENESS IN THE MARRIAGE

In close relationships, justice and forgiveness run on parallel tracks. The tracks usually connect to each other at the point where the personal injustice gaps are felt by the participants.

As Christians, it is our personal and practical belief in God's sovereignty that sets the context for how we respond to relationship injustices. It is not just mental agreement with a doctrine stating God is sovereign that affects us. It is our practical living out of our belief. We might affirm a strict reformed view of God's sovereignty in our belief system. Yet in our relationships we might act as if God were not the King of kings and Lord of lords but rather a minion subject to our judgment. If we want to have a marriage that is infused with God's presence, we need to increase the salience of the structure of our relationship with God. We can do this through daily devotions, daily prayer and conversation with people about God's work in our lives. All of these structures create triggers that are easily activated in most circumstances. When we deal with our spouse over some hurt or transgression, there are myriad triggers that can bring God into the conversation.

Let's take the hypothetical case of Frances and Rod, who are struggling with a troubled marriage. Frances is a good orthodox Presbyterian woman who believes in the doctrines expressed in the Apostles' Creed. She even affirms the sovereignty of God, though she admits she has trouble with doctrines dealing with predestination. Rod has just admitted to having an affair lasting several months, and Frances is mad. The affair was not the first sign of marriage difficulties. She and Rod have been struggling for at least two years, and their relationship has progressively become less imtimate and more characterized by conflict.

Frances is quick to point the finger. She blames Rod for having an affair and being weak. She blames Rod's parents for not raising him to be a more responsible man. Frances is both angry and depressed and has struggled with poor self-esteem all her adult life. She blames her own parents for their lack of supportiveness. Her father was particularly distant; her mother always seemed to be involved in work and never seemed to have enough time to give the children. Frances blames the modern mentality that marriage is like a contract—it is easy to set aside by either party if the other party is perceived as not holding up his or her end of the deal.

Frances says that she is trusting and relying on God, and in many ways she is. She prays for health and mercy. She prays for God's intervention. But she is also disappointed with God for not shielding her from this disastrous marriage, which is destroying her children. She is angry with God. She is bitter toward God about the treatment she feels she does not deserve. "I have been a faithful Christian all my life, for as long as I can remember, yet God seems to show no loyalty to me while still demanding full loyalty from me."

Frances also knows that when she points the finger at other people or at God, the other fingers are pointing back at her. She feels disappointed in herself for not reacting more positively, more lovingly and as a better Christian. Her self-esteem is at a low ebb. She realizes she has failed Rod in many ways throughout their married life, and that the responsibility for their marital troubles is partly her own. "I never thought this could possibly happen to me," she confesses. "I thought I would be able to deal with whatever difficulties I had in a relationship. I am so disappointed in myself that I can hardly stand it." Frances cannot forgive herself for her many failures.

Justice. If Frances and Rod are going to create a better marriage, then they must be concerned with bringing more justice into their relationship. Each one perceives an injustice gap against the other person. The injustice gap that each perceives is made up of thousands of injustices. There are so many injustices, they cannot all be remembered. Only the big injustices are continually brought up and form the center of their ruminations.

Rod perceives a gross injustice because Frances began to pull back emotionally and withdraw sexually from their relationship. He felt it was something Frances initiated and he did not deserve. Frances sees Rod's withdrawal from the relationship as a result of his over-involvement in his work. She felt no sexual desire for him because she felt she was getting no intimacy from him. She was also bitterly hurt when he told her of his affair and was particularly hurt that, even after admitting to the affair, he didn't want to terminate it.

Perceived injustices fuel their relationship difficulties. If they can bring justice into the relationship, it will reduce their perceived injustice gaps. As their injustice gaps are narrowed, they will be more likely to forgive. Forgiveness could occur even in the face of massive injustice. Either or both partners could respond to God's working in their lives and could grant decisional forgiveness, experience emotional forgiveness and communicate their forgiveness to the other. If forgiveness were to occur, each would probably begin to act more justly toward the other person.

Reconciliation. Reconciliation is the restoration of trust in a relationship where trust has been damaged, as in the case of Frances and Rod.[4] God desires reconciliation. In the Scriptures we see that we are to live in peace with all people, "as far as it depends on you" (Rom 12:18). Paul admonishes Gentiles and Jews within the Christian church to break down the dividing wall of hostility (Eph 2:14). Jesus teaches that, if we are at the altar worshiping and we recall that someone has something against us, we are to go confess to them our part and reconcile with them (Mt 5:23-24). That way, our worship can be uninhibited and untainted by bitterness, unforgiveness and guilt for our interpersonal wrongdoings.

God wants to be reconciled with people—and this especially is true in the family. When we hurt a family member, or when we are hurt by one, especially our spouse, we should recall Jesus' guidance. Instead of getting caught up in the triggers surrounding the large injustice gap, fueled by raw emotion, we can try to think of what Jesus would have us do. We can use Matthew 5 as a trigger to turn our eyes toward God and also toward reconciliation rather than getting even.

Implicit reconciliation. There are two ways that people reconcile with each other in human relationships. First is implicit reconciliation. Implicit reconciliation is when trust is restored even though people do not explicitly discuss the restoration of trust or actions needed to restore trust. Most reconciliation in daily life is implicit reconciliation. Namely, we rarely talk about how to restore trust in a relationship. Most of the time we simply set about seeking to bring more justice to our side of the relationship and hope for more justice from the other person's side, reciprocating our efforts.

Rod and Frances might implicitly reconcile, but the cards are stacked against them. Their relationship has slid far down the slope toward divorce. Frances and Rod have been fighting for two years, and Rod's affair probably will not yield to being ignored. They will need to talk about how to reconcile.

Explicit reconciliation. Explicit reconciliation is when people intentionally move through a process of trying to resolve differences and restore trust to their relationship. Using the analogy of building a bridge, I have identified four planks in the bridge to reconciliation.[5] I gave a skeleton summary of each in chapter five, and now we will flesh out the skeleton by applying it to Rod and Frances's marriage.

THE BRIDGE TO RECONCILIATION

Plank 1—Decision. The first plank is *decision*. Decisions are necessary about whether one wishes to reconcile. One does not have to reconcile, and it might not be safe, prudent or possible to reconcile. For example, a woman who is regularly beaten by her husband might decide that she wishes to forgive her husband, but she does not desire to reconcile with him because it is a dangerous situation that is likely to lead to her harm or death. Or a man might hold a grudge against his deceased father. He might forgive his father, but because his father is no longer alive, he cannot restore trust in their relationship and therefore cannot reconcile. In the decision phase, the person also needs to consider how reconciliation might best occur. Will it be implicit or explicit reconciliation? The third decision that must be made deals with the timing of reconciliation. When is the appropriate time to attempt to reconcile?

For Frances and Rod, someone must stand in the gap between them. They recognize their need for someone to intercede and agree to seek counseling. But from whom? Rod wants to go to their pastor. Frances thinks he can't be fair because he plays on the church softball team with Rod. Frances wants to go to a Christian counselor that she had heard from a friend was excellent. But Rod objects. He says he will feel "ganged up on." He already feels guilty about the affair. He wants a counselor who won't be in a "coalition of condemnation" with his wife.

Negotiating the decision plank in the bridge to reconciliation involves several issues of justice. It involves procedural justice. Is there a fair way by which the decision can be made? Is there a fair way by which all the wrongs might be dealt with and forgiveness might take place? This procedural justice is something that will characterize the entire reconciliation process. Therefore, if a person decides that procedural justice cannot possibly occur, then the person may decide not to attempt to reconcile.

The person also must decide whether it is possible to get distributive justice that is perceived to be fair by both parties. Distributive justice is the way that resources are allocated. If the offense has to do with how love or attention or material resources is distributed, then the judgment one makes about whether distributive justice is possible will affect whether the person decides to pursue reconciliation efforts.

A decision to reconcile may also rest on judgments about whether restorative justice is possible. Can the relationship even be restored? Is there a way to have the wrongdoers make amends fairly?

Furthermore, the decision may depend upon divine justice. People enter a decision about reconciling with a wrongdoer or someone with whom they are estranged because, at least to some degree, they believe God will bring about justice. If they believe God will not bring justice into the relationship, then the decision is often made not to pursue reconciliation.

Rod and Frances eventually agree to a compromise on a counselor.

They ask their pastor for a referral. Neither wants to go to a secular counselor. They want their relationship redeemed. Each is wary of being on the short end of a coalition, so neither wants to accept the other's suggestion for a counselor. So they come to an agreement about procedure.

Plank 2—Discussion. The second plank in the bridge to reconciliation is to *discuss*. Discussion involves talking about the transgression and about whether the transgression can be forgiven or accepted or must be forborne or whether it can be justified or excused.

Many issues regarding justice arise in discussions about transgressions. Talking about the transgression often involves distributive justice. Are the pain, suffering and wrongdoing distributed fairly across the two parties? Is forgiveness equal on both sides?

When Rod and Frances meet with Robert, the counselor recommended by their pastor, they both tell their stories. Each naturally sees things from his or her viewpoint, and each describes his or her own suffering. Each is angry with the other because the counselor seems to be listening to both of them equally. However, both are surprised when Robert says, "You have both suffered. I can hear the pain in both of your stories. Clearly there are lots of things that must be done to heal your marriage. I must say, though, that the affair is strictly Rod's responsibility."

"How so?" said Rod. "She did a lot of things that provoked me."

"Yes," said Robert, "but there were many ways you could have dealt with your complaints. When you chose to have an affair, you chose wrongly. That fault is yours."

"But she was refusing me sex."

"Yes, that was probably not a good way for Frances to react to her complaints about you. But still, even if she was totally wrong there, her wrong does not make your wrong become okay."

"So, yeah. I see 'two wrongs don't make a right,' but what can I do? It's water over the dam."

"Certainly, you can bring your sin to God in all sincerity. That's a first step. You might pray about whether you need to confess directly to Frances as well."

"Well, I admitted the affair."

Frances broke in. "But you didn't really confess. I'm not sure you are sorry you did it—just that you got caught."

Discussing the transgression also may involve procedural justice. Can the discussion proceed fairly, or will one partner dominate? Issues of procedural justice can affect whether people continue discussions or even whether they start discussions over transgressions. Frances tended to complain. Rod tended to bully. The counselor had to set some ground rules about how they discussed their conflicts.

Issues of retributive justice arise in discussions over transgressions. Did one person get even but the other person feels at a deficit in their punishment of the other person? Issues of restorative justice also arise. Did each person do what was needed in order to try to restore the relationship? What more should each person do to try to restore the relationship? As these issues of justice arise during the discussion, the injustice gap continually is modified, making forgiveness more or less likely to occur. Over time Rod and Frances continued to negotiate. The first two months of their counseling were characterized by conflict. The turning point came when Rod made an emotional apology to Frances. That did not cure all of their problems, but it seemed to soften each partner.

Even perceived expectations can be treated as a matter of justice. A person can expect the other person to give in, to change, to make concessions or to confess his or her wrongdoing and beg for forgiveness. That seemed to be Frances's expectation, and when it was met, she could release her adversarial stance. If people differ in their expectations, which they almost certainly do, then an issue of justice is introduced. Are the expectations that one holds fair? Are the expectations balanced on each side of the equation, for each person in the relationship? In the case of Rod and Frances, Rod had wronged Frances through his affair. Both partners felt it to be just and fair that he humble himself in an apology.

Overall we can see then that discussions about the transgression continually introduce issues of different kinds of justice. And as those issues pop up and enter into the discussions, or even when the issues are merely thought about, the injustice gap is adjusted in such a way as to make forgiving either more or less likely to occur.

Plank 3—Detoxification. The third stage in explicit reconciliation is *detoxification* of the negative aspects of the relationship. As people unjustly hurt each other, poisons are introduced into the relationship. Detoxification is about removing many of those poisons so that the relationship can be restored to a more neutral balance. Rod and Frances had built up poison for two years during their pre-affair arguments. Now they attempted to recall those hurts, confess them and prayerfully consider forgiving them. In addition, they worked to learn better communication and conflict negotiation skills.

Detoxification of the relationship can raise issues of divine justice. Is God willing to heal the damage done within each person? This might be perceived as a sense of whether God is just or unjust toward each person. Both Rod and Frances worked to trust God. That seemed much easier for Rod than for Frances, and the counselor met several times with her to discern her difficulties in seeing God as a just and loving God.

Detoxifying the relationship usually requires that the parties hold back on any retributive justice. If the parties punish each other, even though they believe such punishment is deserved, that punishment creates negative feelings and thoughts toward the other party. Retribution is almost always perceived as another transgression. Thus the injustice gap is closed to some degree on behalf of the one who punishes, but it is increased on behalf of the other person.

Plank 4—Devotion. In the fourth plank in the bridge to reconciliation, *devotion*, the partners try to restore love to their marriage. They are not only trying to bolster the positive structures already within their marriage but also to build new ones. They try to create triggers that trigger love rather than a return to conflict.

In the devotion stage, major issues around justice concern divine justice and whether God will restore the marriage. Trusting God can enable the partners to trust each other. Failures with each other will inevitably affect their trust in God.

Perhaps Frances and Rod should have been more involved in pursuing restorative justice. After six months, they ended couple therapy, even though the counselor advised them to stay in counseling two months longer. They had done too little to build devotion into their marriage.

Reconciliation and Promoting Just Forgiveness

Let's look at some of the responsibilities of each party in working toward reconciliation. Importantly, reconciliation requires mutually trustworthy behavior. Just as importantly, each person must focus on his or her own responsibility and not on the other's failures.

Our tendency is to zero in on justice. We might think, *Hey, I've been trying to restrain myself from provoking and to act more lovingly, but she [or he] doesn't seem to be taking reconciliation seriously.* It is highly likely that we might think something like that. After all, we are wired for justice, but we are also self-focused.

Self-focus is part of our human nature and part of the Fall. We simply see our own effort, but not the effort of the other person. This is especially true when we are trying to restrain ourselves from acting negatively. If we restrain ourselves, we feel the effort. But when our partner restrains himself or herself, we do not see his or her effort because it is internal. What we see is nothing—because our partner successfully restrained negative behavior. Our limited perspective is simply a product of being human and being in our own skin and not the other person's. However, we have another reason for zeroing in on justice as well. We have had our precious egos wounded, and our sin nature wants to make someone pay. So we distort our perceptions and thoughts and then blame the other person.

It is important not to give in to the merely human. When a person is in a fractured relationship, the Christian's main goal should be first to subject the relationship to the lordship of Jesus Christ in love for the other person. This requires forgiving the other person for wrongdoing against oneself, and also confessing one's own sin so as not to provoke the partner. The person may or may not explicitly or implicitly work to reconcile the relationship. This is true even though the person realizes that God desires reconciliation whenever it is possible, and that God desires people to live at peace with all others, as much as it is up to them to do so.

Given these goals, the person sets off to walk seven parallel paths to promote personal peace. These may involve skill sets such as the following: First, we want to let go of rumination. Second, we try to forbear making responses that are likely to exacerbate the situation. Third, we seek to establish a sense of peace with God by reconciling with God. Fourth, we want to work to bring more justice into the system. Fifth, we wish to reconcile with the estranged person. Sixth, we try to forgive that person. Seventh, we want to forgive ourselves for our own mistakes and misdeeds.

If we pursue these objectives, we make obtaining emotional forgiveness more likely, which can help promote reconciliation. We necessarily want to practice not just *forgiveness,* but a *just forgiveness.* So let's look at bringing justice into the relationship.

Justice and Promoting a Just Forgiveness

In the bridge to reconciliation, the first step is to make decisions about whether, how and when one might reconcile. I showed earlier that these decisions involved considerations of justice. We are continually judging whether our relationship is balanced and whether God's actions are balanced. Humans are fallen creatures. As such, we are deeply sinful and at the same time deeply self-interested. Psychology has shown consistently that we have a self-serving bias. In our own eyes, we are right more than wrong. We work harder than most others. We are smarter than most. Like Garrison Keillor's Lake Wobegon, "All of our children are above average." We perceive ourselves to be more responsible for good outcomes and good behavior and less responsible for bad outcomes and bad behavior.

The way we perceive ourselves will influence the way we perceive a situation. Recall from chapter three the experiment done by Roy Baumeister and his colleagues, in which observers watched a discussion between a victim and offender while trying to see things as either victim, offender or neutral observer.[6] All made the same number of memory errors, but observers as both victim and offender made self-serving mistakes.

In making a decision about whether or under what circumstances to attempt to reconcile, we must realize that our fallen, self-serving nature will predispose us to justify our own actions. We will see the other person as getting more benefits than we are and as paying fewer costs. To heal the relationship, we need to give the other person the benefit of the doubt, because our minds are set up to protect ourselves and therefore work naturally to protect our own interests. Thus, even if we are the victim in a relationship and yet we can see that we did some actions that contributed to our suffering, chances are high we are still minimizing the contributions that we made.

Making a just reproach. When we feel we have been wronged, we make a reproach—a request or a demand for an explanation for the offender's actions. Again, it is easy to see how righteous indignation can rear up within us as we demand that the other person account for his or her behavior. We might feel that we are being fair when in fact we are not being impartial at all. We are merely justifying ourselves. A good reproach usually sounds something like this:

> "Usually you're a very sensitive person. I was surprised that you were so short with me when you did _____. I don't understand what you were thinking. Can you help me understand what led you to respond as you did?"

Making a soft reproach such as this one does not resolve the issue. It merely keeps people talking about the issue and gives them a chance to resolve it.

Giving a good account. Also introduced in chapter five were four types of accounts, or responses to a reproach.[7] *Denial* refuses responsibility for the wrongdoing. *Justification* admits to having done wrong but basically says that the act was still okay because prior events justified it. Usually a justification blames the other person. Frances might say to Rod, "I was justified in withdrawing sexually because you withdrew intimacy from our relationship."

An *excuse* is an admission that the person did the act, but it also provides mitigating circumstances for why he or she did the act. An excuse is not necessarily a bad account of behavior. Timing is everything in determining whether an excuse is harmful or helpful to the relationship. For example, if a reproach is immediately met by a set of excuses, we perceive that the wrongdoer is denying responsibility. If we are the victim, a clumsy excuse from the wrongdoer increases our injustice gap. However, if the offender accepts responsibility for having done the act, confesses his or her wrongdoing, seeks to make reparations and apologize, expresses contrition and remorse, and then asks if it would help the victim forgive if the victim learned what was going on that caused the wrongdoing, the victim might be willing to grant forgiveness.

A fourth type of account is *confession*. It admits to and accepts responsibility and expresses remorse and contrition for having wronged the partner. The offender also seeks to repair the damage through an apology and perhaps through making amends or some sort of restitution for any loss that was incurred. The person might even offer to pay some kind of punitive damages, in terms of material damages or time and effort above and beyond the harm that was caused. I have previously outlined the steps to a good confession using the acrostic CONFESS to help people remember each step (see figure 6.1).

C = Confess without excuse
O = Offer a sincere apology
N = Note the other person's pain (i.e., empathy)
F = Forever value the person (i.e., say directly that you love the person and want to
      reconcile)
E = Equalize (i.e., offer to make restitution)
S = Say "never again" (and mean it)
S = Seek forgiveness (i.e., ask directly)

Figure 6.1. Steps to CONFESS

Making a good denial. It very well may be that a person honestly believes he or she did nothing wrong and has been accused falsely. A denial, even if the person really did nothing wrong, tends to damage the relationship. This is especially true if the denial is a stark, brutal denial or a counter-accusation. Thus if you want to make a denial, you should do it in a way that does not slam the door to more conversation. For example, you might say the following:

> "I see your perspective on this. Let me summarize the way that I hear you describing what happened. [Accurately summarize the other person's point of view.] Am I correctly understanding the way you see things? [Pause for response and correction if necessary.] I see things a little differently. I want to keep talking about this so we can come to some understanding of it. I could be wrong, however, the way that I am looking at this is [describe your own point of view]."

Making a good justification. A justification admits to the act but denies that one did wrong because one was justified in doing so. It is difficult to make a justification that does not turn the other person off and make him or her defensive. Perhaps one of the only ways to do this might be as follows:

> "Yes, I see what you are saying, and I did do what you said I did [describe what was done]. I am sorry that this hurt you, and I wish that I had not hurt you. I feel sad that I harmed you. At the time, I felt I was justified for acting as I did. As I think more about it, I might certainly change my mind on that, but at the time, here is what I was thinking. [Describe how the action felt justified.]"

Working out difficulties in any valued relationship and restoring the all-important emotional bond requires justice, restraint of some of our justice motives, forgiveness, seeking forgiveness and humbly talking about our difficulties.

As I quoted in chapter two, and bears repeating, William Temple said, "Humility does not mean thinking less of yourself than of other people, nor does it mean having a low opinion of your own gifts. It means freedom from thinking about yourself at all." In resolving marital difficulties, perhaps this is at the same time the hardest and the easiest application of humility. On one hand, because of the intimacy of the relationship, challenges from the partner can be the most arousing to our ego. We can try hardest to fight off accusations, especially those we consider unjust (which are most of them). This can make marriage the hardest place to act in humility. We are deeply challenged, and we focus on wounds. It is necessary to attend to our wounds if we are to survive. God built that survival mechanism into humans. So we find ourselves in power struggles with our partner, thinking, *Who does she think she is? She's violating my basic human rights.* We are highly self-focused. It takes superhuman triggers to cue competing mental processes. Fortunately, we have a superhuman God, and we have the Holy Spirit within us to prompt us.

Yet intimate relationships are in some ways the easiest place to get beyond the self. We have invested more time in the marriage relationship than almost any other human relationship, especially if we have been married several years. This time has taught us about the inner workings of the person we love. We can empathize with a person we understand. We also have invested lots of energy and time into the relationship. We are most motivated to work toward bettering a relationship into which we have invested much. True, we might also have been hurt deeply, which can erode our motivation to repair the relationship—if we let it. But we don't have to let it.

JUST FORGIVENESS IN PARENT-CHILD INTERACTIONS

Redeeming a generation. The generation of children called the millennium generation—those who were children or teens during and after the turn of the twenty-first century—seem to be headed down a road that could take them out of the Christian mainstream. This greatly concerns Christian parents. We can feel that we are being tuned out.

The options for electronic input into the lives of millennium-generation youth are legion. With iPhones, iPods, iTunes, access to the Web, music, video games, DVDs and hundreds of cable channels all seeming to play a continual message of sex and violence, it is difficult if not impossible for most parents to keep up with their kids. (As I recently heard someone say, "Even 'we' now has two i's in it." That would be the Nintendo Wii, for those not familiar with electronic games.)

Electronic entertainment media, celebrity train wrecks and the influence of cool or sexy clothes that come from the mass culture trigger attitudes that say adults are irrelevant to the world of the teen and young adult. Thus the adult feels irrelevant to the child, who is busy with his or her own pursuits anyway. But dare we abandon a generation? As we've often heard, at any point Christianity is one generation away from extinction. Sometimes it seems extinction is closer than ever.

If we are to redeem our children, it requires that we as parents strive continually to stay in contact with our children. Parents can, of course, rely on the big guns: "I'll take away all of your privileges." "You'll be grounded until your first child is twenty-one." Or the really heavy artillery: "It's my way or the highway." But those coercive and harsh strategies tend to drive kids to gangs, alternative lifestyles, drug dealers or peers who will accept them. "It's there I feel the love," they say.

Of course, in the limited space of this book, I cannot tackle the complexities of effective parenting. I can only consider one of the most important aspects. Misunderstandings and hurts are bound to happen. That is almost inevitable when parents try to transmit their values to a new generation. It is vital that parents repair the rifts in their parent-child relations. Forgiveness—seeking it and granting it—is essential. Instead of giving a wayward teen the cold shoulder or laying down the law with an iron fist, we need to repair the damaged emotional bond with a warm heart and tender hands.

Forgiveness and seeking it are steps in the right direction. I must say, I find it incredibly hard to utter the words, "I was wrong. I'm sorry." Of course, being a forgiveness researcher has helped. I think about forgiveness, apologies, restitution and making things right all the time. I have many triggers that, in almost every situation, make me eventually think about forgiveness. I say "eventually" because I blush to admit that it isn't always my first thought. By reading this book, you are activating triggers that will stimulate some new thought processes about forgiving that I hope at times will be relevant to dealing with your children, parents, spouse and others. I hope, too, you will build some other understandings of forgiveness, and those will become permanent structures that are waiting to be triggered when you need them.

Family is a great place to admit you are wrong, when you might be. Saying "I'm sorry. I was wrong," is good practice for being a parent. Parents often need to say, "I'm sorry. Can you forgive me?" to lubricate strained relationships with their children. I know that this is important with my wife, too.

We get into the mindset, though, that we are the parents and we shouldn't make mistakes. We think that we will undercut our authority if we admit to mistakes. That simply isn't true. A family is not like a military unit in which obedience must be instantaneous and a leader's orders are never questioned in the field. The authority of a parent is based on love and care for their children. It is based on parental sacrifice that makes children want to sacrifice also. It is based on relational humility that makes the children believe—with good cause—that their parents love them, will treat the children's interests above their own and will not make decisions that advance their own interests above the children's welfare. To make it even more challenging for parents, I don't think most children can learn mutual self-sacrifice well until their brains have finished maturing. And the bad news is, that doesn't occur until around the age of twenty-five.

I believe it is helpful for parents to admit mistakes even if we are not sure we have made a mistake. If the other person perceives me to have made an error or acted harmfully, that is enough for me to make an effort to repair the damage to our relationship. I have never been damaged by saying, "I was wrong," in a close relationship.

A reason to admit to wrongdoing: Relational humility. When we as parents refuse to admit wrong decisions and seek forgiveness, we convey to the child exactly the opposite of relational humility. We convey that we will protect our own ego even if the child has to suffer. Relational humility provokes love in the other person.

This isn't a one-way street. Children do occasionally disappoint us as parents. I thank the Lord that my children have done so little to disappoint Kirby and me. But on the rare occasions when disappointment has occurred, it has been accompanied by a host of emotions. Of course, I have been hurt, angry and sad. But I have also felt more subtle emotions—those I'm not proud of. I have experienced self-condemnation and self-blame, accompanied by regret, guilt and shame. I remember thinking at times, *How could I have been such a failure as a parent?* I easily became swept up in my own experiences of failure, regret, shame and guilt over my parenting failures. That meant that my reactions were usually coming from self-protecting my ego rather than from empathizing with the difficult experiences of my children.

What goes around comes around. The saying "What goes around comes around" is about justice. Love given stimulates love given. Forgiveness given stimulates forgiveness given. This justice is a relational justice that isn't always immediate payback. Sometimes the time frame is extended. We are seeing this now with the huge number of baby boomers dealing with aging parents. We'll see it even more as all of those baby boomers begin to lose their faculties and have to rely on their own children for care and support.

JUST FORGIVENESS IN DECISION MAKING ABOUT ELDERCARE

Many couples—usually in their fifties or early sixties—are becoming members of a sandwich generation, finding themselves taking care of children still at home as well aging parents. Increasingly, they are dealing with the other side of the sandwich—eldercare. Their parents are in poor health, perhaps having experienced a few cardiovascular events, dementia or cancer. The "sandwiched" adults find themselves in the role of caretakers for their own parents. That strains their marriage, their relationships with their siblings over difficult and financially important decisions, and their relationship with their parents. Misunderstandings and hurts abound. Forgiveness is necessary.

In an eldercare situation, one family member may want to keep an ailing parent out of an assisted-living facility. This person may quote the Scripture, "Honor your father and your mother" (Ex 20:12). A sibling who is concerned about the impact of keeping the aging and ailing parent at home may quote, "Each one of you also must love his wife . . . and the wife must respect her husband" (Eph 5:33). Both Scriptures are true. However, for each family member, different needs are important at the time of the discussion. So different needs result in each one giving more weight to a different verse. They may even be able to "hear" the other person's argument and to value the other's point of view, but each may remain convinced that he or she is hearing from the Lord at this moment. They are treating Scripture the same way we treat our inconsistencies in our own personalities. Remember that immediate triggers tend to make us focus on part of our personality and, importantly, ignore the things not in the immediate spotlight.

What is the way out of this dilemma? Both family members may be enlisting God on their side. Both may be tallying Scriptures that support their point of view. Both think with certainty that they are discerning the leading of the Holy Spirit.

This dilemma can only be resolved if (a) one person uses more power than the other, (b) one person gives up, or (c) one or both exhibit humility. Power can be used from a one-up position. Such tactics can be as subtle as arranging the assisted living, which might make the other person feel guilty for undoing the work. Or power tactics can be as crude as coercing the other sibling to cave in at the threat of withdrawing finances. Power can be used also from a one-down position. Guilt is used to sabotage the victor's enjoyment, or nasty retaliation is used in an issue unrelated to eldercare.

One sibling may simply give up. This may be done because the person feels defeated and dejected. Or a person may also give up out of love.

Humility can help resolve the dilemma. One or both siblings may truly seek to put aside their own agendas and try to discern God's will. They may abandon their attempts to bolster their side by using references to God, Scripture or the Holy Spirit. Remember, humility involves reestablishing the perception that a person will treat us with dignity even if our needs, goals and priorities conflict with that person's needs, goals and priorities.

Humility thus requires empathy, sympathy, compassion and love—the positive, other-oriented emotions. Humility also requires a willingness to share oneself. Finally, humility requires that we sense when the other person is in submission to God, to goodness, to humanity and to the needy.

Conclusion

Love is being willing to value and not devalue someone. In the family, just forgiveness is needed at every level. In close relationships, we have many opportunities for forgiveness because we all fail to love so often. We don't even have to fail to love in order to hurt a family member's feelings. Mere perceptions of devaluing can trigger huge injustice gaps in the family member. They can open wounds that we thought were long healed.

All family members are called to love each other. The naked truth, though, is that some family members will love and forgive out of proportion to others. That is the necessity of families in which different ages exist. As romantic partners in a loving marriage, there are times in life when each partner is giving more and the other partner is taking more. It is better not to keep score. Instead, our Christian calling is to lay down our lives for those we love. My father-in-law gave me that great piece of advice on the day I married his daughter: "Over the course of a long marriage, things tend to even out." There have been times when Kirby was very needy, and there have been times when I was. By not keeping score, we deactivate the injustice triggers. By thinking of the family as a place where I lay down my life— for my needy partner, for my needy children, for my needy mother-in-law as she battles dementia—I activate the love triggers. Those triggers keep me focused humbly on love. Those triggers lead not just to justice, but to humble and just forgiveness—the essence of day-to-day love.

JUST FORGIVENESS
IN THE CHURCH

THE CHURCH IS ESTABLISHED AND maintained by God, but let's face it—the church is made up of people and is not yet the church triumphant. Churches divide. Even when they do not divide, they often have raging within them ugly interpersonal interactions that leave deep wounds across congregations and denominations. If we are to find ways that we can promote healing of the deep wounds within the church, we have to understand clearly where those wounds come from.

This isn't the only healing needed within the church. The church has a love-hate relationship with the world. We are in the world but not of the world (Jn 15:19; 2 Cor 10:3). We are to render to Caesar what is Caesar's (Mt 22:21). We are to honor the worldly authorities (Rom 13:1) but use our conscience as a church and as individuals within society not to get swept up in honoring authorities and pursuing peace at any price (1 Pet 2:16).

Finally, we are need healing in our relating to other religions and to those people who are hostile to Christianity. Healing does not mean we treat other religions as equal paths to God (Jn 14:6). Nor does it mean that we merely treat Christianity as one of many religious voices, striving to live and let live, to agree to disagree. No, Christians believe we are living within the truth (Jn 14:6). On that we cannot compromise. But we can have respectful dialogues with those of other religions and with those hostile to Christianity (see Acts 17:22-31). We can join with those of other beliefs at times (see Lk 9:50; 11:23), but at other times we also draw the line in the sand (Mt 12:39-45).

In this chapter, we will examine what we can do to help heal the church. We will address each issue, but we'll find that the clue to our behavior comes, not surprisingly by now, in the humble application of just forgiveness.

HEALING DIVISIONS WITHIN CHURCHES

Let's strip it down to the very basics. Wounds happen in the church because of two fundamental reasons: Either people differ on doctrines or people treat each other poorly.

God calls us to be pure in doctrine. There is a legitimate justification for not maintaining fellowship with a body of other Christian believers because important doctrines differ. This is the basis of denominationalism in Christianity.

However, I believe that most wounds in the church do not result from doctrinal differences. They are the result of how people treat each other. Doctrine is too often used as a club to bludgeon our enemies into submission. Failures in humility seem at the core of most church conflict. As disciples of Christ, we are commanded to love other Christians and even to love our enemies. When we do not practice love, then division, separation and further sin occur. There are deep, psychological reasons why people do not treat each other well that are rooted in human anthropology. My advice here cannot be boiled down to a simple "Can't we all be nice?" or "Can't we all get along?" We must recognize the complexity of human motivations and personality to understand why deep wounds are experienced within congregations and to be able to heal those wounds effectively.

Sociology, doctrine and interpersonal patterns. Sociologist Max Weber wrote around the turn of the twentieth century. He suggested a brilliant sociological analysis of denominationalism and of what prevents it.[1] He distinguished between churches and sects. He used the term *church* broadly, referring to believing communities rather than specifically Christian communities. He used the term *sect* to refer to any group of religious believers organized around charismatic leadership. *Charismatic* refers to gifted leaders, not to what we think of as the charismatic renewal, which is built on God's grace-gifts to believers.

A church is a community of religious believers who engage in established practices. But a church does not spring into existence fully grown. All churches begin as sects. Sects usually arise in opposition to an established church and organize around a person. Abraham left Ur and eventually founded a family group, the Israelites. Moses congealed Judaism around the law. Jesus was (among other things) a charismatic leader who organized a sect of followers, which was later organized by Peter, James, Paul and the other apostles after Jesus' resurrection and ascension. Muhammad organized Islam around his leadership.

As sects grow, they become unwieldy and unable to operate on the basis of charismatic leadership. We are familiar with Jethro advising Moses that he would need to set up a hierarchical structure (Ex 18:14-26; Deut 1:15-17). Similarly, with Christianity, house churches proliferated across Asia Minor, but eventually a structure had to be imposed (Acts 6:1; 11:1-4; 15:1-35). Five centers of Christianity were named, by acclamation, and councils began to decide matters of doctrine that had until then been decided by local elders. At that stage, argued Weber, the sect became a church. Leadership was no longer vested in charismatic leaders but in *offices*—pastors, bishops, councils. The office was said to have authority, not the person who occupied the office.

Inevitably, however, differences of opinion and personal agendas create dissatisfactions within any church. Like-minded dissenters begin to coalesce and demand change. If they are defeated in their change attempts, they might break away and form a sect.

According to Weber, some churches have developed ways to handle differences within their boundaries. Others are not as flexible. The Roman

Catholic Church has tended to be flexible. There are orders (e.g., Jesuits, Benedictines, Franciscans), monasteries and different aspects of the church in which dissenters can remain Roman Catholic and yet have a different identity and emphasis. Two failures in Roman Catholicism were the split with Orthodoxy and the Protestant Reformation. The Protestant Reformation began as a sect. Its emphasis on doctrine, however, was inflexible. Thus when dissenters to Lutheranism (such as groups rooted in the Reformed theology of Calvin) or to the Anglican Church (such as Wesley's Methodists) occurred, they tended to become sects, which then became churches, which spawned new sects.

We can look at differences in doctrine at different levels of generality. At the broadest level, of course, there are differences across religions. There are also important differences even within Christianity. The divisions between Roman Catholicism and Orthodoxy were the earliest major divisions. Protestantism later split off. After Protestantism's split, with its emphasis on doctrine, the Protestant denominations proliferated. Each of the Protestant denominations believes important doctrinal differences exist that justify forming a separate denomination from others within Protestant Christianity. Doctrine is clearly important, and doctrinal differences provide reasons and justifications for splits. Today the worldwide Anglican fellowship may rupture. But consider this: Long before 2009, the same differences existed within the Anglican fellowship. Yet people coexisted despite the differences. Why then have the differences become so crucial that numerous churches have left the fellowship?

Though doctrinal differences are real, they are usually red herrings in explaining splits in churches. People of conscience will necessarily make decisions about their doctrinal beliefs and will gravitate toward different religions or denominations. We are attracted to denominations or congregations by similarities. However, churches that divide or experience conflict do not do so because of doctrinal differences. Usually people in a church have relatively uniformly self-selected doctrines. When a church split occurs, people may agree on ninety-nine out of a hundred important doctrinal issues, but the one salient issue is used to justify splitting the congregation. We have to ask, then, how does such an issue gain the power to divide a congregation? I believe it usually has more to do with the way people treat each other than the importance of the issue. People tend to hurt each other through two basic patterns: power struggles and failure to act in love.

Power struggles. A *power struggle* is a division over an issue, but the real dynamic behind the disagreement is not the issue.[2] The real dynamic is disagreement over who has the say in the issue. In marriage counseling, I have often seen partners in the midst of power struggles. They will literally reverse their positions on issues from time to time because really what is being negotiated is who has the power in the relationship. For example, a woman might complain that the family never goes anywhere for summer vacation. The man justifies his position by saying he works hard, is under a lot of stress and doesn't want the added stress of travel. However, if the man were to come home and say, "Let's go to Yellowstone National Park this summer," the wife is almost certain to object. She might not actually say she wants to stay home, but she might say, "No, let's go to Yosemite National Park." At issue is who has the say about what the family will do.

This frequently occurs in churches too. Churches might divide over a doctrinal issue. Or one member of the congregation might be acting offensively, and people line up in support for or against that member. The issue usually is a negotiation of power.

Power struggles develop over conflicting emergent goals. (Note that this is a term used by couples therapists and has no relationship to "emergent churches."[3]) When issues arise and there is underlying tension within the relationship, the partners focus their tension, and thus their attention, onto the new issues. They act out their conflicts around those new issues. Because the new issues are undecided, the patterns are not already fixed. Conflicting parties see the new issue as a chance to gain power—to have the say. Old issues recede into the background. Power struggles often come to a head when the sides take incompatible positions and vow to make their position the only one.[4] They forget that their declared position is likely only one of many positions that could meet their interests. The power struggle is over which position will prevail.

During power struggles, people's empathy for each other decreases. People focus on winning, not on the other people. Partners or sides in a church disagreement may hurt each other and inflict wounds that they ordinarily would not inflict.

Failure to act in love. This leads to the second major reason that church members hurt each other. People do not act in love toward each other. I have defined love as being willing to value the people on the other side and being unwilling to devalue people.[5] As a conflict heats up and the issue takes a prominent place in the church's life, people focus on winning and on their own ego needs. They devalue or do not value people who disagree. This is not one-sided. Furthermore, even if the people are indeed treating each other with respect and valuing each other, people on the other side may perceive themselves to be devalued.

People tend to hold irrational unspoken beliefs. For example, most people believe something like this: "I deserve for everyone important in my life to love me, regardless of what I do and how badly or how well I act." Or people might believe that "I deserve to be heard or listened to." Others might believe "I deserve to be recognized as wise, and therefore others should allow me to be influential in making decisions."

It is easy to see, then, that if two sides in a church disagree with each other, people on either side may perceive that they are not being valued. Their irrational beliefs are not being acknowledged by people on the other side.

WOUNDS INFLICTED DURING CHURCH CONFLICTS

In chapter four I outlined a model of forgiveness and relational spirituality (see figure 4.3). That model is particularly important when we are dealing with hurts in the church. Those wounds often are perceived as desecrations (in figure 4.3, the TS relationship). Psychologists of religion at Bowling Green State University in Ohio have studied the severity of response when we feel that something sacred has been lost or desecrated.[6] If I prize the unity of feeling and thought in my local church, and if disagreement disrupts and destroys that, then it can harm not only my relationship with the offenders (in figure 4.3, the VO relationship), but it can also put kinks in my relationship with God (the VS relationship).

Even worse, I might feel that my beliefs in God have been treated profanely or desecrated. If I believe, for example, that according to Scripture men should be elders, but not women, then a congregational vote that goes against my belief might leave me feeling like my sacred beliefs have been trampled under the boots of an overzealous women's movement. Similarly, if I believe fervently that Scripture clearly teaches that women should have equal access to leadership as men, a congregational vote that goes against this belief will likewise be seen as a desecration. After such decisions and the power moves that accompany them, the blow of experiencing a desecration at the hands of the beloved brothers and sisters in my own congregation is virtually impossible to simply put aside or forgive easily. The desecration is not only a sacred loss but a deep desecration and betrayal.

Such losses and desecrations make me reevaluate the character of my fellow church members. I might come to perceive them as not really brothers and sisters after all, or at least as estranged family members. If you refer back to figure 4.3, you'll see that I have rethought the OS relationship. That is, I now see the offenders as having a different type of spiritual relationship with God than I do. Thus it is harder for me to forgive.

Accumulation of injustices. People perceive a deep sense of injustice when they experience conflict with each other and when power struggles or unloving acts are perceived to be taking place. And as we see, these perceived injustices are exacerbated when the struggles are within the local church community. Let me deal solely with the remaining human aspect for a moment—the wounds that arise from interacting with other people in a power struggle.

Injustices usually accumulate. People on "one side" in a church dispute keep an internal accounting of offenses by the "other side" as an injustice gap, in the same way they do when individuals harm them. Anyone on the other side who harms, insults or doesn't respect a person contributes to the injustice gap. Then, a big sinful event—a quantum change—can occur. Of course, after people make a quantum change in their perception of the relationship, the injustices seem to accumulate rapidly. When someone on the other side does something nice or appears to be understanding, that does not reduce the injustice gap as much as a small injustice increases the injustice gap. It takes a lot of understanding and empathy by people on the other side to begin to close that injustice gap.

Hurt feelings. People who believe they have been misunderstood get their feelings hurt. When we have been hurt, we look to hurt back.[7] Hurt feelings trigger payback strategies (see figure 5.1). Physical pain creates anger and fear, and the pain of hurt feelings is similar.

Blows to the ego. Another wound that occurs within the congregation is the blow to the ego from simply losing the power struggle. Nearly half of the people in a divided congregation will end up losing. This is especially true if a public vote is taken within the congregation. Sometimes, if a congregation depends on ruling elders, then everyone might get angry with the elders for making a decision they believe does not value them properly.

Guilt and self-condemnation. Throughout a power struggle within a congregation, people often behave in ways they are later ashamed of. This creates a sense of guilt, regret and self-condemnation that can wound a person's personality. Perhaps the guilt and self-condemnation feed poor self-esteem. The person might simply feel bad about himself or herself and want to leave the congregation to escape a situation that reminds him or her of a painful past. On the other hand, the person might feel guilty and self-condemning and seek to deal with those feelings by being defensive, justifying his or her behavior and maintaining obsessive correctness in behavior.

Seeking vindication. Sometimes people endure division in a congregation and do not leave the congregation after the division is settled. But whether they're on the winning or the losing side, they may desire vindication. They look desperately for proof that they were, after all, right. For years afterward they look for vindication and refer to the events of the past, seeking to have everyone vindicate their behavior.

Negative memories. Certainly people who go through painful conflicts within a congregation are plagued by negative memories. Reminders will stimulate them to anger, depression or anxiety. The natural tendency, then, is to escape from or avoid the situation that provides such reminders. Thus after a church has had a painful division or conflict, it is not uncommon for many members to leave the church, regardless of which side they were on in the conflict.

Past actions leave people feeling wounded. They might have experienced betrayal by others whom they thought were supporters, or not enough support from those who were simply not aggressive enough in arguing the issue. They may feel antagonism, resentment and hatred for people on the other side because of the harmful behaviors that went on.

As a result, after the conflict dies down, people simply may no longer feel at home in the congregation. The memories and reminders are too raw or too persisting. They have experienced a big sinful event or a quantum change. They may worry about the influence of other people with differing doctrinal beliefs on their children, or they may resent the pastor for teaching objectionable doctrines. Altogether, the wounds experienced from conflict, which seem to have come from many directions, differ in depth from superficial to deeply disturbing and life changing.

GROUP DYNAMICS IN CHURCH CONFLICTS

Groups of people behave in ways that individuals would probably never behave if they were not in the group.[8] These patterns must be overcome if we are to heal the rifts within congregations that have gone through conflict.

Limiting contact with the other side. When an issue divides a congregation, people in each group tend to meet with like-minded folks but exclude those who differ. They do this for two reasons.

First, there is group pressure to think similarly to people we hang out with. Classic experiments in social psychology show that people will converge on their judgment if the situation is ambiguous.[9] People want to have consensus. They modify their own individual opinions to be like others in the group. So they seek out like-minded folks with whom they can agree on whom the bad guys are (i.e., them, not us) and what wrongs the bad guys have committed.

Second, other social psychology experiments show that people will go along with the group even in cases where an objective difference from the group opinion exists. Solomon Asch asked participants in his studies to judge which line out of three standard lines was closest in length to another given line.[10] Each participant was grouped with five to seven other people, whom the participant thought were also participants in the study. Actually they worked with the experimenter. Their job was to collectively give the wrong answer to the question at strategic points during the study. The single participants, faced with group agreement on a wrong answer, would often go along with the group. Why? There is great pressure to conform to group judgments and perceptions.

Encouraging negative out-group biases. As a result of these two group effects—convergence on judgments of unclear happenings and a desire to fit in with the group—a bias against the out-group can easily develop. As we learned in chapter four, group members perceive the offenders' relationship with the Sacred (OS in figure 4.3) as different from their own.

People meeting exclusively with members of their own group share stories and judgments about the many wrongdoings the other group has inflicted. That shapes people's attitudes and judgments to reinforce the bias against that group. They create triggers that stimulate structures and processes that magnify in-group and out-group differences (see figure 5.1).

In addition, we are all ego-driven. We believe that we are right. Thus people who agree with us must therefore also be right and share some of our wisdom. A positive in-group bias tends to develop, as well as a negative out-group bias. The in-group bias sees people who agree with us as wiser, stronger and more virtuous than people who disagree with us. The out-group bias sees people who disagree with us as different from us, and frankly not quite human.

Portraying out-group members as nonhuman or subhuman. Robert Sapolsky, a biologist, evolutionist and cultural anthropologist, tells an interesting anecdote.[11] When Middle Eastern tribes, and sometimes countries, go to war, they paint a picture of each other showing the inhumanity of the other group. The stark differences that are highlighted fuel the hatred that sustains the war. Then when peace is being brokered, leaders of the two tribes or countries must find common ground. Sometimes they sit and talk with each other for hours, at the end of which they "discover common relatives." So the other side is not an alien animal after all but just a distant relative. Then they can reconcile.

This attempt to portray the other side as nonhuman is not unknown in the United States. In the Gulf War of the early nineties, just before Congress voted to authorize the war, a supposed Kuwaiti nurse testified that Iraqi troops had come to her Kuwaiti hospital and removed three hundred fragile children from incubators in order to take the incubators back to Iraq. In the vote to authorize the war, which passed by five votes, seven people cited that case of horrid barbarism of the Iraqis as the reason for their yes vote. Later it was discovered that the testimony of the "nurse" was bogus, presented to arouse sympathy for going to war against Iraq. (We saw the same thing happen in the unfruitful search for weapons of mass destruction in Iraq during the war that deposed Saddam Hussein. But the WMD accusation served its purpose. Who would use WMD but those who are nonhuman? So the United States went to war.)

Hiding in anonymity within groups. Social psychology experiments have also shown that groups provide a sense of anonymity. Because we are part of a group, we feel like we will not be singled out to be responsible for all of our actions. When people believe themselves to have anonymity, they often will do more harmful behavior than if they were responsible as individuals for their behavior.

Using spirituality as a weapon. Christians are not immune to power struggles and power agendas. In groups people form alliances and coalitions to accomplish their goals. Often their goals are about power and influence. These power agendas are not usually aimed at something like taking control of a Fortune 500 company. Power in Christian churches, even the biggest and wealthiest, doesn't usually translate into riches or control over people's lives. Power within churches is usually about having our way. We invest our lives and finances in a church, and we just want to have a say in how it is operated. We want people to look up to us. Often this power game is played by being the most spiritual person in the church. We know these kind of people. They always say, "Let's pray about it." They spiritualize most conflicts, drawing attention to their own humility. Yet despite the spiritualizing, it seems that they keep the attention focused on themselves. Here power is the ability to focus attention on oneself.

How can complex and diverse Christians settle on remarkably similar agendas despite their differences? It is virtually impossible to predict the behavior of groups by looking at the individual members. Yes, the members of any local congregation are likely to be more similar to each other than to individuals in a different congregation. But within the congregation, there are almost certainly people with individual differences in interests, goals, methods of accomplishing goals, preferences, coping and defensiveness. Because of the vast differences, the group seems to behave in ways that are influenced by subtle triggers that activate structures within the church and translate into behavioral interactions. A group, with its collective memory, is like an individual with a history. The personal memory of one's history is a powerful structure that has numerous triggers attached. A church's collective memory includes how the congregation worships, what people talk about after church and even what types of clothes members wear to church. Churches seem to have a worldview. Often some member may have written that worldview down as a mission statement. These established structures drive the behavior of the church. They establish the norms for the church's operation. When someone violates one of those norms, the disapproval is palpable.

When a potential split begins to take shape within a congregation, each side claims God is on its side. This is not unique to church conflicts. Virtually every country or faction within a country, when it goes to war, will claim that God is on its side. In a congregational conflict, this often shows up as a difference in the way Scripture is interpreted. The argument can turn on a single verse or on which verses are the relevant ones—the ones that "count."

In a family system, family members in a power struggle form coalitions across hierarchical boundaries. One person (for example, one child) triangulates a third party, gaining power by enlisting the third party on his or her side. In churches, group dynamics are similar. Factions try to triangulate God on their side. This is particularly toxic within the church because the implications of winning the theological debate might mean that the other side is treated as heretical. Words like "heresy" or "blasphemy" are used. Wounds from theological arguments can be particularly vicious. Whereas the purpose of theology is to rightly understand the Word of God to promote Christian living, during church power struggles theology is used as a weapon against brothers and sisters. Then those very brothers and sisters begin to be seen as heretics or blasphemers and not as Christian brothers and sisters. By dehumanizing—as most in-groups do when having serious conflict with out-groups—it is easier to fight and hurt the other.

There are many reasons why people might feel wounded and in need of healing after a conflict within a congregation. True, many of these go back to the fallen nature of humans—their need for power, influence, love and respect from everyone around them. Certainly people are likely to behave badly because they can take comfort in group anonymity within the group or feel stronger because they think the group will approve of their behavior.

HEALING WOUNDS IN CHURCH CONFLICTS

Wounds and betrayals and resulting resentment and negative memories characterize the aftermath of a conflict. Yet people want to escape negative situations as quickly as possible so they won't be reminded of the conflict and pain. So let's ask the tough question: How can we help wounded people in an injured congregation heal?

Love is the best preventive medicine. The best healing, of course, is to prevent significant wounds from occurring. Because the major human desire that is thwarted in congregational conflicts is love—feeling valued and not devalued—the best preventive strategy is to seek to value all people. People in the congregation should strive to treat each other with respect and love, to treat each other as a pearl of great value (see Mt 13:45-46). Christians will be together throughout eternity, so it is important to be able to see that we are interacting with a family member with whom we disagree. The flip side is to stifle devaluing of those on the other side of any issue. The leadership in the congregation can try to keep gossip about the other side from multiplying by cautioning people against that tendency.

Have a goal. If a Christian church community is to be healed, it must have a goal. The goal is to restore a sense that people on the other side are precious brothers and sisters. As such, they are worthy of our love and care, are mutually beneficial because of complementary gifts (1 Cor 12:12-31) and are safe from our attacks. These perceptions won't simply develop. We must consciously plan ways to reach this goal. Those are the very conditions that make for healing, redemption and reconciliation.

Pray. Prayer changes things. The leadership should challenge all members to pray for discernment of their own part in conflicts and for ideas of how to rebuild unity. God can use such prayers to soften hearts.

Educate the Christian community about in-group and out-group dynamics. It can help if people are told about the development of in-group and out-group biases. They can be educated about how groups tend to behave in more hurtful ways than individuals do, because in a group responsibility is divided.

Resolve conflicts before they get out of hand. Conflict resolution strategies should be put into motion as soon as possible. It might be possible to forge a win-win situation by using programs such as Ury and Fisher's *Getting to Yes: Negotiating Agreement Without Giving In.*[12]

Find a mediator. The best person to mediate a problem-solving or conflict-resolution program might be an elder who is respected by both sides. If the congregation is already hotly divided, it might be necessary to bring in a mediator from outside the congregation.

Develop the qualities needed for healing. It is not always possible to prevent conflict and prevent wounds from occurring in the midst of conflict. The conflict may have run its course, leaving behind it a battlefield littered with wounded hearts. In the same way that empathy, understanding, listening and valuing stand the best chance of preventing conflict, those same qualities are most likely to heal the wounds that arise from power struggles and unkind acts within congregations.

Allow public small-group meetings. Early in the healing process, it is usually not a good idea to get the whole church together *for discussion,* though the church can be brought together *for education.* After education, healing will occur fastest in small groups that incorporate people from each side. Structured groups are better than unstructured discussions in the early phases. It is too easy for unstructured discussions to lead to further disagreements and hurts, or to be perceived as merely the rehashing of old wounds. People might be reluctant to attend such meetings. After structured groups complete fixed curricula, less structured get-togethers can be arranged. People often want to have floor time. The leadership of the church might want to meet with individuals who were heavily involved in the conflict. The meetings should be pastoral rather than accusatory or corrective.

Encourage churchwide prayer. Churchwide prayer can be directed toward specific trouble spots and toward providing a positive vision for restoration.

Reach out to those who are still upset. After a series of small-group and congregational meetings are carried out and churchwide prayer has been practiced for healing, it is necessary to wait and see what kind of fallout will occur. There may be people who wish to leave the congregation. It is a good sign if people keep reaching out to those potential changers. In one church disagreement with which I was involved, my wife and I reached out to a disgruntled couple. They left the church eventually, but later they mentioned that we were the only couple in the church who seemed to care whether they left. I know that many people in the congregation were concerned that this couple would leave, but they were reluctant to talk to them because they were afraid others would perceive them as taking sides.

Moving on versus processing the past. When churches go through hard times, some people stay, and some move to other churches. Soon new members trickle in who did not go through the turmoil. Most of those who stick around but still have hurt feelings usually do not believe that the past conflict was "processed" well. *After all,* they think, *how well could it have been processed if my feelings are still hurt?* They want to talk more about the conflict. New members can't understand why we don't just "move on." The old members caution against allowing wounds to fester. This tension can be eased (but probably not completely avoided) if church leaders provide a statement that brings closure. Then they declare the matter as settled as possible. This cannot occur too soon after a conflict, or people with hurt feelings will feel muzzled, and pressure and resentment will build instead of decline.

Making a wise decision to split. What if a split is in everyone's best interests? Let's face it. Sometimes people just cannot live together. If they continue to try, they will probably kill each other. I have seen congregations divide over contentious, seemingly irreconcilable differences such as gay marriage; abortion rights; ordination of gays, lesbians and bisexuals; and the inerrancy of Scripture. Acrimony becomes so intense that the sides cannot live or worship together.

As we discussed in chapter five, Jacob and Esau were so at odds that Jacob feared for his life, even after sending ahead of him great restitution for his past offenses. Then Jacob wrestled with an angel of God, who so humbled Jacob that he became a broken man. Jacob and Esau reconciled, yet in wisdom they did not try to live together.

This is the missing step in most church splits. The only effort to reconcile is to offer to graciously accept the other side's sword at our feet. Usually both sides are similarly "willing" to be so gracious. Thus no reconciliation occurs.

Yet is it possible, in Christ's power and love, to reconcile. Then, in

Christ's wisdom, a decision might still be reached to split. This can only happen if one side takes the initiative to treat the other side not as apostates or enemies but as brothers and sisters in Christ. This requires being vulnerable, counting the cost and taking up Jesus' cross. Can we follow?

Below I summarize a dozen suggestions for healing. The principles involve justice, forgiveness and peace and are rooted in the Christian virtues.

1. Hostilities must stop. A cease-fire is needed. All parties need to cultivate love and a desire for peace.

2. Enlist as many people as possible on both sides to pray for peace and for those who differ from them. Pray a blessing on them. This is even more necessary if particularly harmful acts have already occurred than if hostilities are still latent.

3. Conflict management and communication need to be taught, preached and practiced amid an attitude of respect. All parties need to cultivate a desire for justice. The focus should be on helping others feel that justice is being served as well as it can be. "What can *I* do to help *you* feel that repairs have been made?" is the question each should ask.

4. The people need to relate to each other more than to the opinion leaders. Often congregations split because of conflict between a few key players who drag others along for support. Before long, groups of people are fighting. To free a congregation from conflict, the faction leaders need to be disempowered, and some of the people on each side need to work for reconciliation.

5. People need to tell their stories in small groups that include members of both sides of conflicts or misunderstandings. Empathy can be initiated by hearing of the suffering of others. All parties need to cultivate love.

6. Parties need to confess their own wrongdoing. Also each party must grant decisional forgiveness to others and, where possible, express that forgiveness. They must commit to practice both confession and decisional forgiveness.

7. The new people who want to move on must develop empathy for the people who want to process the past. The new people must tolerate the old business. Similarly, the old members must have empathy for those who did not experience the misunderstanding. They must not inflict repeated rehashing of old business on the new members. All parties need to cultivate empathy and love.

8. Forgiveness and reconciliation need to be promoted and practiced. This can be done through public rituals and programs, often through small groups.

9. Repeated interaction with like-minded and different-minded believers must be aimed at. The people formerly on the other side need to be accepted and included. If both sides continue to interact, the congregation can be brought back together.

10. With all being done, we must accept that we will never know, understand or resolve everything. We must expose as a fantasy that, if we could only understand what happened, we could put it behind us, have closure, never think of it again. The fact is, a painful event will be remembered. It should be. Remembering the pain helps us not make the same mistakes again.

11. A leader should publicly declare the matter substantially resolved, urging tolerance if some are still unhealed but encouraging the congregation to move forward. A ritual congregational response should be formulated.

12. If possible, lessons learned should be written down. It would even be helpful to articulate them aloud within the congregation.

One of the worst parts of life in the church is that we hurt each other. Power struggles not only damage people's faith by disillusioning them in their view of other Christians, but power struggles also are a bad witness to people not in the church. Christians need to repair the damage done as quickly and as thoroughly as they can. This is our calling, to be healers and to reconcile people to God as well as to each other (2 Cor 5:18-20).

HEALING DIVISIONS BETWEEN
THE CHURCH AND THE WORLD

Let's shift our focus away from conflict within the church to conflict between the church and the world. Certainly there are many instances in which the church as a whole or those who have authority to speak for the church have taken a position at odds with other communities or nations. Sometimes in looking back we see that the church has gone awry. How does the church end up doing violence?

Wrong-headedness about means and ends. We have heard of instances in which church members who oppose abortion have aggressively impeded and intimidated women on their way to abortion clinics. People have murdered physicians who perform abortions. We also have heard countless times about the unwillingness of the church to oppose wrongdoing. For example, the Pope recently apologized for the church's failure to try to stop the Holocaust. The church in South Africa did not oppose the apartheid policies of the nationalist government. The list goes on.

How does the church—whose champion is Jesus, whose mission was to preach the good news to the poor, to announce pardon for the prisoners and recovery of sight to the blind, to set the burdened and the battered free and to announce the year of the Lord (Lk 4:18-19)—get to the place where it will either do violence or stand by and not interfere with oppression? Often it is because we see clear ends and think that the means do not matter.

Focusing on righteous ends hides unrighteous means. Let's take an example. Suppose we think that abortion is taking lives, so we think that stopping abortion justifies acting in oppressive, coercive, even violent ways. We focus on the one truth and obscure other considerations (i.e., coercing someone else acting in accord with our own conscience). Using our model in figure 5.1, the triggers fire our righteous indignation, which sweeps us along some of the mental processes that focus attention on belief structures. However, as we have repeatedly seen, when we focus emotionally on one set of processes and structures, it usually means we are not focusing on other important structures. It is precisely when we feel the most righteous, the most caught up in doing good, that we must force ourselves to ask, what truths are being hidden by these righteous feelings and motives?

Focusing on righteous means hides unrighteous ends. Similarly, we might use biblical, even forgiving, means, yet not attend to the ends. The church in Germany during World War II, in South Africa during the apartheid era, and in the United States during slavery or the internment of Japanese Americans during World War II, focused on biblical means. They said, "We must obey the civil authorities. We should turn the other cheek. We must love our enemies." But those Christian means likewise sent their thoughts and actions down a pathway that caused them to ignore justice.

Not acting in humility. We get in trouble when we seek to bring about righteousness under our own power. We are deeply sinful. We know this, but we do not always let that knowledge guide us. We think that we know what is right. We say to ourselves that we are God's hammer to pound out justice. When we think that, alarm bells should be furiously ringing in our heads. We should be thinking not just about righteousness, but about what God would have us do: do justice, love mercy and walk humbly with our God (Mic 6:8).

HEALING DIVISIONS WITH OTHER RELIGIONS

The Crusades stand today as perhaps the biggest blight on the church in history. How could the Crusades have happened? No doubt there were sincere religious motives. But there were more secret psychological seeds. Though admittedly this may oversimplify the case, the three principal seeds included fear, greed and the triumph of power-lust over love.[13] Those seeds still grow spiritual weeds today.

Fear. A social psychology theory called Terror Management Theory (TMT) explains how fear can lead to schism and violence against other religions.[14] TMT doesn't condemn Christianity. It explains how people act when they face a crisis of existence. If our way of life is threatened, we fear losing our existence. We defend ourselves. If our faith is challenged, we bolster our own faith and put down another faith. Sometimes when we are very threatened, we take up arms to show how strong our faith is. Sometimes we feel attacked and believe that to defend ourselves, we must fight back. TMT tells us that oppressive faith happens because we are anxious about our very survival.

Greed. It is no secret that part of the shame of the Crusades was the goal of plundering the treasures of Muslim cultures. This was not the main reason, and probably was rarely referred to during the Crusades. Nonetheless, greed was not an insignificant motivation. In the present, the United States characterizes its struggles in the Middle East as a struggle against Muslim terrorists and tyrants. Indeed, in addition to a true fight against terrorism and tyranny, fear and greed for oil (and the freedom it buys) certainly play a part.

Power versus love. My favorite author is Malcolm Muggeridge, a major communications celebrity of the 1970s and 1980s, who brought Mother Teresa to the eyes of the world.[15] Having lived at the pinnacle of power, he was keen on the distinction between love and power as motives for our behavior. In his latter years he gave up a celebrated atheistic stance and converted to Christianity, even becoming a popular Christian apologist in his last twenty or so years. He joined the Roman Catholic Church rather than a Protestant or Anglican church because he saw in the crucifix the humility of Jesus. In the empty cross of Protestantism, he saw the power of Jesus. While he knew that each emphasized one part of the true picture of both love and power, he wanted to identify with love more than power.

God did exert his power over death in the resurrection, power over disease in healing, and power over suffering because, as Paul argues, this present suffering is not worth comparing with the glory to come (Rom 8:18). Furthermore, in the end, Jesus will come again in power. But God also does not eliminate suffering. He is with us in the furnace of persecution, pain and privation. He comforts us so that we can comfort others. We are to pick up our cross and walk humbly, laying down our life, as Jesus did. We are to die to self. We are called to love God above all, and secondly to love others. We are to let love be our aim.

When we look at other religions and see a red flag, this is our lust for power. Instead we should look and see needy people. We need to be in dialogue with the people in that religion, not simply respond to a red flag. The red flag of power triggers fear, which leads to defensiveness and attack. But God is sufficient to protect his church. Yes, we sometimes must be willing to go to battle and be the instruments God uses to protect his church. But I believe that occurs less often than we think.

In this chapter we have been talking of two problems. In one, we have divisions in the church. We seek to tear apart our brothers and sisters. In the other, we have divisions between the church and the world. We do not bless the world or other religions but instead seek to crush them. In both problems, we are deviating from authentic Christianity. We are doing what the flesh requires of us, not what the Lord God of heaven requires of us.

In his essay "The Church's Great Malfunctions," Yale theologian Miroslav Volf argues that such problems are due to two malfunctions in the church.[16] Volf called these malfunctions "idleness of faith" and "oppressiveness of faith." We fail due to idleness of faith when we see faith as mere deliverance and blessing, not as how we must live day to day as men and women of faith. Our faith is too thin, too surface-level, not deep enough. We fail due to the oppressiveness of faith when we use power to fight evil while we ignore love. We make this mistake for three reasons: First, we see in Revelation Jesus coming again in power, and we assume that we should emulate him. Instead, we miss the deeper truths that we should imitate him in his humility (Phil 2:5-11); imitate the martyrs; imitate Paul, who lived the Christian life without oppression or violence. Second, we use our faith merely to bless what we already want to do. We do not seek the hard teaching under the real truth that God supplies our needs, is merciful to us and blesses us with rich grace. Third, we are unwilling to walk that narrow path when we see it. Our failure is our unwillingness to submit our character to the fiery furnace of God by acting out love-based instead of power-based Christianity.

Kirby and I have belonged to Christ Presbyterian Church for more than thirty years. In the late 1990s, one of those hot-button issues that has split congregations and denominations emerged in our beloved congregation. Tensions mounted weekly. As conversations multiplied, it became clear to me that Kirby and I would probably end up on the short side of the congregational vote, which we ultimately did. Yet this issue did not split the church, and it did not drive Kirby and me away.

Two events made all the difference. One night Pastor Doug McMurry and an elder on the session came to our house to talk. By the end of the night, I still felt that our reasoning was not being listened to. But I was honored that we were visited by the pastor and allowed to engage in a dialogue. It wasn't necessary to visit us in our home, as the vote was fairly well determined by then. But Doug cared about losing two of the sheep entrusted to his pastorate.

The second incident involved an extended conversation between Kirby and one of the elders, Steve Sandage, who championed the other side of the issue. At the time, Steve was a doctoral student in the Ph.D. program at VCU. In fact, I was Steve's dissertation supervisor, and he was in mid-dissertation. If ever there was the potential for a vulnerable position, that was it. But Steve initiated a long conversation with Kirby. Afterward she described it as one of the most mature, honoring conversations she had ever had in the midst of a disagreement. Steve really listened to Kirby, took her reasoning seriously, and treated her with enormous respect and Christian love. He did not change Kirby's mind, nor did Kirby change Steve's mind. But that interaction was what Christian love was all about.

Steve was courageous in speaking his position in truth and love. He honored me by trusting that I would not respond with coercion at school. And he created a relationship of real understanding and mutual honor.

Kirby and I lost the battle. But Doug, Steve, Kirby and I won the war. Love was more important than power.

Twenty-three years ago, I attended a citywide worship service in Richmond. The attendees were about half black and half white. Up front sat the church pastors. The worship was emotionally moving, and numerous times I cried.

I knew that there had been racial tensions in Richmond for hundreds of years. Richmond was one of the main ports where slaves were sold on the blocks down in Shockoe Bottom. It was the capital of the Confederacy. Richmond was, if anything, a symbol of racial and ethnic differences. And that symbol was strongly evident in the churches, which continued to be ethnically segregated except for a few individuals. So this early morning worship felt to me like a historic event.

There was a lull in the worship, and as we prayed, one of the white pastors got up and walked out. He soon returned with a basin of water, and he proceeded to wash the feet of a black pastor with whom he had some bitter interactions in the past.

I have never felt, before or since, such a sense of unity within the church. It is not the act of foot-washing that is important. It is the attitude of foot-washing, of humble service, of stepping down from our high horse that helps people run together, brings peace between them and helps them share communion.

Traditional wisdom says that if I still feel an injustice gap after a long-ago wound, I should wait for the other person to close it through apology, restitution or reparation. That isn't always the math of the kingdom. Jesus was the offended one, yet he was the one who washed his disciples' feet, not the other way around.

JUST FORGIVENESS IN
COMMUNITIES AND SOCIETY

Miroslav Volf suggests that Christianity is about more than merely receiving redemption and blessings.[1] It includes, just as importantly, making it possible for others to know God personally through Jesus and the Holy Spirit. That is, we all have at least one divine mission—to infuse the communities we live in and the society we belong to with the aroma of God so that others can be drawn to the Lord. One way of describing the divine mission is the Great Commission. We are to go into all the world, teaching and making disciples of all people (Mt 28:18-20). Paul said it in another way: we have a ministry of reconciliation—reconciling people to God (see 2 Cor 5:18-20).

We carry out our ministry of reconciliation by living and working in community. In the previous chapter, we considered the special community of the church. In this chapter we look more broadly toward our lives in other communities. Not surprisingly, relationships run awry in those communities just as they do in the church—perhaps even more easily.

Christian traditions differ in the degree to which members are encouraged to interact with society. For some, the goal is to be separate from the world, which is one of the original fundamentals of the faith from which fundamentalism originated. Even the most ardent fundamentalist, though, usually lives in and interacts with numerous communities daily. Others, such as the evangelical tradition that has always appealed to me, embrace the ideal that we should live thoroughly in the world to infect the world with Christianity while relying on God to keep us from being hooked by the world into worldly lives.

The Amish at Nickel Mines, Pennsylvania, had their world invaded on October 2, 2006, when Charles Carl Roberts IV executed five schoolgirls, wounded five other children and then turned his gun on himself.[2] Police, hospitals, counselors and reporters quickly got involved. Even now writers revisit the events in that community, as I am doing.

The Amish, of course, gave a wonderful example of Christian forgiveness. Even before the sun had gone down on the murders, Amish families had visited the family of Charles Roberts, offering forgiveness. Yes, they grieved. Yet the structures of the Amish community made decisional forgiveness and the expression of forgiveness givens, not something to be debated. At the killer's funeral, there were as many from the Amish community as there were from the surrounding community.

As theologian Colin Gunton has described, we were created as communal creatures by a communal trinitarian God.[3] Therefore, we must get along in human community. Broad community interaction is not something we are sentenced to; it is something we cannot and should not avoid. We were created for community living. How else can we carry out Jesus' great commission or reconcile people to God unless we live within the fabric of society? And that requires darning the holes in that fabric.

In this chapter, I look closely at Christian living in two important communities. First I look at just forgiveness in the workplace because it is there that we spend so much time. Then I look at whether forgiveness has any place in the justice system, because this is where we might hope to find some combination or justice and forgiveness.

JUST FORGIVENESS IN THE WORKPLACE

We spend about one-third of our waking time at work. Based on sheer time, our relationships with our boss, subordinates, colleagues and workplace support systems (e.g., technical support, administrative support, human relations) are important. It is the work setting, often our boss in particular, that has virtually total control over our survival needs and many of our esteem needs. We deal hourly with people we trust (more or less) and who we hope care for us and will take care of us. Peter Hart found that up to 13 percent of the variability in life satisfaction was accounted for by job satisfaction.[4] It is not surprising, with this much time to relate and with the importance of the workplace for our happiness, that the people we work with inevitably let us down. They violate our trust, fail to meet our expectations, and do things out of spite, envy or meanness to aggravate or undermine us.

Thus the workplace is a rich source of transgressions. Most workplace literature emphasizes justice—distributive and procedural justice—and is concerned with preventing and dealing fairly with violations of justice.[5] These infractions can be due to power abuses by supervisors; coworker disagreements; corporate decisions that affect pay, promotion or downsizing; and numerous others. In the workplace, workers, customers, customer-service personnel and competitors interact. There are many opportunities for people to offend and hurt each other.[6]

However, it is not mere proximity and amount of time that might make the workplace a breeding ground for unforgiveness. Most workplaces are cultures of competition. (To their credit, many workplaces are now trying to minimize internal competition, though the marketplace will continue to emphasize external competition.) The workplace is the focal point of much of our emotional experience.[7] There is competition between and within companies. Employees compete for attention, resources, and success—even in so-called noncompetitive work settings. They are often rewarded with differential salaries. Employees invest their ego in their work, so pride in one's performance is likely to be high around work-related behaviors. In addition, people place different degrees of importance on success, which is often a factor that enhances competition and might exacerbate the negative effects of hurts and offenses. Power differentials exist. This is obvious in generally hierarchical corporate systems, but even in cooperative work settings some people are simply more influential than are others. Finally, perceived discrimination due to race or gender can stimulate unforgiveness.

Transgressions in the workplace. What kinds of transgressions occur in the workplace? First, there are transgressions done by businesses that affect their customers and shareholders. These are important and can affect huge numbers of people. For example, when it was revealed that racism was occurring at Texaco, the company apologized publicly many times.[8] On the other hand, when a Union Carbide plant in India suffered an explosion resulting in many deaths, the company's wrongdoing was not promptly dealt with. In Texaco's case, many customers were probably retained. But Union Carbide's response probably cost the company money and reputation.

Let's look at the case of the Toro Company, which manufactures lawn care products. Toro Company is often sued when people misuse power equipment. Before 1991 the company policy was to litigate all claims. Then from 1992 to 1996 Toro Company changed its policy. It expressed sympathy for personal injuries and offered restitution. In those five years, it is calculated that Toro Company saved $54,329,840.[9]

Importantly, while promoting the granting and seeking of forgiveness is good business (as in Texaco's and Toro's cases), it is not *merely* good business. It is often the *right* thing to do. It is also an alternative that is often vastly superior, for many reasons, to denial of wrongdoing, holding grudges, seeking revenge or remaining emotionally hard toward either victim or transgressor.

Although such acts by businesses can have widespread personal effects, I am going to focus on what we are more likely to experience day to day. Most people were outraged at the Enron accounting scandal, but they didn't lose sleep over it unless they lost money. But when my boss treats me unfairly or when my colleague hurts my feelings, those are the kind of workplace transgressions that matter, the kind I might lose sleep over.

Several types of workplace behaviors and conditions can set the stage for unforgiveness. First, negative evaluations by supervisors, or even the hint of a negative evaluation, can trigger unforgiveness toward supervisors.[10] Sometimes this has roots in childhood ("Mom always liked you best"), sometimes in school ("I didn't get the part in the play because she's teacher's pet"). We don't like to be evaluated negatively by authorities. Second, supervisory decisions with which employees disagree ("Why do we have to work on Sunday? That's not fair") can result in unforgiveness. Third, some people may earn more or get more perks than others for what seems like the same work. We can feel bitter toward our coworkers and administrators when unfairness happens. Fourth, disciplinary actions ("I was late for the third time this month, and now I'm now on probation and have to watch myself every minute. I think he's out to get me") can result in unforgiveness. Guilt and shame trigger defensiveness. Fifth, supervisory decisions for assigning different workloads and unpleasant duties can stimulate resentment ("He always gets the plumb assignments"). Sixth, hiring and firing provide many situations around which people experience transgressions. When downsizing occurs, certainly we would be angry if we were let go, but we might get just as upset if our friends are terminated.

To complicate matters, often it is not safe to talk about one's unforgiveness toward an employer, supervisor and sometimes even coworkers. It is not a good idea to gossip anyway. As Christians, we certainly want to avoid being gossips or even being thought of that way. But even legitimate discussion of what is going on in a company can be fatal to a career or a job. Power differentials result in real consequences for expressing dissatisfaction. Therefore, unforgiveness often must be dealt with alone or with a support system outside the workplace. Conflict management skills could prevent a few transgressions, but many perceived transgressions are not likely to be addressed interpersonally, especially when they cross hierarchical boundaries.

Consequences of unforgiveness in the workplace. If workers harbor chronic unforgiveness in the workplace, they may have poor morale—feelings of resentment, bitterness, hostility, hatred, mistrust, suspicion, anger and fear.[11] Poor morale can affect their productivity. They might call in sick because work isn't a happy place. Unhappy workers sometimes get "hurt" and take time off according to disability laws. By spending time ruminating about workplace conditions and past transgressions, workers might produce less and put themselves at risk for physical injury or mental health problems. So workers might really be ill or injured more often because of the health impact of chronic unforgiveness.

Workers with workplace grudges might simply not cooperate with each other or management.[12] When workers get hurt in the workplace, they often get sad or mad, and that usually leads to getting even. They make up their losses. They strike back at the business or boss through *property deviance* (e.g., theft, fraud, embezzlement, sabotage or vandalism). Or they get even through *production deviance* (e.g., wasting resources, underperforming, wasting company time). They may also strike back through *political deviance* (e.g., gossiping, showing favoritism or undercutting the boss's authority). Finally, they may get even through *personal aggression.* This can include physical or verbal abuse, sexual harassment or making it unpleasant for the transgressor to continue to work there. Personal aggression can also occur in groups. Perhaps a few employees don't like Gretchen. She is surly, negative and abrasive. Over time she has hurt lots of feelings. So workers decide to "mob" her. They make Gretchen's days hell, hoping that finally she will quit.

Workers might also change jobs themselves to escape from situations characterized by unforgiveness. Job changes reduce productivity for everyone. The trained employee takes valuable knowledge and skills to a competitor. The job is vacant or filled by a temporary, undertrained person until a new employee is hired. New people must be trained, taking trainers' time and continuing to fill the position with a less competent worker, at least until the learning curve rises to the level of the previous worker.

Justice and workplace transgressions. Often workers are concerned with managers' violations of distributive or procedural justice or both. Distributive justice involves equitable distribution of resources. Procedural justice involves following stated processes. But in a recent study of abusive supervision, Bennett Tepper argues that the voluntary turnover of workers seems better predicted by violations of interactional justice than by violations of procedural or distributive justice.[13] Scientific studies of on-the-job transgressions have dealt with *interactional justice* or *relational justice.* These forms of organizational justice focus on the quality of interpersonal interactions at work.[14] They are not about workplace procedures or distributive justice but about a fair relational climate—how all workers treat each other.

Dealing with unforgiveness in the workplace. Many human relations departments try to prevent unforgiveness. They provide training in communication and in the resolution of differences. Leadership training can help supervisors become less likely to provoke subordinates to fear, anger and unforgiveness.

Human resources departments have devoted less attention to repairing relationships once a transgression has been experienced. They may provide counseling by employee assistance programs (EAPs) or transfer disgruntled workers to different work units or locations. Usually hurt feelings and emotional pain are simply ignored. Workers are expected to "deal with it" or to seek employment elsewhere. In an environment as large and complex as many businesses, transgressions are inevitable, regardless of how much preventive training is available.

Benefits of forgiveness in the workplace. People respond to transgressions with anger, fear of being hurt again, or both. People may later ruminate about transgressions. As we discussed in part one of the book, workers have lots of options for handling hurt—accepting and moving on, forbearing, seeking justice or forgiving.

Each of these ways of reducing unforgiveness involves the elimination of negative emotional states. Only forgiveness, however, can result in a positive emotional state. Decisional forgiveness, followed by emotional forgiveness in which negative emotions are replaced by positive other-oriented emotions (i.e., empathy, sympathy, compassion or love) provide the only coping strategies that can reduce unforgiveness and move beyond the neutral state to yield a net positive emotional state.

A worker might decisionally (or even emotionally) forgive but still not trust a manager. Ideally, forgiveness stimulates reconciliation, but it might not. On the other hand, reconciliation might occur without forgiveness. In business settings, people might restore trust through working together on common tasks. However, they might hold a grudge for years as a result of a past transgression. This is the usual occurrence when transgressions occur. Trust on work projects is restored more easily than forgiveness is granted.

This is a challenge for Christians, who want to bring their Christianity into every aspect of their lives until their character is transformed and people are drawn to Christ. They need not always forgive to the extent that they become the company doormat. Justice is a part of Christian character just as much as forgiveness.

Forgiveness is an act of mercy and grace. When a person transgresses, he or she builds up a social and perhaps economic debt. The injustice gap probably cannot be eliminated through justice alone. Forgiveness is at the same time an act of mercy, which is not giving someone what he or she deserves, but also an act of grace, which is giving something he or she does not deserve. So relational justice, I believe, is possible—as we have seen—by pursuing fairness in one's interactions, being humble enough not to misuse power or always insist on one's own way and by forgiving perceived transgressions. A short individual ethic is summarized in Romans 12:9-21, especially the following verses: "Love must be sincere. Hate what is evil; cling to what is good. Be devoted to one another in brotherly love. Honor one another above yourselves. . . . Do not repay anyone evil for evil. Be careful to do what is right in the eyes of everybody. If it is possible, as far as it depends on you, live at peace with everyone" (Rom 12:9-10, 17-18). If even one-half of all workers lived by that ethic, what a workplace it would be!

BUSINESS ETHICS AND CORPORATE SOCIAL RESPONSIBILITY

Let's shift gears a minute and look at transgressions from the standpoint of the business rather than the worker.

Business ethics is concerned with how businesses deal with society and with employees. Businesses transact publicly with customers, shareholders and people in the broader social arena. But business ethics also deals with how people treat each other within the workplace. Let me suggest that businesses deal ethically with transgressions in the public arena (e.g., with customers, larger communities, shareholders and policy) differently from the way workers deal ethically with workplace transgressions. My colleagues and I have called these an *ethics of the mind* versus an *ethics of the heart.*[15]

Ethics of the mind. Traditionally, ethics has been approached in a rational, principle-driven and abstract way. Ethical issues are typically treated as problems to be solved. Solutions are thought of in terms of applying ethical principles to the problem. The best known of them are (1) do no harm (i.e., non-malfeasance), (2) do good (i.e., benevolence), (3) fairness or equal treatment (i.e., justice), and (4) balancing autonomy and choice against duty and responsibility.

Thus most business ethics involves discussions about principles. Some debates are *consequentialist*. That is, the dilemma is discussed in terms of benefit versus harm to various people. Decisions are made on the basis of the most positive or least negative net consequences. Other ethical theories approach ethical discourse as *deontological*. In such theories, people do their duty or do what is right according to a set of guiding principles, regardless of the consequences to self or to others.

Ethical discourse is primarily an activity of theorizing philosophically about dilemmas, rationally analyzing ethical principles and expecting that people can and will apply these principles when they face difficult decisions. To assist them, ethics casebooks consider real-life examples that can help people rationally apply ethical principles.

Ethics of the heart. In an alternative approach, ethical decisions are made because of life in a community. This distinction was raised in a classic book by Michael Oakeshott.[16] He observed that people acquire *habits* by living with people who habitually behave in a certain manner. We acquire habits in the same way that we acquire our native language. He argued that one way of understanding ethical behavior is to understand the habits that characterize a community. These might be called habits of the heart.[17] Such an approach to ethics is contrasted with abstract ethical principles used to make individual decisions that guide our behavior.

The fundamental questions that I am raising about the daily practice of business ethics boils down to these: Is ethical discourse and analysis, which is largely principle focused, actually the way that people make ethical decisions? Or do people make ethical decisions differently? Furthermore, *should* ethical decision making be primarily rational? Or *should* it be contextualized by community?

The application of ethics of the mind, which involves rational, principle-driven analysis, depends on (1) recognition that the case at hand requires an ethical decision, (2) recognition of the principles that are applicable and (3) reasoning about which principles should be applied if several principles compete. On the other hand, ethics of the heart involves sensitivity to interpersonal and emotional context, although it is not completely divorced from principles.

In chapter four I described decisional and emotional forgiveness. Decisional forgiveness was primarily rational. Emotional forgiveness was dominated by the emotional parts of the brain and body. Similarly, personal ethical decision making is not always analyzed abstractly and rationally. Instead, emotion can override reason. Not only does brain functioning differ, but the decisions also differ dramatically. This suggests that the decisions from rational, principle-driven, ethical, decision-making exercises might differ in brain processes and in actual outcomes from emotion-driven, hands-on decisions.

Let's consider Stanley Milgram's classic studies on obedience.[18] People were urged by an experimenter to give what they thought were painful and dangerous electric shocks to a learner who was actually a confederate of the experimenter. No shocks were actually given to the learner. Many participants delivered what they thought were high levels of shock. The mere pressure of a white-coated experimenter triggered their obedience. Participants ignored their compassion for the victim because they focused on the virtue of helping science or being a responsible research participant.

In another aspect of Milgram's work, people were given a description of the study but did not actually go through it themselves. In this case, they applied principle-driven ethics. Almost all said they would not administer the shocks. When people were put in the actual situation, however, most of them gave shocks—lots of them. People responded strongly to their closeness to or the distance from the experimenter (an experimenter in close proximity elicited more obedience) or to the learner (a learner who was at a greater distance elicited more obedience). Personal ethics and principled ethics differed.

At Manchester University in England, neuroscientist Tom Farrow and his colleagues have used functional MRIs to scan people's brains while the people made judgments of the forgivability of a response.[19] Farrow found that when people reasoned about the fairness and justice of transgressions, much of the neural activity occurred in the prefrontal cortex and frontal lobe (which are associated with controlling oneself, overcoming the desire to do the easy thing, and with reasoning). However, when people considered whether they might forgive the transgressions, brain activity occurred less in the cortex and more in the limbic system (in which structures like the amygdala, hippocampus and hypothalamus process strong emotional responses) and the anterior cingulate gyrus (which is a portion of the cortex involved with monitoring internal conflict, having empathy for people and engaging in thought about emotionally arousing issues).

Let's draw these studies together. When dealing with transgressions, two types of thinking are involved. One type of thinking involves rational analysis and judgment about whether events are fair or just. In those cases ethical reasoning might be helped by logical, philosophical discourse. People benefit from having thought through difficult decisions and from examining cases that could be pivotal in helping make a general decision. This promotes ethics of the mind, and it can lead to decisional forgiveness, though reasoning might not lead as directly to emotional forgiveness.

However, we also find that the more personal the transgression, the more likely it is that a person will respond by using emotional processes rather than by applying rational, principle-driven analysis. Reasoning is involved, but primarily it is limbic-system activity that *conditions* how we respond. In the same way that Oakeshott has argued about ethics, the way people make personal decisions has much to do with habits of the heart rather than habits of the mind.[20] Many transgressions take place within workaday business environments. These might be between boards of directors and management, between management and workers, and between workers. These transgressions are up-close and personal. Thus they engage people's emotions. If we are to behave ethically in this community, we must consider an ethics of the heart and deal with our emotional unforgiveness through experiencing empathy, sympathy, compassion and love toward our community of coworkers.

If you are a business leader, then consider this. One task of leaders is to provide a means of shaping corporate culture such that an ethic of responding with empathy, altruism, forbearance and forgiveness might be promoted. The role of the middle manager in modeling such behavior is crucial. A manager who advocates an ethic of forbearance, tolerance and forgiveness yet who vindictively punishes his or her workers for transgressions, or allows such interactions to occur, will likely not produce a community that values positive responses to transgressions. People are highly attuned to situational triggers. Your behavior is all-important.

A Christian response. If we take our Christianity seriously, then responding to transgressions with the ethics of the heart should not be as much of a stretch as it might be for people who highly value justice but seem to have little use for granting forgiveness (although they might be more than eager to receive it). Forgiveness is at the center of Christianity. We of all people should be putting it into practice in the trenches where we work.

As I've stated throughout this book, we cannot be a doormat. We aim at just forgiveness, which is rooted in humble discernment. *What would God have us do in this case?* we must ask ourselves. Then when we are most convinced that justice and retribution is the godly response, we need to use that thought to trigger a prayerful examination. Yes, there are times for focusing on justice and laying aside mercy. It's just that they occur far less frequently than we usually think.

To summarize, businesses must deal with transgressions because transgressions are a part of being human and because we spend much of our lives at work. Ethical discourse, or an ethics of the mind, has a role in shaping ways people handle wrongs inflicted upon them and others. However, we must not be content to look just at ethical principles. Instead, I suggest we need a relationship ethic, an ethics of the heart, which sets the communal tone for the ways people deal with personal transgressions. Decisional and emotional forgiveness are associated with the ethics of the heart and with ways managers and workers treat each other. This is our trinitarian-based way of handling forgiveness in the workplace.

JUSTICE AND FORGIVENESS IN U.S. SOCIETY

Most of us think of Christianity as a religion of peace. It advocates turning the other cheek, forgiveness and reconciliation. Justice seems to lurk silently in the wings. This is a warped view of Christianity, however, because justice has always been of concern. With Rome enforcing its law with its undefeatable army, early Christian writings didn't highlight justice issues the way Judaism and Islam have. But even from the early days, when Ananias and Sapphira tried to cheat the Christian community, God exacted divine retribution (see Acts 5:1-11). That no doubt had a restraining effect on the community. As the church grew, larger tribunals evolved to decide questions of faith and doctrine (see Acts 15:6-29).

The Puritans were the dominant religious group in the founding of the United States. The Puritans had been persecuted in England and elsewhere, and they came to this continent with the notion that a state religion—such as existed in England, where the Anglican Church and the king were joined—was a dangerous idea to religious freedom. In most colonies, state religion was forbidden.

The development of justice in the United States. Justice in the United States has been influenced by the Christian Scriptures. Most early leaders came from Christian roots or had a strong sense of natural theology. So inevitably the shape of the civil legal system was influenced heavily by Christian thought. A Christian-based legal system is built on discernment of God's law as it applies to civil discourse. However, reflecting on Calvin's authoritarian governing of Geneva gave the founding leaders pause. John Knox's influence suggested a system of procedural and structural checks and balances. Those from British backgrounds brought a tradition informed by the Magna Carta, taking rule from the king and investing it in laws.

The modern justice system is set up to govern civil and criminal disputes. Civil disputes involve contested claims regarding property, rights and responsibilities. Criminal disputes deal with breaking of laws in which someone experiences actual or potential harm, either to their person or their property. Both can involve hurt feelings, perceived injustice and resentments.

What role, if any, does forgiveness play in the justice system? A glib response is "None. The system is about justice, not forgiveness."[21] This is not quite strictly true on the face of it, and becomes less true as we delve into the system a bit. First, law enforcement is supposed to be governed by discernment that a crime has been committed. However, police officers do in fact use discretion at how vigorously they pursue an alleged wrongdoer. Forgiveness by a police officer might occur in a particular incident, with the result that a case might not be vigorously investigated. Judges are supposed to be impartial triers of fact, regardless of their own views. But judges are human. Their opinions can affect numerous judgments before and during trials—both civil and criminal. Juries are also supposed to be impartial triers of fact, but jury members are human too. Their views about crimes or property disputes necessarily enter discussions within the cloistered jury room. Forgiveness can affect individual members or even entire juries. Even in sentencing, victim impact statements are often made. Victims can attest to their own forgiveness—or to the damage incurred and their strong desire for justice—and can advocate for mercy in sentencing, dramatically introducing forgiveness into court proceedings. Prisons employ personnel who are human—and act like it. Throughout history, prisons have also been called *penitentiaries* (from the same root word as *repentance)* and reform schools, and even now they are called correctional facilities. These labels convey a richer and deeper notion than mere imprisonment. Governors occasionally commute sentences or pardon offenders, which is becoming increasingly common as DNA evidence can provide after-the-fact information in the case of many convictions.

So throughout both civil and criminal proceedings, there are in fact many times when individuals can be triggered to focus on justice, harm and retribution on the one hand, or compassion, forgiveness and mercy on the other hand. The myriad people involved have different value hierarchies, with different structures as the most salient. Thus different structures are most easily triggered. What seem to be the most innocuous cues can trigger the biggest reactions. For example, if a defendant dresses well and arrives at court with a fresh haircut and nice suit, a jury might be more likely to be predisposed toward mercy.

The justice system is aimed at providing fair procedures and laws to guide the conduct of society and settle disputes, enforcing laws, trying alleged crimes and carrying out judicial decisions. In one respect, justice is independent of forgiveness. Justice is one way of balancing social, economic and criminal injustices. Justice might prevent or reduce unforgiveness, though that is not the primary concern of justice.

In another respect, though, parties will inevitably feel that unfair decisions have been made. Many will develop unforgiveness toward people in the justice system (e.g., police officers, judges, attorneys, criminals, plaintiffs, witnesses, corrections officers), procedures that aggravate or frustrate (e.g., court delays) or other disputants.

Dealing with injustices in the justice system. Can we deal better with our perception that failures in the justice system have occurred? After a final decision by a judge or jury, societal justice may be settled, but individual perceptions of injustice may linger for the rest of someone's life.[22]

Because of pride, greed and justice motives that demand wrongdoers be held accountable and punished, lawsuits happen. Throughout the lawsuit, hurtful things are said, allegations are made, lies may be told, one's character may be assassinated and one's arguments denigrated. In short, lawsuits and criminal trials will both provide many opportunities for even more transgressions than the original perceived injustice. I would hypothesize that all parties finish a lawsuit with more resentments, grudges and unforgiveness than when they began the lawsuit.

Often much is at stake in trials. Lives are lost. Memories are disrespected. Fortunes change hands. Public humiliations ensue. People live with the consequences of the legal action and might personally hold grudges and communicate their feelings to their family, friends and a wider public. My purposes below are to consider the experience of an individual going through a criminal and a civil case, examine the sources of possible unforgiveness and describe ways people can cope with those sources of unforgiveness.

When wrongs are perceived during legal proceedings, the biggest obstacle to forgiveness is not knowing whom to consider forgiving. I have frequently told the story of my mother's murder on New Year's Day, 1996, and my forgiveness of the murderer.[23] Let me examine briefly just a few of the incidents that occurred in the aftermath of her murder.

The police botched up the evidence in the investigation of my mother's murder, but who messed up? I don't know, so there is no single person to consider forgiving. On the other hand, the police certainly investigated the crime vigorously, and they even caught a suspect. I am grateful to the police officers who pursued the truth. But I don't know to whom I should be grateful. Then the grand jury did not bring back a verdict to indict the young man accused of the crime. Should I be angry at the members of the grand jury? Should I forgive them? I don't even know who was on the grand jury. The list of transgressors could continue—the young man's lawyer, victim advocates who did not keep us well informed, newspaper and television media who raised our expectations of a conviction.

The young man apprehended for the crime confessed but later recanted. Should he specifically be forgiven? He has not been clearly shown to be guilty, even though the police were confident he was guilty. Still, there was no trial. Someone had murdered Mama, and I could forgive the person who committed the crime in general, even though I didn't confidently know his identity. Would that be enough to set me free from hostility?

My mother's death and my forgiveness of her murderer was one of the most difficult experiences of my life. Yet God gave me the grace to forgive, opening my eyes to my own hatred and violent motives toward the murderer, and showing me that I could be forgiven, even in the darkness of my own heart. I had to forgive to pass that mercy on.

My brother and sister and I arrived at the same decision within weeks. We felt that we must forgive the murderer, though it was clear that he needed to be incarcerated (if he could be convicted) so that others would be protected from his inability to control violent impulses. The decision to forgive was similarly difficult for each of us because it raised the question of whether, by forgiving, we were betraying our mother. Each of us independently concluded that by forgiving, we were instead honoring the values she taught us—to be compassionate to the needy and to forgive those who have harmed us.

God has been so gracious to me throughout dealing with this murder. First, I realized that I had studied forgiveness for about ten years when I was called on to put my learning to the test. I marveled—how could others come upon such violence and evil without preparation, and yet forgive? Yet God had been merciful in preparing me to deal with the issue. Second, my mother had told me just a few weeks earlier that she was worried she might have cancer. Because she had cared for my father as he was dying of cancer, she was deathly afraid of having cancer. The murder was undoubtedly terrifying and painful for her. But it was quick. I wonder whether, had she been able to choose how she would die, she might not have chosen the quick though brutal murder instead of the slow but painful journey through cancer. Third, my mother had solid Christian values, but she spent almost her entire life in East Tennessee. Yet after her death, I have carried her values to literally millions of people through having had the privilege of sharing her story on television, in movies and in print interviews.

Pain from the crimes and issues that people litigate, or sometimes don't litigate, cascades down through the years. Almost ten years after Mama's murder, my brother, unable to shake persistent depression and posttraumatic stress disorder, committed suicide. The family had all of the wounds of Mike's suicide to forgive, but his death also opened all of the memories of the murder and its lack of resolution.

Dealing with unforgiveness in the justice system. Forgiveness—or unforgiveness—is aided by the situations we expose ourselves to that trigger either unforgiving ruminations, forgiving thoughts or merciful images. If we talk a lot about how unfair the justice system was, we probably won't forgive. If we tell others our story of forgiveness, then forgiveness will feed on itself. Similarly to the way we dealt with other topics throughout this book, we must intentionally look to creating or exposing ourselves to the triggers that build our faith instead of challenge it.

I could find benefits in ways that my brother, sister and I dealt with our attitudes toward the murderer. I could find benefits in the death being just the way it was, though that did not make the act less horrifying or less evil. But more than merely finding benefits, I found God walking with me throughout the entire murder investigation, forgiveness and telling others the story of forgiveness. Finding that God walks through the fire with us frees us to forgive.

Restorative justice. In recent years a rehabilitative model of criminal justice has been virtually abandoned, replaced by a system of justice that emphasizes punishment and protection of society from repeat offenders. This has colloquially been called "Trail 'em, nail 'em and jail 'em." While this strategy is partly responsible for the reduction of violent crime, it has resulted in overburdened court and prison systems.[24] More than 1.3 million people are incarcerated in the United States today. Furthermore, victims often are frustrated. Crimes are considered to be crimes against the state, and victims are often cut out of the process.

Another approach to criminal justice, called restorative justice, has emerged within the last thirty years.[25] In restorative justice, perpetrators (often youths and young adults) who have been charged with a crime or have already been sentenced are brought face-to-face with the injured parties. Usually community representatives also attempt to mediate an agreement. The agreements seek to restore perpetrators to good standing with the community instead of merely incarcerate them.

When it is successful, restorative justice benefits the perpetrator, who receives less harsh punishment, is given the opportunity to apologize and make restitution, and receives help reintegrating into the community and getting rehabilitative work. Restorative justice also benefits the victims, who might be the recipients of restitution. Restorative justice benefits society by allowing offenders to be restored to productive work rather than become a burden on society, which funds incarceration and incurs costs from the secondary problems that arise from exposing offenders to hardened criminals. Restorative justice programs are often run relatively inexpensively using community volunteers. Participants might or not meet with their attorneys present.

Yet restorative justice is justice, not forgiveness. True, it is a kinder and gentler justice than punitive justice. Therein lies the connection to forgiveness. Because it provides an opportunity for offenders to apologize, make restitution, be restored to the community and experience some redemption, restorative justice stimulates forgiveness.

Whenever misdeeds or misunderstandings become highly harmful, they often cannot be resolved by simple agreement between the parties. The legal system is a societally proven way to resolve such difficulties while ensuring procedural justice. The goal is to provide a balance of distributive justice and retributive justice with a guarantee of fair procedural justice. Nevertheless, the legal system often produces solutions to the societal issues but simultaneously damages the psychology and mental health functioning of the people operating within the system. The system is designed without any attempt to minimize suffering; rather it is all about fairness and justice.

People who are involved in that system as victims, criminals or as plaintiffs in civil lawsuits must consider not just the social justice aspects but also their own mental health aspects and the effects of the cases on people who know them and other members of society. Decisions must be made on a personal level, which may not maximize individual benefit and more societal justice, but in fact may contribute to more positive ongoing interactions within all of society and certainly a better emotional balance across society.

As with much of what I've presented in this book, we can make lasting changes only if we change what is lasting—the structures of our lives, the triggers that provide access to those structures, and the processes that connect thoughts, behaviors and situations. Changing society to be more godly is not only a lifelong work for individual Christians, it is a community effort by congregations and a societal effort by the body of Christ in a worldwide coordinated effort. That work will not just happen spontaneously. It requires making the effort to promote justice—in humility, not arrogance—and being quick to promote forgiveness as well.

JUST FORGIVENESS
IN THE WORLD

ON AUGUST 31, 2005, A HORDE OF Muslim Shiite pilgrims were crossing a bridge over the Tigris River when something set off a stampede. In their panic to get away from the violence of mass hysteria, hundreds of people jumped into or were forced into the Tigris. Young Sunni men were observing from the eastern bank of the river, and several dived in to help. One of those was Othman al-Obeidi, who rescued six Shiites. Then, exhausted, he could not save himself.[1] Not all the Sunnis who saw the stampede leaped in to help. It is reported that some cheered as the Shiites drowned and trampled each other.

Muslim Shiite-Sunni sectarian violence is not unique. Roman Catholics and Protestants have had their bloodbaths—think Northern Ireland or the Counter Reformation. Christians and Muslims have slaughtered each other in Beirut, as have Hindus and Muslims in Pakistan and northern India. Buddhist priests were slaughtered in Tibet to quell political dissent as recently as 2008. Nonreligious groups have perpetrated violence on each other too. In Rwanda, tribal killings reached a death toll of eight hundred thousand in one hundred days. The people in the Balkans have killed each other for centuries. The Chinese still resent the Nanjing massacres by the Japanese during World War II.

Up to this point, we have examined individual experiences of forgiveness and justice as well as applications within families, churches and communities. In this chapter we move the last step toward forgiveness in global society, looking at relations between groups. We may never be personally involved as a combatant in war. We pray that we will never be involved in ethnic violence such as the kind that has occurred in Rwanda and other countries throughout Africa. We hope to never encounter combatant factions like the leftist, rightist and centrist police and militia of Colombia, or the Shiites and Sunnis of Islam. Yet as a country, we are currently involved in peacekeeping efforts in Afghanistan and Iraq after wars that stripped away established rule and left factions vying for power. So chances are high that we will indeed experience at some level the effects of armed intrastate or interstate conflict. In recent years virtually all conflict has been intrastate conflict. Only about two out of twenty-five conflicts involved countries at war with each other. Most armed conflict occurs within a country.

In this chapter I try to help us understand the roots of those conflicts. I examine why some cultures are especially violent, why there is prejudice, why societal violence occurs and why it persists. Then I ask what we might do to prevent, mediate or diminish such conflict when it occurs.

VIOLENT CULTURES

It is a simple fact of life. Some people are more violent than others.[2] Some cultures are more violent than others. Among primitive societies, hunter-gatherers tended to be more violent and less forgiving. They tended to enforce boundary violations through violent retribution. This makes sense for their survival. For hunter-gatherer groups, resources were scarce. Animals moved, and their population changed with seasons, droughts or times of abundant rain.

Nomadic people also tended to be violent. Their resources often involved raising sheep, cows or goats, which could easily be stolen. Therefore, much effort was expended hunting for scarce resources like grazing land. Violence was used in raiding other territories. Territories were patrolled, and violence was used to punish border violations.

In agrarian societies, however, people were less likely to steal land or crops. The people were tied to their crops and their land, so there was little incentive to raid other people groups. If they did, they were easy to find and easy to retaliate against. While there might have been internal squabbles over ownership, those were relatively infrequent. Everyone in the group knew whose land was whose and whose crops were whose. Thus, overall, agrarian societies—and those located on fertile ground—were less oriented toward violence and aggression than were hunter-gatherer or nomadic societies.

In addition, virtually any society that came into contact with other societies developed some reconciliation or forgiveness-like rituals for making up after a conflict within the group. In small communities that had virtually no contact with the outside world, blood feuds tended to develop, and cultures of honor existed. Because there were few external threats, there was little reason to evolve a social mechanism for affecting reconciliation. Members had to be punished or retaliated against when they broke group norms. Reputations had to be maintained lest one be seen as a doormat. Only punishment or revenge deterred future violations.

If interactions with particularly hostile external groups existed, though, survival dictated that members must reconcile quickly after a transgression. If they didn't, the divided group had less chance of defending itself. An ostracized member would probably be killed by enemies. The group had little choice but to work out a way to forgive or reconcile to keep its numbers strong.

Anthropologists Martin Daly and Margo Wilson sampled sixty cultures around the world in an anthropological study of revenge.[3] They found that 95 percent of the cultures employed revenge—feuds, retaliatory wars and private vendettas. Michael McCullough, for his book *Beyond Revenge*, relocated written sources about those sixty cultures that Daly and Wilson had previously studied.[4] He found that 93 percent of those cultures that Daly and Wilson had shown to employ revenge also, surprisingly, employed some variant of forgiveness or reconciliation. Those were written sources in which forgiveness and reconciliation were mentioned explicitly. Some of the other 7 percent of the sixty cultures took forgiveness and reconciliation for granted. Their literature did not mention it because it was assumed. McCullough concluded that almost every culture held within it a mechanism for forgiveness and reconciliation as well as for revenge, but how each one manifests depends on the conditions. A large part of the conditions involves the other people with whom the group interacts regularly. In a large, complex society, like most developed nations, there will be attitudes that govern relations with many of the groups of people that must be dealt with daily.

PREJUDICE

Prejudice is seeing and treating people the same because they are members of the same group, race, country or ethnicity, and treating outsiders as somehow inferior to our in-group. Prejudice is similar to discrimination, though discrimination is giving one group priority over another through actions or through dispensing resources or aversive duties. Prejudice is attitudinal. Discrimination is acting on prejudices to favor one group.

However, all prejudice is not created equal. Arizona State University psychology professor Steven Neuberg has studied prejudice, stereotyping, discrimination and stigma throughout his career. He suggests that some prejudices are rooted in fear and anxiety.[5] These come about because we feel that our safety and security are threatened. Other prejudices are rooted in anger. These develop because we have a belief or experiences to suggest that the groups might take resources from our in-group. Still other prejudices are disgust-based. They arise because the other people are seen to threaten the health and welfare of our in-group. Other prejudices center on other negative emotions, like sadness (those people make our group feel helpless and hopeless), contempt (they don't pull their weight but try to freeload off the group's resources without giving back to the group), jealousy or envy, and the like.

Not all prejudice is bad. It depends on the degree of real danger. For example, in Rwanda during the hundred days of genocide in 1994, Hutus killed over eight hundred thousand Tutsis because of prejudice and discrimination. The prejudice of Hutus resulted in the murder of Tutsis. However, for Tutsis who were being hunted during those hundred days, it was adaptive for them to be prejudiced against Hutus. The objective threat was real. Many (but not all) Hutus were willing to kill any Tutsi. So it was adaptive for survival for Tutsis to play the percentages and remain wary of all Hutus. But generally it is important to seek discernment from God in the specific cases in which we may face danger.

Prejudices can be overcome. Biologist Robert Sapolsky describes a study in which people's brains were scanned when they saw pictures of people of the same race and others of a different race.[6] When people of a different race were seen, the amygdala—which is an innerbrain limbic-system structure that governs fear and anger—became more active. At first people interpreted this as evidence of a biology of prejudice. *Aha*, they said, *our brain is wired to treat people differently according to their race or ethnicity.*

However, this study doesn't tell where the increased amygdala activity originated. It may have had genetic contributors, been taught by parents, been learned through one's own experience, or derive from a combination of all of those. This biology of prejudice, however, was quickly shown to be modifiable. If people were told something about the person ("He is a Christian" or "She goes to your university") before seeing the picture, then the amygdala did not activate. Seeing a person as similar to ourselves can squelch prejudice—if we let it.

While prejudices can be overcome, they often exist—just buried beneath the veneer of civilization. They can lay dormant for years, perhaps even decades or centuries. Then a trigger event sets off a violent action.

ORIGINS AND TYPES OF SOCIETAL VIOLENCE

People like Ervin Staub, professor of psychology at University of Massachusetts-Amherst, have devoted their lives to studying how societal conflicts result in one group's willingness to act violently toward another group of fellow citizens (intrastate violence), kill huge numbers of them (mass killing) or try to kill all of them (genocide).[7]

Most conflicts have a history, and usually both sides have different versions of it. They can each point to a big sinful event (see chapter one) that they use to define the relationship. So different current events trigger different mental processes and activate different memories and action patterns.

Let's take the religious conflict in Iraq as an example. For many people in the United States, the occupation of Iraq has been a mystery. We don't understand the religious histories and the current events in Iraq (and even its neighbor Iran) that have led to today's conflict. Permit me, then, to illustrate the political, religious-based conflict by briefly summarizing the conditions in Iraq.[8]

Two major branches of Islam. The world is now seeing much Sunni-Shiite violence—especially in Iraq and Iran. Most Muslims in the world are Sunni (followers of the Sunna, or "the way of the prophet"). However, in some countries Shiites (followers of Ali, son-in-law and cousin of Muhammad) are in the majority, such as in Iran, Iraq, Bahrain and Azerbaijan, with smaller concentrations in Afghanistan, Saudi Arabia, Pakistan, Lebanon and other scattered countries.

History of Sunni and Shiite Islam. In 632 Muhammad died without naming a successor. Ali and Abu-Bakr (his father-in-law and friend) were contenders. Abu-Bakr had the most support and became the caliph. His followers eventually became the Sunnis. Abu-Bakr was murdered in 661 by a heretic, which again left the succession in dispute. At that time most Sunnis backed Muawiya and his son Yazid. The followers of Ali, later the Shiites, backed Ali's son, Hussein. In a battle in 680, Hussein was killed and beheaded by the Sunnis. Hussein became a martyr, which strengthened the Shiites. The Shiites still commemorate this event when they celebrate Ashura each year. There is usually a parade, and sometimes devoted Shiites flagellate and cut themselves in honor of Hussein.

For Shiites, the big sinful event was Hussein's murder and decapitation. For Sunnis, the big sinful event is what they perceive as the idolatry of the

Shiites—their reverence for Hussein, the pictures of Ali that adorn their houses and mosques, their naming of Ali in the daily calls to prayer. Sunnis stamp Shiites as heretics.

While the conflict between Sunnis and Shiites is not primarily a religious conflict, religion is a badge that identifies the sides. In our model of forgiveness and relational spirituality (see figure 4.3), Sunnis see Shiites as being spiritually different from them (the OS relationship). Thus when any new transgression occurs on either side, the other side is exceedingly difficult to forgive.

Different stories of prejudice and discrimination are told by Sunnis and Shiites to their children and to each other. Both suggest that one can never trust the other side. Each group can point to graphic, usually bloody reasons that justify such caution, give evidence of historic inequity, and provide motives for retaliation if structures make retaliation possible and if triggers ignite retaliation.

Modern history in Iraq and Iran. In Iraq, Sunni leader Saddam Hussein built a national guard of mostly Sunni soldiers. He fought the Shiite government of Iran under Ayatollah Ruholla Khomeini from 1980 to 1988, and he repressed the Shiites of Iraq.

However, with the defeat of Saddam Hussein in the 1991 Gulf War, the Iraqi majority Shiites saw a weakening in Sunni control. For Sunnis, the protective structure (i.e., the mostly Sunni army) was weakened. The weakened structure was highlighted by Saddam's defeat on the world stage. This ignited a Shiite uprising against Sunni control. Saddam responded with typical ruthlessness. Some have estimated that he killed more than three hundred thousand Shiites. His army reasserted a physical structure that, in addition to Saddam Hussein's own purging of Shiites, kept religious tensions under control until the second U.S. invasion of Iraq.

After the most recent Iraq war, the United States and its allies disassembled the Saddam-controlled, Sunni-dominant army, which weakened Sunni control in Iraq. Sunni-Shiite violence soon resumed. Sunnis boycotted the first post-Saddam election in January 2005, which gave political control to the numerically dominant Shiites.

Violence was engineered by militia on both sides. The violence was capped by the Sunni destruction of the Shiite golden-domed mosque at Samarra. That triggered Shiite reprisals against Sunnis in August of 2005, leading to more violence between Shiites and Sunnis. Then Saddam Hussein (a Sunni) was hung at the hour of morning prayers on the first day of the Sunni celebration of Eid al-Adha. The Shiites did not start the celebration of Eid until the following day, so for them it was not a holy day. But for Sunnis, this was a contemptuous kick in the teeth. The hanging of Saddam and the badgering he was subjected to at the scaffold provided another trigger for violence. Only the "surge" of additional U.S. troops and the building of walls between the communities—two new structures—have been able to stem the violence.

We can see that it is not the explosion that kills five and wounds twenty in Iraq that is the real problem. Bringing peace to a victim or supporter of a bombing victim is not as simple as making a treaty to stop the killing, forming new structures or deactivating some hot triggers. It is not as simple as promoting forgiveness in the wake of loved ones being killed. There are 1,376 years of historical memories, shaped in narratives that selectively recall big sinful events, that must be forgiven. That requires some heavy lifting of unforgiveness.

THE PERSISTENCE OF SOCIETAL VIOLENCE

Gerald Patterson reviewed more than fifty years of scientific research on violence and found that for individuals, the possibility of violence can be detected early.[9] As early as seventeen months of age, a child's behavior could predict later violence. Children who hit, kicked and physically responded to parents had a larger chance of developing into violent preschoolers, school-aged and adolescent children than did less violent seventeen-month-olds. In most families there is some conflict every sixteen minutes on average. But in most families it is resolved by talking, redirecting, laughing, discussing or more direct verbal direction. In families at risk for rearing violent adults, though, parents may themselves use coercion or force to resolve conflict with children or between themselves.

And, importantly, parents give in to a child's physical coercion, which rewards the child and makes future use of physical coercion more likely. Violent teens and young adults have learned in the family that violence can get them their way.

In school these children are quickly ignored and cut out of interactions with less-violent peers. They gravitate toward other deviant peers—either similarly violence-prone kids or otherwise socially maladjusted youth. These peers direct the child's violent tendencies toward real violence-prone behavior such as fighting, stealing, mugging, drugs and gang violence.

Violent youth, then, tend to be nonsystematically trained within their home and peer groups toward violence. They are typically noncompliant from early childhood, have a propensity for violence, are rewarded by parents and other children who give in to their bullying, and have poor social skills.

In societies the picture is similar, but it differs in important ways. Politicians and military leaders lead groups into violent conflict, but soldiers who volunteer or are drafted from the population must do the actual fighting and killing. Patterson shows that planning for war is highly predictive of initiating conflict. Planning involves making strategic alliances and allocating resources to the military. Bruce Bueno de Mesquita, in *The War Trap*, shows that initiators of conflicts usually win.[10] That is, violence usually pays off for the one that starts it. Also, Bueno de Mesquita shows that most decisions to initiate conflict are cognitive, though not necessarily rational. This is important, and it is what I have argued throughout the book. Rational decisions involve (a) weighing costs and benefits, (b) basing the decision on accurate assessment of all the major data, and (c) making choices on the basis of what is most probable. The field of cognitive psychology, however, is a testimony to the fact that people seldom make rational decisions.[11] Rather, their decisions are often based on triggers that set their thinking down different roads than a rational analysis would. Triggers can include emotion (e.g., greed, sexual lust, anger, fear, envy, lust for power), political considerations (such as a leader who is about to lose an election or be deposed) or need for resources. Leaders (even when advised by a cabinet representing multiple points of view) usually do not tabulate all costs and benefits. They ignore entire lines of thought. This was demonstrated in the groupthink before the Bay of Pigs invasion of Cuba; Lyndon Johnson's decision to commit to heavy engagement in Vietnam, anticipating quick victory; and the second Gulf War, in which the prospect of a quick and decisive military victory (fostered by U.S. experience in the first Gulf War, which did not include completely dismantling Iraq's social structure) focused attention on military conquest rather than on the costs and difficulties of restoring peace to an occupied country.

Leaders lead groups into wars, as I mentioned earlier, but soldiers—official armed services or unofficial militia—must do the fighting. Good soldiers are well trained, disciplined and well socialized. They are not usually violence-prone individuals, who are in fact more prone to go absent without leave or disobey orders.

After World War II, a study by the U.S. government found that only 25 percent of combat soldiers actually fired their weapons during combat.[12] This was interpreted at the time to mean that soldiers retain a strong moral aversion against killing in spite of the rigors of military training. This turned out not to be the case. Failure to fire was found to be the result of poor training rather than hesitancy to kill due to moral scruples. With improved training under simulated battle conditions, between 90 and 95 percent of combat soldiers fired their weapons in combat during Vietnam. However, as an encouraging note, in the infamous My Lai massacre of Vietnamese men, women and children noncombatants, over 50 percent of the soldiers refused to obey orders to fire into the groups of unarmed civilians.

We see again that strong situations can trigger retribution, revenge and violence. In this case, training in lifelike combat situations is a strong structure. Emotion—primarily fear in combat situations—can trigger the most available mental structures, which (if military training is good) aim the soldier toward violent acts under orders of commissioned or noncommissioned officers.

Still, there is another important piece of the puzzle. People are likely to perpetrate violence against those they see as out-group members. We are members of literally dozens of groups. I am a Christian, a Caucasian, a sixty-three-year-old, a member of Christ Prez, a family patriarch, a psychologist, etc. So what is important is not that we are a member of a group, but *which of the groups to which we belong* is the focus of our attention right now. What are the triggers that focus our attention on a particular in-group/out-group difference?

In the military, triggers include identification with one's buddies. Soldiers are directed to fight or continue to fight when odds are desperate (a) because they are rewarded by their buddies and (b) because they are punished by their buddies for incompetence. Soldiers in a work group or squad are like family. They are a band of brothers (and now sisters as well). We never leave comrades on the field of battle. We sacrifice for our comrades. Responsibility and duty to comrades are the values that are triggered continually in combat. When groups of soldiers are depleted by deaths and their superiors combine units, those units rarely become effective combat units. There is no sense of in-group membership with such a thrown-together unit. On the other hand, incompetence is punished. I was a naval officer during the Vietnam era and heard stories of "blanket parties." If a sailor did not act responsibly, was noncompliant or put the group in jeopardy, then some night someone would throw a blanket over his head and the group would beat him. In Vietnam anecdotal stories suggested that as many rookie officers were killed by friendly fire (i.e., shot in the head by their own troops) as by enemy fire. Incompetence that might lead the band of brothers (and sisters) into danger is punished.

Wars, once begun, are maintained because wars are functional for the leaders. They provide political leaders and often military leaders with rewards, glory and a place in history as a champion for their in-group. Rarely do common soldiers get the kind of glory that will sustain fighting. They get camaraderie, and on a different (more abstract) level, a sense of patriotism and service. The conflicts won't end because the triggers and structures persist.

Visible structures persist. There are societal reasons that wars are difficult to end. Societal structures continue to favor war. The presence of armies, public statements by leaders and repressive policies are societal-political structures that keep the conflict hot on everyone's minds and make triggers out of seemingly innocuous events.

Hidden structures exist. Some structures are more hidden. Parental teaching has usually programmed adults since childhood with group differences and prejudices. The group memories of historic wrongdoing by the other side may have been discussed for years.

Prejudice appears to maintain safety. Remember, prejudice is adaptive if one really isn't safe. In the United States we have ethnic prejudices despite living in a society where ethnic tensions rarely explode (and when they do, they tend to be localized, not national). Detroit was the site of ethnic conflict in the 1960s. Los Angeles was the site in the 1990s after the Rodney King police-brutality incident and the subsequent acquittal of the police officers, which triggered riots, and after the O. J. Simpson murder trial and not-guilty verdict. But overall, most of us feel relatively safe. Even in the conflicts just mentioned, the National Guard did not slaughter the perpetrators of violence or innocents just because of their ethnicity. Such prejudicial spread of violence is often the case in conflicts in the Balkans, in Lebanon or some African states, which have long histories of unsafe ethnic relations.

Beliefs are rehearsed and repeated. Old hurts keep being retold. "We must never forget we're getting a raw deal." Both sides are likely to say that they are unfairly treated. They focus on evidence that the other side usually doesn't consider valid. "We've been terribly wounded and will suffer interminably." Both sides can point to the pernicious effects on their lives (personally or as a group) of abuses at the hands of the other side.

Present inequities continue. Both sides can always trot out evidence of the effects of inequity. Furthermore, real inequity and real persecution might continue. Often neither side is aware of it. Mona Sue Weissmark wrote a book titled *Justice Matters,* in which she described bringing together Holocaust survivors and ex-Nazi soldiers to talk about their experiences of the war.[13] Holocaust survivors said things like, "Life was all about

surviving the death camps, getting enough to eat, not getting sick or injured (which could put oneself at risk of being put to death)." One said, "I
didn't even realize there was a war until I was a teenager."

The ex-Nazi soldiers told a different story. They might say, "The bombing of Berlin was not even a nightmare. It went on day and night. No
respite. Millions were killed. We were afraid that death would fall out of
the sky at any moment. Bombs were so impersonal." Some would say
things like, "I did not even realize there were death camps until I was a
teenager." Both groups were focused on their own survival needs. The
death camps and the bombings were going on at the same time, but neither side was focused on that which did not affect their own survival.

Fear of the future. People lose hope. They do not expect things to
change. Any reminder of a past harm can trigger fear. A survivor of trauma
might say, "When I see history starting to repeat, my mind rushes to the
worst conclusion." *Fear* drives people toward conflict, not love. When
people respond from fear, however, they do not usually make good self-
controlled, long-term decisions.

Our brain structures tell the story. The prefrontal cortex in many ways
acts as a brake on the runaway emotional reactions that are signaled by
our amygdala. When we react before engaging the prefrontal cortex, our
reasoning is mostly emotion-based reasoning. To defeat fear thinking, we
need emotional healing that will give us the necessary time it takes for the
prefrontal cortex to inhibit the knee-jerk protectiveness of the amygdala.
Our positive emotions of empathy, sympathy, compassion and love arise
from being able to take the other person's perspective. They require time
to develop.

John says, "Perfect love drives out fear" (1 Jn 4:18). But we cannot experience love for someone we are afraid of unless something triggers empathy. Perhaps the trigger is well-rehearsed Scripture. Perhaps it is seeing
some compassion-inspiring event. Perhaps it is some conscious reminder
we have built into our family, our church, our community or our national
identity. But defeating fear requires conscious action in advance of seeing
the triggers of fear thinking.

Emotional conditioning. Over time we are programmed to respond with fear, anger, sadness, disgust, contempt, envy or jealousy. Emotional conditioning programs us to respond with prejudices based in those emotionally conditioned emotions.

Reactive people keep reacting. Many people are simply emotionally reactive. They respond by jumping at the sound of loud noises, reacting to the smallest slight as if it were a major betrayal and freaking out over major betrayals. In society those people make a lot of noise anytime something happens.

RESOLVING AND HEALING SOCIETAL CONFLICTS

Most armed conflicts in the world are intrastate (within a nation) rather than interstate (between nations). As a result, throughout the world people kill and hurt their countrymen, kin and former friends. They ignore many similarities. They focus on in-group versus out-group differences. When fighting or mass killing that might lead to genocide or ethnic cleansing occurs, efforts first must be made to broker an uneasy peace. I will discuss three mechanisms for resolving political conflicts. The first two are well established in the world of peacemakers and are called track-one diplomacy and track-two diplomacy. The third I call track-three diplomacy.

TRACK-ONE DIPLOMACY

Track-one diplomacy[14] involves efforts by officials to create peace on paper, agreements between governmental and appointed leaders, cease-fires, negotiated peace. In many ways, though it is essential to any negotiated peace settlement, track-one diplomacy is an attempt at a rational solution to an irrational problem. It rarely succeeds in bringing real peace. At best, it restores a lack of hostility.

Peacemaking efforts often fail in violent intrastate conflicts. The world community waits too long, ignoring the signs of potential violence, conflict and war. The world community closes its collective eyes to ethnic cleansing, mass killing and other atrocities. Then the world community intervenes, often with expensive and inefficient military attacks. In track-one diplomacy, leaders meet and agree to a cease-fire. Perhaps they divide up territory and material resources. Peace is imposed rationally. It is monitored, perhaps by United Nations peacekeeping forces, which quell rebellion and violence. It involves the visible: leaders, words, agreements, issues, statements of interests, demands.

But as I said, it is a rational solution to an irrational problem. What's irrational about it? Leaders are the defenders of each side and must be "strong." The idea is that strong leaders can negotiate peace and persuade weak people (the other side) to accept it. Both sides stake out their positions, which become demands, which are incompatible with the other side's demands. Whereas there are probably lots of ways that both sides could satisfy their interests, framing the problem as a strong leader persuading a weaker one to accept the demands of the strong side virtually dooms the "negotiation" from the outset.

Based on justice, which is seen from two sides who necessarily do not see things similarly, no mutually just solution will be possible. Arriving at a compromise requires each leader to give up something. Giving up something is interpreted by each leader's constituency as weakness—the leader must have been forced to give up some of their side's "demands."

THE CYCLE OF AGGRESSION

There is a natural cycle of aggression that pushes groups toward violence and aggression. The cycle has three phases (see figure 9.1). Aggression is followed by suffering, which is followed by coping, which is followed by aggression, closing the cycle. Coping involves two strategies: trying to bolster weaknesses and enacting strength. Aggression is one of the ways of coping. Let's look more closely at the cycle.

Aggression. People act aggressively. They might think they are defending against actual or potential violence, or they may be trying to demonstrate that they are strong enough to take care of themselves and are not dependent on others. Perhaps they are on jihad, acting righteously against the unfaithful. Perhaps they see themselves as defending tarnished honor. Violence occurs. As Patterson showed, violence is rewarded. It gets people what they think they want.[15]

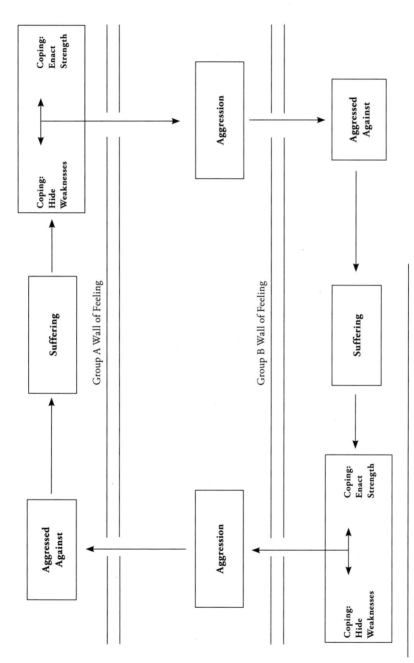

Figure 9.1. The cycle of aggression

Suffering. However, both sides in armed conflict (and often in other political conflicts) suffer. They suffer injury, pain, shock, panic, loss, grief, threat to survival. Dave Grossman, in his book *On Killing*, detailed the huge costs of harmful conflict—even among the winners.[16] Even if we look only at veterans returning from conflict, the costs are enormous. About 20 percent have long-term emotional disorders. About 18 percent have posttraumatic stress disorder. In one study 56 percent of returning veterans exposed to heavy conflict were either dead or chronically ill by age sixty-five. Veterans who have participated in combat also have higher rates of divorce, marital problems, alcoholism, joblessness, heart disease and ulcers than noncombatants. Samuel Marshall showed that since the Napoleonic Wars, more civilians are killed than combatants.[17] That difference is widening in modern years. Besides all of the personal suffering, society suffers from the diversion of resources from productive living toward the taking of life.

Coping by hiding weaknesses. When we feel threatened or weak, the stress response kicks in. We typically freeze. We try, through immobility, to allow the stressor or predator to pass us by. If that does not succeed, we flee. If it looks as if we are going to fail, we fight.

Another way we try to suppress our feelings of weakness is by getting angry. Anger sends adrenaline and cortisol coursing through our bodies, and those hormones empower us. Feelings of weakness can also make us feel shame and humiliation. When we believe we have been shamed and humiliated, we want vindication. Thus we demand justice. We compile a case for how we have been mistreated and unfairly dealt with, and our justice motive is aroused. Instead of feeling shame, we feel as if we must be the caped crusader for justice.

When we feel weak, we usually experience a loss of identity. Our group or individual identity has been threatened, and we tend to draw toward others like us for communal strength. We may do this physically, but we also do it simply by bolstering our sense of identity. Instead of hiding our identity, we proclaim our identity loudly.

Coping by enacting strength. We also cope with unjust aggression and suffering by creating shows of strength. We demand—not request—uncompromising justice. We vow no mercy in the conflict. Even if we get a measure of justice during conflict, it is never enough.

The shame and humiliation we feel are not just converted into a desire for vindication. We usually set out to actually eradicate the source of humiliation and shame. To engage in this holy war, we need a justification. So we create a conflict history. In this story the other side is (virtually) completely at fault. We are (virtually) completely right. We were forced to defend ourselves. *It's not our fault, don't you see?*

Our anger and condemnation might easily be generalized toward others. We might take vengeance on groups similar to the oppressing group. (Think about the Japanese Americans confined during World War II.) We might rail against those people or groups who are not preventing the harm and injustice against us. We might even act against innocent victims by hurting, destroying or emasculating them through the same types of one-up and one-down power plays I discussed in chapter six.

If we understand the structures for conflict and war and the triggers that activate those structures, we might be able to create triggers to activate mental processes that turn on structures for just forgiveness.

World War I was a particularly savage war, with armies entrenched and shelling and shooting each other at every hour. But one Christmas Eve, peace broke out. Christmas is a Christian holiday that was celebrated in the countries of both sides of combatants. That evening became a trigger that stimulated goodwill and good feelings. Troops on both sides emerged from the trenches and laughed, ate, drank and sang together. The officers had to order the soldiers back into the trenches.

Other temporary truces broke out locally. Robert Sapolsky tells how the sides signaled that they wanted a temporary peace.[18] One side would get its best gunner to lob a shell a hundred yards behind the enemy trenches. Then he would repeat the shot continually. The other side would get its best gunner to reciprocate. Lots of shooting would be going on, but it would be a signal for temporary peace, not conflict. Sometimes, though, an inexperienced soldier might shoot into the other side during one of the unofficial truces. That was handled by a reciprocal arrangement. The offending side would allow a free shot without reprisal. Then the truce would resume.

Game theorists, headed by economist Robert Axelrod, found a similar pattern.[19] Using the game *The Prisoner's Dilemma (PD)*, Axelrod and his colleagues studied forgiveness and justice in a mock situation. *PD* is a game between two parties in which cooperation results in modest gains for each. Betrayal rewards the betrayer with a large payoff if the opponent chooses cooperation. But if both sides choose to betray, both suffer. Axelrod invited mathematical economists to submit strategies that would maximize winnings. A competitive strategy that seeks to maximize winnings in the short term might involve a couple of easy betrayals, but it is quickly met with punitive betrayals in return—usually until the gains and losses have been equalized. The best strategy turned out to be tit for tat. The player begins with a cooperative move, and if the opponent cooperates, the player also continues to cooperate, and both partners benefit.

If both people are playing tit for tat, though, what happens if someone makes a mistake, intending to cooperate yet betraying instead? Or what if a machine malfunctions, making an unintended signal? Life is full of mistakes beyond our control. That mistake will still trigger a betrayal, which will in turn trigger a betrayal from the other player. So to handle signal errors, a "forgiving tit for tat" turns out to be a good strategy. In forgiving tit for tat, the opponent is allowed a free mistake. With the first betrayal, a cooperative response is still made. With the second, however, betrayal is returned. Forgiving the first betrayal—giving the opponent the benefit of the doubt—keeps people cooperating, even though an inadvertent error has occurred.

In subsequent modifications, *PD* has been used to study all sorts of strategies. If a group of people play each other and are allowed to communicate, anyone who tries to take advantage soon gets a bad reputation. The group shows no mercy. In fact, people might even try to exploit him or her. *PD* has even been used to allow a betrayer to communicate an apology between rounds. Predictably, that creates a tentative forgiveness.

We see that people can insert triggers to signal justice and forgiveness.

Justice is signaled by embracing a strategy that, while it might give the person the benefit of the doubt initially, will punish wrongdoing and keep on punishing wrongdoing until fairness has been reestablished. Forgiveness, however, can also be signaled—whether it is emerging cautiously from our entrenched positions because we share a Christian structure (like the WWI troops did on Christmas Eve), or allowing a free shot when one's side took advantage of vulnerability, or a forgiving tit for tat in the *PD* game.

Forgiveness triggers might include saying, "We are alike, not different; look at our similarities," as with the Christmas Eve truce. They might say, "We won't take advantage," as with allowing a free shot. They might say, "We will give you the benefit of the doubt, this time," as with forgiving tit for tat. Can any of these strategies be used on the world stage to help groups heal from harms they have inflicted and suffered in the past? This leads us to track-two diplomacy.

TRACK-TWO DIPLOMACY

Relationship. *Track-two diplomacy* involves the bringing together of opinion leaders of conflicting sides to hear each others' stories of pain, hurt and offense, and the forging of a will to reconcile.[20] It is based on the principle that reconciliation is relational, not rational. Thus building trust is central, and a third party is usually necessary.

Accompaniment. Reconciliation of conflicting parties usually requires accompaniment by a third party. Accompaniment sends the message, "I will be with you. I will work alongside you." Accompaniment is not leadership, taking over, pushing, protecting, pulling, cheerleading or motivating by the third party. Accompaniment requires humility. The third party is best thought of as a mediator or consultant.

Humility. All parties must be characterized by some humility. The opposite of humility is arrogance—believing one has the full truth, that one knows best. Reconciliation fails when we believe (whether we are helper or participant) that we have no more to learn. People must have the humility to self-examine. We must take the log out of our own eye so we can see well enough to help the other get the splinter out of his or her eye.

Attunement. People must build their own reconciliation process rather than apply a rote process. This requires engagement, attunement (requiring commitment and trust), sharing of oneself and ideas, letting people build their own ways, and sometimes letting people go their own ways. This does not mean that we cannot give very specific guidance, but it means that we cannot expect our guidance to "work" every time.

Connection. Track-two diplomacy requires that we see complexity; keep discussants in contact; keep them connected; balance truth and mercy, justice and peace; and help people build the bridge to reconciliation from both sides (see chapter six).[21]

Wandering together. To use a different metaphor, reconciliation is wandering in the desert. Reconciliation is at the same time both a destination and a process. We want to be reconciled, but we are in different places at different times in the process to reconciliation. There is a rush away from where we felt we were in captivity and a rush toward the promised land. But there is a lot of desert between captivity and the promised land. To get there we must take seriously the need for community and personal preparation and look through a long-term lens.

TRUTH TELLING

Often societies hold public hearings to get at the truth. Most peacemakers believe that if the truth is not known, the stories of societal conflict will continue to be prejudicially one-sided. That plants the seeds for future violence and aggression.

There have been a number of such societal experiments since World War II. War crimes tribunals seek to try people in international court for crimes against humanity. Truth commissions seek to uncover the truth by soliciting testimony from perpetrators and victims. Usually the culmination of the truth commission involves a publicly released report.

The South African Truth and Reconciliation Commission (TRC) was a bold experiment that might have transformed post-conflict efforts at societal healing. The TRC consisted of three types of hearings. *Human rights hearings* sought to solicit testimony from people whose human rights had been violated. The intent was to document the extent of the violation of human rights that had occurred on the part of the Nationalist Party under the apartheid philosophy. These hearings dealt with crimes that were politically motivated, not cases of individual criminal behavior for nonpolitical purposes. Also, testimony was sought regarding violation of human rights on the part of various groups who perpetrated political violence. *Amnesty hearings* involved perpetrators of politically motivated crimes. Amnesty was given in exchange for testifying truthfully on all matters. *Reparations hearings* were to decide on fair reparations for damages incurred by politically motivated violence. All three types of hearings by the TRC have been criticized.[22] Human rights hearings were criticized because some witnesses said they felt pressured to offer public forgiveness. Amnesty hearings were criticized because they did not attract testimony from the leaders of the various groups, especially the Nationalist Party. Reparations hearings were criticized because of the small reparations awarded for major losses such as death or total loss of property.

In Rwanda a solution such as the South African TRC hearings would have been impossible. More than eight hundred thousand killings were estimated to have occurred in one hundred days. To have public hearings to investigate that number of crimes or to subject the court system to those trials would have kept the courts bogged down for the future. Instead, the Rwandan gacaca (gah-cha-cha) trials were a uniquely Rwandan response to the genocide of 1994.[23] Trials were conducted in local villages.

In Colombia conflict had been occurring for years, with many people involved in the violence. Colombia instituted a limited amnesty program. In return for fully cooperating and telling the truth, perpetrators were not granted full amnesty; instead, they were guaranteed that regardless of the number or seriousness of the crimes they had committed for political purposes, a maximum of eight years of incarceration would be sentenced. The Colombian solution avoided the criticism that perpetrators got off scot-free, yet there were still incentives for perpetrators to surrender and testify.

Though such commissions, trials and hearings have been criticized, they have helped to shape a public narrative of the events within each country. Certainly, the full story is not known, but more of the story on each side of the conflict is made public. Each side still tells its prejudicial version of the events, no doubt; but the public discussions within and around the hearings make it more difficult for either side to accept a completely one-sided view of the conflict. The hope is that less next-generation hatred will come out of the recent conflicts because of the public testimonies.

Commissions have suffered from a variety of weaknesses that should be targets for improvement in future commissions, hearings and trials.[24] First, because the testimony is public, witnesses are vulnerable to coercion and threats of violence (or actual violence), either in reprisal for damaging testimony or to intimidate against giving damaging testimony. Second, not everyone comes forward in public trials and hearings. Thus the idea that the full truth can be learned is admittedly unrealistic. Third, some of the people who do not come forward are usually the ones who have benefited most from the violation of human rights. They are powerful and wealthy enough to insulate themselves from damaging testimony. The common people bear the brunt of the costs in such hearings and commissions.

TRACK-THREE DIPLOMACY

The third mechanism is what I call *track-three diplomacy*. If track-two diplomacy is aimed at having opinion leaders of each side meet together for personal, empathy-building conversations (usually in groups), then track-three diplomacy is aimed at opinion leaders influencing opinions on their home turf. Track-three diplomacy involves opinion leaders working with their constituencies to bring about changes in attitudes that foster and maintain peace and reconciliation. They can effectively transmit peace, teach forgiveness and reconciliation skills, promote the valuing of forgiveness and reconciliation, and employ a variety of methods to do each of these with the people with whom they work on a daily basis.

Track-three diplomacy might involve a local congregation in forgiveness and reconciliation groups. There might be attempts to help congregants understand and empathize with the other side. Many resources could be employed to assist pastors (and other opinion leaders in the broader community) to promote pro-peace values and skills.

Track-two and track-three diplomacy seek to engender learning, which changes structures in the environment. By changing our mental structures, we supplement modifications by leaders and politicians and states, which presumably have helped begin to change physical structures. To promote healing, forgiveness and reconciliation, we must do what we can to change the environment—even if it is an environment of memories inside people's heads.

If lasting peace is to be returned to the damaged community, then people and environments must change. We change people by prayer, which can free supernatural intervention. We also change people by our own example, illustrating Christian love in our daily lives. We also change people by changing the environment. But let us realize that we, too, are people in that environment. So in living out our responsibility as peacemakers, we, too, must be and will be transformed.

As we have learned throughout this book, political violence—like societal injustice, failures of the church to function as God's called people, dysfunctional families and handling pain inflicted on us as individuals— cannot be resolved through justice alone. To heal, societies require not just justice but divine *justification*. In justification, God brings justice and mercy together in a laser beam focused by Jesus Christ. Divine justification works in us directly and also through our application of justice and forgiveness in humility before God.

As Ephesians 2:10 says, "[God] creates each of us by Christ Jesus to join him in the work he does, the good work he has gotten ready for us to do, work we had better be doing" *(The Message)*. God has prepared a place for us to be ambassadors of justice and forgiveness through humility. May we have the spirit to discern what our mission is, eyes to see the goals and the paths to get there, and courage of heart to carry out our mission in spite of the inevitable obstacles we will face along the way.

WHAT CAN WE DO?

THE FILM *THE END OF THE SPEAR* IS A fictionalized account of the real events involving Elisabeth Elliot and Rachel Saint with the Waorani tribe in Ecuador.[1] The Waorani were portrayed in the movie as a morally depraved culture—lawless, refusing to submit to the government, killing others, even killing each other. After they killed a group of missionaries, two of the wives of the martyred men did the unthinkable—they went to live among the Waorani. The spirit of forgiveness exhibited by Rachel and Elisabeth transformed the Waorani, who began listening to the message that the missionaries had preached and that their widows were now preaching and living. The message was about a God who does not seek retribution; instead, God's own Son gave his life that the offenders could live. The Waorani laid down their spears, and the culture was transformed. It is simply amazing that the sacrificial love and courage of those women could transform a culture from violence to peace.

There have been critiques of this account (easily findable through Web search engines) that suggest a much more complex story than the one the movie told. That story would indeed include themes of forgiveness and reconciliation. But it would also tell about the mistakes on the side of the missionaries—a shooting that killed a Waorani man, Rachel Saint's agonizing decision about vaccination that may have cost lives. In light of this, the forgiveness by the Waorani is remarkable, as they became Christian.

MOTIVATIONS TO SEEK JUSTICE AND FORGIVE

The injustice gap feels subjectively real. People have a well-developed sense of injustice when they experience something that seems unfair or unjust. That gives rise to their justice motive and creates directed thinking about how to bring more fairness or justice or balance into this system that has been upset by an injustice.

Some of the earliest cries we hear from very young children are "It's not fair!" or "That's not right!" Children appeal to this inner sense of morality and fairness. Theologians attribute this inner sense to people being created in the image of God. Evolutionary psychologists point to the survival value of having a sense of fairness and morality and boundaries. Social psychologists posit an equity theory that suggests people behave in ways that seek to maximize their personal gain.

Thus people have strong justice motives, and those motives are built into the fabric of human nature. However, like poorly woven patches of fabric, there are imperfections and stresses that also are built into human nature. Those cause the justice motive to be perverted and twisted into the service of self-interest. From one perspective, we are constantly at war within ourselves to manifest a justice motive that is pure and godly and to defeat the sin nature within us, to overcome unrighteousness. This can be done in the flesh, attempting to impose a will upon our human nature, but it is often futile. However, this battle can also be waged in the spirit, in which case we join with God's desire to make us purified in our motives. Generally that purification involves strengthening other motives that God has built within our human nature.

Grace and mercy motives. Life is not fair. In the end, God is a fair judge who will bring justice to all of existence. But while we are on earth, our life simply is not ever going to be balanced, just or equitable. Part of this is because we are fallen, and thus self-interest is an ingrained quality in our nature, so life doesn't *seem* fair. But merely seeing life as warped and unfair is only part of the problem. The other part is that life really is not fair.

Because life isn't fair, it doesn't seem logical that God would leave us to stew with unfulfilled justice motives raging within us. In fact, he hasn't. He has given us two other motives that help balance the justice motives and help us want to close that injustice gap in ways that do not simply trade harm for harm and good for good. *Mercy* is not pressing for the justice that an offender deserves. *Grace* is giving people gifts that are not deserved. Both mercy and grace motives are ways humans have within them to ease the tensions arising from a large injustice gap and the justice motive to eliminate that gap.

Altruism or agape love. A third positive motive that combats our self-righteous sense of injustice is the motive of altruism or agape love. *Altruism* is acting unselfishly to benefit another person. Altruism often happens because we are related to other people and are in close relationships with them. This has been called *kin altruism* by evolutionary psychologists.[2] It is well established that people will act more altruistically for their own offspring or mate than for people who are distantly related to them. On the other hand, people will still act altruistically and self-sacrificially on behalf of people with whom they have virtually no kinship at all. They will even rush into danger to save a dog that does not even belong to them. This altruistic motive is built into people as part of the characteristic of God that is love. In Christianity, we know it as *agape love*. Paul, John and other New Covenant writers tell us that agape is the ideal love to emulate because it is the love that is closest to God's love.

Though altruism can be simply kind and loving behavior, when it is self-sacrificial, we think of it as motivated by God's work in our lives. We see his distinctive fingerprints. We call self-sacrificial altruism agape love.

Keeping motives in balance. When people experience injustices and have a large injustice gap related to a transgression, they seek to close that gap because it is unpleasant to experience a sense of injustice. It generates negative emotions such as anger, fear, resentment, hostility and hatred. It erodes trust and makes people untrusting.

People are thus motivated to restore peace. This peacekeeping motive is a strong push to do whatever it takes at whatever cost to restore harmony. But peacekeeping can be detrimental to long-term good relationships. Jesus does not call people to be *peacekeepers* but rather to be *peacemakers*.

Peacemaking is trying to establish a just peace. It balances the motives for justice against those for mercy, grace, altruism and love. It does not give up one set of motives for the other. Micah sums up our duty as a peacemaker: "What does the LORD require of you? To act justly and to love mercy and to walk humbly with your God" (Mic 6:8). Acting justly seems to be more natural for people than loving mercy and walking humbly with God. Namely, we indulge our injustice motive, often harshly, often in our own self-interest.

That is why Jesus frequently throughout the New Testament admonishes people to indulge the love or altruism motive, the grace motive and the mercy motive. He says, "Do not judge, or you too will be judged" (Mt 7:1). "Blessed are the peacemakers, for they will be called sons of God" (Mt 5:9). "Love the Lord your God with all your heart and with all your soul and with all your mind and with all your strength [and] love your neighbor as yourself" (Mk 12:30-31). Who is your neighbor? Your neighbor is someone like the good Samaritan (see Lk 10:25-37), who was of a different religious persuasion and even ethnicity, yet treated the needy person as a neighbor. Jesus admonishes people who detect that someone has something against them to leave their gift at the altar and go and be reconciled, as much as it is up to them, with that person (Mt 5:23-24). That is, he admonishes people to take the first step, even when they have wronged the other person, or especially when they have wronged the other person. Paul tells us to be ambassadors of reconciliation, reconciling people to God (2 Cor 5:18-20). He tells people to break down the walls of hostility across ethnicities (Eph 2:14-18), to tear down the wall dividing Jew and Gentile. We are told not to be anxious by John the apostle (1 Jn 4:18), Paul (Phil 4:6) and Peter (1 Pet 5:7).

We therefore are armed with these characteristics that God has built within our character, and we are called to respond to transgressions in ways that deal justly yet lovingly with the transgressor. There are three primary principles that govern our behavior:

First, seek God.
Second, take responsibility for reducing tension.
Third, pursue pathways to peace.

These principles can be applied at every level we have considered throughout this book—in the divine, the world, the community, the interpersonal and the individual levels.

THE DIVINE

Seek God. We are to be reconciled to God and to help reconcile others to God. That is our calling as Christians. To do that, we need to seek God with all of our heart. That involves seeking not just justice, not just love, but also God's loving justice. God forgives on the basis of Christ's paying the just penalty for sins. We must accept that and go to God for that just forgiveness whenever we are needy.

Take responsibility. We can be tempted to blame God for injustices that happen and for any of life's circumstances that seem unfair. Yet God is calling us not to give in to bitterness but instead to reach out to others in our own pain and frustration—like Rachel Saint and Elisabeth Elliot did—and to lead others to him for their restoration. In so doing, not only do we take responsibility, but we also find God. God has taken the initiative and placed a desire in our hearts to be deeply connected to our Savior. We are to respond to that by seeing ourselves as sinful and taking responsibility for our sins, imperfections and shortcomings. We throw ourselves at the feet of Jesus in love, and we place our sword at his disposal. He will give us a mission, and at the same time he will lavish mercy and grace upon us so we can help others receive the same love, mercy and grace.

Pursue pathways to peace. There are many ways to be close to God. We do not all have to do the same ritual behaviors, pray for the same amount of time in the same way, use the same biblical or church language, or act like a clone of the perfect Christian. It is important that we pursue pathways to peace with God in the way that God made us, using the personalities he gave us.

THE WORLD

Seek God. In society, it is our individual duty and obligation to seek God regarding how we can help to bring about a just and peaceful society. The Christian Scriptures do not advocate state religion. Christianity grew up in a time when Rome ruled the world, so the emphasis could not be on a Christian society or Christian government. Instead, the emphasis was about being part of the kingdom of God. Thus, while Christians want to transform society into a society more consistent with Christian principles, this is a political agenda. It is not really a Christian's highest calling, which is to know and seek to love God. Nevertheless, as Christians we seek God's will for ourselves and for our neighbors, and participate with other citizens in transforming society. This is often the very way we live out our highest calling.

Take responsibility. Even though the Christian's main call is not to form a political governing body, when societies are in tension, the Christian is still to take responsibility to move the portion of society that he or she touches into more godly activities. Thus we are to take responsibility.

For example, when tensions arise between Muslims and Christians, Christians should not be thinking about defeating Islam with power and might. The battle is the Lord's. It is not ours to execute violence against people who disagree with us. Christians did not take up arms against Rome, even though the Romans were oppressing them. The Christian stance, then, should be aimed more at seeking God's participation, acting in ways that prevent and restrain violence but do not succumb to peacekeeping. Rather, peacemaking is the mode of operation within societal conflicts.

This means that it is also not in a Christian's best interest to blame the past or to blame God. Focusing on past injustices won't help bring about a just society. The people who have perpetrated injustices are called to reconcile with people who have something against them. Therefore, rather than having a victim mentality, people should strive to have the mentality of one who seeks to make a just peace happen.

Pursue pathways to peace. There is no one way to bring peace about in societies that are in conflict. Instead, there are many pathways. These may involve communication to prevent additional differences, resolution of conflict to end hostilities, and acts of forgiveness and reconciliation to heal the effects of past conflicts. We are to seek pathways to peace that are acceptable to other people in other societies or other portions of society, and we are to seek to bring about those pathways that are acceptable to all participants.

THE COMMUNITY

Seek God. People behave and live in groups. Groups serve two important functions. They support each other, and they also hold each other accountable for group standards. We are to seek God in the groups to which we belong, whether these are work groups, church groups or community groups. We want to hold each other accountable not only to group standards but to group standards that are consistent with Christian belief and practice. We support people by showing love within the group.

Take responsibility. When change is needed in a group, when there is conflict or discord, rather than blaming other group members, each person is responsible for initiating that change. This is not something we do naturally. We believe that we are right and on the side of justice, and we hang back, waiting for the person who wronged us to make the first move. Christians are called, however, to be active, not passive, in taking responsibility for bringing about peace.

Pursue pathways to peace. There are numerous injustice gaps that exist within groups who have conflict. Each person perceives issues differently. Different actions have a different impact on each person. Thus there is no single way to balance all of the injustice gaps. Having public events to mark reconciliation or permit open communication will often keep the harms more public. However, sometimes people merely need to be loved, and some reconciliation happens in private as people confess their sins to one another and are healed.

THE INTERPERSONAL

Seek God. We are in many important primary relationships, and in each one we need to seek what God's will is in that relationship. We try to bring our knowledge of God into that relationship and show love, grace, mercy and altruism, as well as try to establish a just and fair relationship.

Take responsibility. We must keep short accounts within relationships. When problems arise, we need to attempt to resolve those problems quickly. This does not always mean saying "I'm sorry," but it means being sure that the other person knows that you feel remorse or contrition. Usually this boils down to asking the person directly what they're experiencing or feeling. In relationships the work of forgiveness and reconciliation takes place. People make requests for explanations for the other person's behavior. They must give loving and accurate accounts of their own behavior. People are coached to seek, grant and accept forgiveness in ways that their pride and self-interest sometimes would not direct them to do. We are told to give others the benefit of the doubt, to practice good communication and conflict resolution and to seek the level of intimacy appropriate for that relationship.

Pursue pathways to peace. There are many ways that people can have peaceful relationships with each other and still maintain justice within their relationship. Usually, though, these boil down to acting lovingly toward the other person. We are to be more concerned with showing mercy and walking humbly with God than with getting strict justice for the injustices we experience. Micah does not tell us to get justice, but rather to "act justly." We are to act justly in relationships and be more concerned about our acting justly than about finding ways we have been victimized and what others need to do to act justly.

THE INDIVIDUAL

Seek God. Individually, if love is our aim and we love God above all things, it will empower us to be able to love others. We are told to lay down our life for others as Christ laid down his life for the church. We are called to self-sacrifice and altruism, to mercy and grace. All of these, including forgiveness and justice, derive from our relationship to God.

Take responsibility. We are also called to live above our own self-interests. We are to take responsibility any time we feel an injustice has happened, not to righteously proclaim how this injustice has been perpetrated on us but to take responsibility for bringing peace into the situation. We are called to pursue just forgiveness.

Pursue pathways to peace. As we have seen throughout this book, there are many pathways to peace. Our call as Christians is to pursue the just forgiveness that heals relationships and makes us able to live out the redeemed character we have in Christ.

Specific Things Individuals Can Do

Let's look at some specific things that each of a couple of stakeholders can do.

The Christian.

Rely on God. Tune in to the Holy Spirit. Use Jesus as a model. Trust that God is sovereign, and remember that he cannot be put in a box. God redeems, protects, heals, enriches, keeps us safe, cares for us. Things do not always happen the way I would have planned it. I usually see God's hand in retrospect rather than in the moment.

Change personal values to live humbly as a child of God. Even if my attachment relationships with my parents and with God have been damaged by my upbringing to date, one message I have repeatedly given: we aren't stuck in the past. We can take responsible and loving action in the present. Find the structures in our lives that do not contribute to just forgiveness. Reconsider them in light of knowing God. Change the structures. Set up triggers that cue godly memories, thoughts and relationships. The setting of those triggers is part of reexamining our values in light of knowing God.

Teach peace to the next generation. I can commit myself to teach just forgiveness to the next generation. Whatever generation I am in, there is someone younger. Even if you are reading this book in your high school years, you can contribute to teaching forgiveness and mercy and proper use of justice to younger siblings, children you baby-sit for or even fellow students who might not be acting lovingly. As an adult, you can teach just forgiveness in many arenas. The schools can educate for peace. Programs can be instituted within the schools to help children think about how peace can be kept while maintaining a fair sense of justice. Essay contests can help children think about peace and forgiveness, forbearance and conflict resolution. Writing assignments and reading assignments can aim to inform children about forgiveness and justice. The schools can teach the basic academic disciplines and still keep those disciplines within an atmosphere that trains children to be less aggressive, less oriented toward retributive justice, and more oriented toward forgiving. Violence prevention programs in the schools can provide training for alternatives to violence. Children learn computer skills in schools and also experiment with those skills at home. Technology can be harnessed to promote forgiveness as well as to promote violence. Currently computer games are aimed mostly at combat and competition. Games, however, could be created to promote a sense of competition of the game player in resolving conflict. Sport is a great vehicle for teaching youth positive values. Many adults are youth sport coaches. Not only can coaches coach their sport, they can also teach children how to act in just forgiveness.

Set up just and forgiving structures (personal, social and societal) and triggers and do not presume that we know exactly what should work and how. Rather, in humility rely on God to give discernment, which he will often do through Scripture or through Christian community.

Cultivate humility. Cultivate virtue in general, but in one sense, the main virtue is humility—the humility of seeing myself in right relationship to God and others. I must strive to know who I am. As my friend, psychologist David Myers, says, "There is only one God, and it isn't me." Yet I strive not in a self-serving way, but in a way of hungering and thirsting after righteousness. I must know who God is. He is the loving, just and forgiving Sovereign. I must actually know God. This involves a personal knowledge based on lived experience. I must trust God even though I may not see the big picture. In humility, I must try to promote justice. But at the same time, I must realize how very sinful and self-absorbed I am. I will most often try to justify why I was wronged and why I should be pursuing justice. I must try not to be led down that path. I am wise to assume I've done wrong and to seek forgiveness. But if I still feel that I have been wronged, I must try to forgive as a default position. I must look for the surprise of God's redemption. I am only sixty-three, but I have found that I see God's hand when I'm looking back more than I see it when I'm looking forward.

Develop skills for virtuous living. In addition to humility, other helpful virtues include sensitivity, empathy, sympathy, compassion and conscientiousness-based and warmth-based virtues.

Make and act on a plan. As the old saying goes, we cannot steer a stationary boat. So we need a navigational plan. We need a mission in life and objectives to accomplish that mission. For over thirty years I have had a mission based on what I thought God wanted me to do at that phase of my life. At first I tried to help people experience less pain. That served me well when I was doing a lot of counseling. Then I felt God directing me to promote better marriages and families. After my mother was murdered, though, God gave me the mission of promoting forgiveness in every willing heart, home and homeland. I still want to help people have less pain in life, and to help promote better marriages and families. Those were worthy goals. But now I see those as objectives to accomplish my mission of promoting forgiveness.

Having a clear, written mission statement helps me navigate toward the big, unmistakable landmarks. That way I don't get led down small tributaries or find myself running on the rocks or the shoreline.

The citizen.

Make your family a just forgiving family. This begins with husband and wife. The husband's role is to lay down his life for the wife as Christ did for the church. He should be thinking first about forgiveness—seeking it and giving it. Only then should he consider justice. In most cases, if the husband is willing to seek forgiveness and grant it quickly, issues of injustice will take care of themselves. The wife's role is similar. Ephesians 5:21 says, "Submit to one another out of reverence for Christ."

If the husband and wife are living a life characterized by love, that will help them create a just forgiving family. They can strive to act justly, forgive and seek forgiveness quickly, and see themselves in humility as children of God. That will help them orient their relationships with their children, their own siblings and their parents in loving, just and forgiving ways. They can teach just forgiveness with authority because they are living it.

Mobilize the church community. Churches have it within their missions to promote forgiveness. In the United States, churches reach the majority of people in the country. If churches could be excited about promoting forgiveness, it could begin a grassroots movement. Small groups, Sunday schools, adult programs, youth ministries and worship activities might be targeted toward dealing with problems requiring humble just forgiveness.

Mobilize the broader community. Local community organizations could be mobilized to promote forgiveness. It is not unreasonable to expect that many Christians would participate in such programs outside of the church. Thus a Christian might organize a book club at the public library, which would allow people within the community to interact around common ideas. Both fiction and nonfiction books that support forgiveness could be subjects of book clubs, which could induce people throughout the country to converse about forgiveness. State or federal government could sponsor national reading recommendations that might induce people throughout the country to read similar things during the course of a year and engage in conversation about those books.

Movie clubs might be even more popular than book clubs. We now seem to have a video-minded attitude. Movies have become part of the national language. Many excellent movies have forgiveness as a theme, such as *Les Misérables, Unforgiven, A Time to Kill, You've Got Mail, Casablanca* and many others. Movie clubs could discuss a movie each month.

Some effort to coordinate movie clubs nationally could be made to create a public conversation about forgiveness.

Excite leaders to provide positive leadership. Grassroots leaders able to help people mold opinions in a variety of organizations throughout the country. Government agencies or nonprofits could produce programs to train grassroots leaders on how to promote forgiveness. Leaders might help promote forgiveness and contribute to peace and common welfare.

Personal philanthropy. Perhaps God has gifted you with great resources. You can make a difference by focusing your philanthropy where it can have an impact. In some cases that means funding treatment programs. However, consider supporting research in forgiveness. At the beginning of the twentieth century, when John D. Rockefeller was deciding where to make philanthropic donations, he first thought of investing in making medical treatments more widespread. His financial adviser, Frederick T. Gates, suggested that he invest in medical *research* instead. Through the strategic philanthropic investing of Rockefeller and others, modern advances in medical research were greatly enhanced. Today we could do the same thing with studying forgiveness and reconciliation in individuals, churches, communities and the world.

CONCLUSION

Pursuing peace in the name of Jesus can be costly, as Rachel Saint and Elisabeth Elliot found in Ecuador and as Immaculée Ilibagiza found in Rwanda. It might involve profound suffering. It must involve courage. I don't want to glorify suffering. It clearly will end when we are ultimately with the Lord. But even suffering has the power to transform individuals and entire cultures.

Edward Schillebeeckx, a Roman Catholic theologian, argues that when we talk of evil and suffering, we do not have to deny God's power.[3] There is a power to disarm evil through suffering. It is through divine humility that divine power becomes most effective. Power means the ability to bring about important consequences. Self-sacrificial love accomplishes such significant changes. Obviously, this power often results in fatality for an individual, as it did when Jesus lay down his life for others.[4] But it changes and overcomes evil.

Pastor Otis Moss, in a talk at Chautauqua, New York, admonished his listeners to speak truth to power.[5] I've summarized his words here, reconstructed from my own notes:

> We need prophets of truth and apostles of justice. Listen to them. We need ministers of mercy and philanthropists of forgiveness. See their vision. We need disciples of love, teachers of reconciliation and ambassadors of peace. Tread in their path. If we do these things, then we will surely break through the thickets of hatred, injustice, deceit, violence, discord and judgment. We can all speak truth to coercion, speak love to power. Can we suffer without retaliating? Can we forgive when we are grievously wronged? In suffering, we may feel that we are losing. But those who see us suffer and remain true will be won to the truth.

James 3:13-18 says,

> Who is wise and understanding among you? Let him show it by his good life, by deeds done in the humility that comes from wisdom. But if you harbor bitter envy and selfish ambition in your hearts, do not boast about it or deny the truth. Such "wisdom" does not come down from heaven but is earthly, unspiritual, of the devil. For where you have envy and selfish ambition, there you find disorder and every evil practice. But the wisdom that comes from heaven is first of all pure; then peace-loving, considerate, submissive, full of mercy and good fruit, impartial and sincere. Peacemakers who sow in peace raise a harvest of righteousness.

Life is not fair. But God is good. God's will shall ultimately prevail. Things that don't seem right and just on this earth will be put right ultimately. Still, we live on this earth and must follow where life leads us. We have a choice: Will we follow the strands of justice and forgiveness in biblical light to where they intertwine with humility? That will lead to peace with God and peace among humans. Or will we seek personal peace at any price? Will we seek justice through payback, retaliation or revenge? Trying to follow the single strand of personal peace—mercy without justice—or the strand of personal retribution—justice without forgiveness and the love of God—or even trying to enact just forgiveness without the humility of knowing whose we are will lead to a dead end. It will lead us to torment, disappointment with God and bitterness with others. The threefold cord—justice, forgiveness and humility—knitted and braided by a trinitarian God who understands such intimate interconnections, will lead us home to humble just forgiveness and peace.

ACKNOWLEDGMENTS

The newest ideas in this book are three: (1) a model of how forgiveness and justice relate to each other primarily through humility, (2) a general concept that to make change permanent, we must change permanent (mental or physical) structures, processes or triggers that direct our attention to those structures and processes, and (3) applications to resolving hurts and conflicts in family, church, workplace and the world.

My interest in how justice and forgiveness can be joined through humility owes a great debt to my interactions with Charlotte Witvliet (to whom I dedicate the book). Also, I am grateful to Donnie Davis, who picked up the ball at studying humility scientifically and ran downfield, dragging me along on his coattails. He did this in spite of difficult family health problems. He has been a model of humility even as he has studied it academically.

The general concept of making change permanent through modifying structures, processes and triggers has arisen through doing invited talks around the world. I put the model together and presented it for the first time in Hong Kong, so I owe a particular debt of gratitude to Eadaoin Hui, who invited me to Hong Kong for the first time in 2006, and to the many wonderful friends, scientists and government servants I met during those travels.

These applications again have grown up by reflecting about difficult situations. Having seen churches suffer painful splits and others in which conflict was present yet members were able to resolve differences in love, I wanted to organize what we know so that more congregations might resolve differences in love. Workplace applications of forgiveness came about through advising Evan Brownstein's honors thesis and through a chapter invited by Bob Giacalone for the book *Positive Psychology in Business Ethics and Corporate Responsibility*. My thanks to Bob for giving me the opportunity to write about our studies and my theorizing.

Similarly, in my travels around the world, I have experienced cultures in which historic conflicts have occurred. In the process I have learned a lot about forgiveness and reconciliation on the world stage. Some of the very helpful people in bringing me into those experiences include Mervin and Hildegard van der Spuy (South Africa), Fred and Heather Gingrich (the Philippines), Danny Ng and Tony Ting (Singapore), Eadaoin Hui and Wai-sze Lui (Hong Kong), and others who have invited me to write about or speak about international applications (e.g., Rodney Petersen, Ray Helmick, Jennifer Garvin-Sanchez and Erin Martz).

The new applications in this book rest on ongoing collaborations concerning forgiveness research and writing with my graduate students—Katie Campana, Donnie Davis, Aubrey Gartner, Joshua Hook, Jeff Jennings, Shay Mann, Andrea Miller, Michael Scherer and Goli Sotoohi—and colleagues like Steve Sandage, Mike McCullough, Nathaniel Wade, Charlotte Witvliet, Julie Exline, Jennifer Ripley, Jamie Aten, Mark Rye, Jo-Ann Tsang, Wendy Kliewer, Barbara Myers, Eadaoin Hui and David Watkins. I am also highly indebted to my brilliant personal assistant, Nicole Frohne. All have shared in the development of our understanding of forgiveness, reconciliation and their applications.

Finally, research today cannot exist at a level that seems to have much impact in the world without generous philanthropy. I am deeply indebted to the John Fetzer Institute (#2254.01, #2266, The Fetzer Forgiveness Research Network and the newly awarded Forgiveness in Christian College grant), the John Templeton Foundation (Grant #239) and the NIH through VCU's General Clinical Research Center 5MM01RR1 00065-410535.

Having a life mission like I do—to do all I can to promote forgiveness in every willing heart, home and homeland—entails lots of travel and speaking. Kirby, the love of my life, has been continually supportive and tolerant of all of my travel and time spent at work. She inspires me. My children and grandchildren likewise are an inspiration to me, and I can only hope that this book contributes a microscopic part in making their worlds more livable.

Introduction

[1]Kurt Lewin, quoted in D. Cartright, ed., *Field Theory in Social Science: Selected Theoretical Papers* (Chicago: University of Chicago Press), p. 169.

[2]Immaculée Ilibagiza with Steve Erwin, *Left to Tell: Discovering God Amidst the Rwandan Holocaust* (Carlsbad, Calif.: Hay House, 2006).

Chapter 1: Tensions and Questions

[1]Malcolm Muggeridge, *Confessions of a Twentieth-Century Pilgrim* (San Francisco: Harper & Row, 1988), p. 49.

[2]N. T. Wright, *Evil and the Justice of God* (Downers Grove, Ill.: InterVarsity Press, 2006).

[3]J. B. Phillips, *Your God Is Too Small: A Guide for Believers and Skeptics Alike* (New York: Touchstone, 1998).

[4]Simon Wiesenthal, *The Sunflower* (New York: Schocken Books, 1998).

[5]Everett L. Worthington Jr., *Forgiveness and Reconciliation: Theory and Application* (New York: Brunner-Routledge, 2006).

[6]Malcolm Gladwell, *The Tipping Point: How Little Things Can Make a Big Difference* (Boston: Little, Brown, 2002).

[7]William Miller and Janet C'de Baca, *Quantum Change: When Epiphanies and Sudden Insights Transform Ordinary Lives* (New York: Guilford Press, 2001).

Chapter 2: Humility

[1]See Immaculée Ilibagiza with Steve Erwin, *Left to Tell: Discovering God Amidst the Rwandan Holocaust* (Carlsbad, Calif.: Hay House, 2006).

[2]Ibid., p. 91.

[3]Ibid., pp. 151-55.

[4]C. S. Lewis, *God in the Dock: Essays on Theology and Ethics,* ed. Walter Hooper (Grand Rapids: Eerdmans, 2001), pp. 240-44.

[5]Andrew Murray, *Humility: The Beauty of Holiness* (New Tappan, N.J.: Revell, 1997).

[6]Malcolm Muggeridge, *Confessions of a Twentieth-Century Pilgrim* (San Francisco: Harper & Row, 1988), pp. 48-50.

[7]Fyodor Dostoyevsky, *Crime and Punishment*, trans. Sidney Monas (New York: Signet Classics, 1968).

[8]Everett L. Worthington Jr. et al., "Forgiveness and Health," *Journal of Behavioral Medicine* 30 (2007): 291-302.

[9]Oswald Chambers, *My Utmost for His Highest* (Uhrichsville, Ohio: Barbour, 1935).

[10]Everett L. Worthington Jr., *Humility: The Quiet Virtue* (Philadelphia: Templeton Foundation Press, 2007), p. 105.

Chapter 3: Justice

[1]John Grisham, *A Time to Kill* (New York: Island Books, 1989).

[2]Ibid., p. 422.

[3]Lawrence Kohlberg, *The Philosophy of Moral Development: Moral Stages and the Idea of Justice,* Essays on Moral Development, vol. 1 (New York: Harper, 1981).

[4]Carol Gilligan, "In a Different Voice: Women's Conceptions of Self and of Morality," in *Caring Voices and Women's Moral Frames: Gilligan's View,* Moral Development: A Compendium, ed. Bill Puka, vol. 6. (New York: Garland, 1994).

[5]Melvin J. Lerner, *The Belief in a Just World* (New York: Plenum, 1980).

[6]Frans De Waal and Jennifer Pokorny, "Primate Questions About the Art and Science of Forgiving," in *Handbook of Forgiveness,* ed. Everett L. Worthington Jr. (New York: Brunner-Routledge, 2005), pp. 17-32.

[7]Lerner, *Belief in a Just World.*

[8]John Darley, "Just Punishments: Research on Retributional Justice," in *The Justice Motive in Everyday Life,* ed. M. Ross and D. T. Miller (New York: Cambridge, 2002), pp. 314-33.

[9]Everett L. Worthington Jr., "Unforgiveness, Forgiveness and Reconciliation in Societies," in *Forgiveness and Reconciliation: Religion, Public Policy and Conflict Transformation,* ed. Raymond G. Helmick and Rodney L. Petersen (Philadelphia: Templeton Foundation Press, 2001), pp. 161-82.

[10]Ibid.

[11]Ernst Fehr and Klaus Schmidt, "The Economics of Fairness, Reciprocity and Altruism—Experimental Evidence and New Theories," in *Handbook of the Economics of Giving, Altruism and Reciprocity, Vol. 1, Foundations,* ed. S. C. Kolm and J. M. Ythier (New York: Elsevier Science, 2006), pp. 615-91.

[12]Ernst Fehr and Simon Gächter, "Altruistic Punishment in Humans," *Nature* 415 (2002): 137-40.

[13]Michael E. McCullough, *Beyond Revenge: The Evolution of the Forgiveness Instinct* (San Francisco: Jossey-Bass, 2008).

[14]Darley, "Just Punishments."

[15]John Darley, Kevin Carlsmith and Paul Robinson, "Incapacitation and Just Deserts as Motives for Punishment," *Law and Human Behavior* 24 (2000): 659-83.

[16]Roy F. Baumeister, A. M. Stillwell and S. R. Wotman, "Victim and Perpetrator Accounts of Interpersonal Conflict: Autobiographical Narratives About Anger," *Journal of Personality and Social Psychology* 59 (1990): 994-1005.

[17]Roy F. Baumeister, Ellen Bratslavsky and Catrin Finkenauer, "Bad Is Stronger Than Good," *Review of General Psychology* 5 (2001): 323-70.

[18]Scott R. Stanley, *The Heart of Commitment: Cultivating Lifelong Commitment in Marriage* (Nashville: Thomas Nelson, 1998).

[19]Edward E. Jones and Richard E. Nisbett, "The Actor and the Observer: Divergent Perceptions of the Causes of Behavior," in *Attribution: Perceiving the Causes of Behavior,* ed. Edward E. Jones and D. E. Kanouse (Hillsdale, N.J.: Lawrence Erlbaum Associates, 1987), pp. 79-94.

Chapter 4: Forgiveness

[1]I have written much about forgiveness, which may interest those who want a more detailed account. For a self-help book, see Everett L. Worthington Jr., *Forgiving and Reconciling: Bridges to Wholeness and Hope* (Downers Grove, Ill.: InterVarsity Press, 2003). For a professional counseling model, including summaries of supportive research, see Everett L. Worthington Jr., *Forgiveness and Reconciliation: Theory and Application* (New York: Brunner-Routledge, 2006).

[2]Everett L. Worthington Jr. et al., "Forgiveness and Health," *Journal of Behavioral Medicine* 30 (2007): 291-302.

[3]Loren Toussaint and Jon R. Webb, "Theoretical and Empirical Connections Between Forgiveness, Mental Health and Well-Being," in *Handbook of Forgiveness,* ed. Everett L. Worthington Jr. (New York: Brunner-Routledge, 2005), pp. 349-62.

[4]David Stoop, *Real Solutions for Forgiving the Unforgivable* (Ann Arbor, Mich.: Servant, 2001).

[5]Chris Carrier, "I Faced My Killer Again," *Leadership Journal* 11 (January/February 1998): 73.

[6]F. LeRon Shults and Steven J. Sandage, *Transforming Spirituality: Integrating Theology and Psychology* (Grand Rapids: Baker Academic, 2006).

[7]Don E. Davis, Joshua N. Hook and Everett L. Worthington Jr., "Relational Spirituality and Forgiveness: The Roles of Attachment to God, Religious Coping and Viewing the Transgression as a Desecration," *Journal of Psychology and Christianity* 27 (2008): 293-301.

Chapter 5: Dealing with Wrongdoers

[1]This model is summarized in my two books *Forgiving and Reconciling: Bridges to Wholeness and Hope* (Downers Grove, Ill.: InterVarsity Press, 2003), and *Forgiveness and Reconciliation: Theory and Application* (New York: Brunner-Routledge, 2006).

[2]The manual is available for free download at <www.people.vcu.edu/~eworth>. Many research studies on the REACH model with general participants (not just Christians) are summarized by N. G. Wade, Everett L. Worthington Jr. and J. Meyer, "But Do They Work? Meta-Analysis of Group Interventions to Promote Forgiveness," in *Handbook of Forgiveness,* ed. Everett L. Worthington Jr. (New York: Brunner-Routledge, 2005), pp. 423-40. Studies involving a model particularly directed at helping Christians forgive

include Carey Lampton et al., "Helping Christian College Students Become More Forgiving: An Intervention Study to Promote Forgiveness as Part of a Program to Shape Christian Character," *Journal of Psychology and Theology* 33 (2005): 278-90, and Steven P. Stratton et al., "Forgiveness Interventions as Spiritual Development Strategies: Workshop Training, Expressive Writing About Forgiveness and Retested Controls," *Journal of Psychology and Christianity* 27 (2008): 347-57.

[3]Michael E. McCullough, *Beyond Revenge: The Evolution of the Forgiveness Instinct* (San Francisco: Jossey-Bass, 2008).

[4]Ibid.

[5]Frans de Waal, *Peacemaking Among Primates* (London: Penguin, 1989).

[6]Worthington, *Forgiving and Reconciling.*

[7]Scott R. Stanley, *The Heart of Commitment: Cultivating Lifelong Commitment in Marriage* (Nashville: Thomas Nelson, 1998).

[8]Pumla Gobodo-Madikizela, *That Night a Human Being Died: A South African Story of Forgiveness* (Boston: Houghton-Mifflin, 2003).

[9]Charlotte van Oyen Witvliet, Thomas E. Ludwig and D. J. Bauer, "Please Forgive Me: Transgressors' Emotions and Physiology During Imagery of Seeking Forgiveness and Victim Responses," *Journal of Psychology and Christianity* 21 (2002): 219-33.

[10]For additional studies that found similar results but used different methods, see Mark R. Leary et al., "The Causes, Phenomenology and Consequences of Hurt Feelings," *Journal of Personality and Social Psychology* 74 (1998): 1225-37; Jeanne Zechmeister and C. Romero, "Victim and Offender Accounts of Interpersonal Conflict: Autobiographical Narratives of Forgiveness and Unforgiveness," *Journal of Personality and Social Psychology* 82 (2002): 675-86.

Chapter 6: Just Forgiveness in the Family

[1]Frank Viola and George Barna, *Pagan Christianity?* (Carol Stream, Ill.: Tyndale House, 2008).

[2]Lee A. Kirkpatrick, *Attachment, Evolution and the Psychology of Religion* (New York: Guilford Press, 2005).

[3]Susan M. Johnson, *The Practice of Emotionally Focused Couple Therapy: Creating Connection* (New York: Brunner-Routledge, 2004).

[4]Everett L. Worthington Jr., *Forgiving and Reconciling: Bridges to Wholeness and Hope* (Downers Grove, Ill.: InterVarsity Press, 2003).

[5]Ibid.

[6]Roy F. Baumeister, A. M. Stillwell and S. R. Wotman, "Victim and Perpetrator Accounts of Interpersonal Conflict: Autobiographical Narratives About Anger," *Journal of Personality and Social Psychology* 59 (1990): 994-1005.

[7]Peter Schönbach, *Account Episodes: The Management or Escalation of Conflict* (New York: Cambridge University Press, 1990).

Chapter 7: Just Forgiveness in the Church

[1]Max Weber, "The Social Psychology of World Religions," in H. H. Gerth and C. Wright Mills, *From Max Weber* (New York: Oxford University Press, 1958).

[2]Jay Haley, *Strategies of Psychotherapy* (New York: Grune and Stratton, 1963).

[3]Frank D. Fincham, Judith Hall and Steven R. H. Beach, "Forgiveness in Marriage," in *Handbook of Forgiveness*, ed. Everett L. Worthington Jr. (New York: Brunner-Routledge, 2005), pp. 207-25.

[4]William Ury and Roger Fisher, *Getting to Yes: Negotiating Agreement Without Giving In* (New York: Penguin, 1981).

[5]Everett L. Worthington Jr., *Hope-Focused Marriage Counseling: A Brief Therapy*, rev. ed. (Downers Grove, Ill.: InterVarsity Press, 2005).

[6]Annette Mahoney, Mark Rye and Kenneth I. Pargament, "When the Sacred Is Violated: Desecration as a Unique Challenge to Forgiveness," in *Handbook of Forgiveness*, ed. Everett L. Worthington Jr. (New York: Brunner-Routledge, 2005), pp. 57-72.

[7]Michael E. McCullough, *Beyond Revenge: The Evolution of the Forgiveness Instinct* (San Francisco: Jossey-Bass, 2008).

[8]Donelson R. Forsyth, *Group Dynamics,* 5th ed. (Belmont, Calif.: Wadsworth, 2008).

[9]Muzafer Sherif, *Social Interaction: Process and Products* (Oxford: Aldine, 1967).

[10]Solomon E. Asch, "Opinions and Social Pressure," *Scientific American* 193 (1955): 31-35.

[11]Robert Sapolsky, *Biology and Human Behavior: The Neurological Origins of Individuality,* 2nd ed., lecture by the author (Chantilly, Va.: Teaching Company, 2005).

[12]Ury and Fisher, *Getting to Yes.*

[13]Meic Pearse, *The Gods of War: Is Religion the Primary Cause of Violent Conflict?* (Downers Grove, Ill.: InterVarsity Press, 2007).

[14]Jeff Greenberg et al., "Terror Management and Tolerance: Does Mortality Salience Always Intensify Negative Reactions to Others Who Threaten One's Worldview?" *Journal of Personality and Social Psychology* 63 (1992): 212-20.

[15]Malcolm Muggeridge, *Confessions of a Twentieth-Century Pilgrim* (San Francisco: Harper & Row, 1988).

[16]Miroslav Volf, "The Church's Great Malfunctions," The Christian Vision Project, November 29, 2006 <http://www.christianvisionproject.com/2006/11/the_churchs_great_malfunctions.html>.

Chapter 8: Just Forgiveness in Communities and Society

[1]Miroslav Volf, *Free of Charge: Giving and Forgiving in a Culture Stripped of Grace* (Grand Rapids: Zondervan, 2005).

[2]Donald B. Kraybill, Steven M. Nolt and David L. Weaver-Zercher, *Amish Grace: How Forgiveness Transcended Tragedy* (San Francisco: Jossey-Bass, 2007).

[3]Colin E. Gunton, *Father, Son and Holy Spirit: Essays Toward a Fully Trinitarian Theology* (London: Continuum International, 2003).

[4]Peter M. Hart, "Predicting Employee Life Satisfaction: A Coherent Model of Personality, Work and Non-Work Experiences, and Domain Satisfactions," *Journal of Applied Psychology* 84 (1999): 564-84.

[5]Daniel P. Skarlicki and Robert Folger, "Retaliation in the Workplace: The Roles of Distributive, Procedural and Interactional Justice," *Journal of Applied Psychology* 82 (1997): 434-43.

[6]Howard M. Weiss and Russell Cropanzano, "Affective Events Theory: A Theoretical Discussion of the Structure, Causes and Consequences of Affective Experiences at Work," in *Research in Organizational Behavior: An Annual Series of Analytical Essays and Critical Reviews,* ed. Barry M. Staw and L. L. Cummings (New York: Elsevier Science, JAI Press, 1996), pp. 1-74.

[7]A. P. Brief and Howard M. Weiss, "Organizational Behavior: Affect in the Workplace," *Annual Review of Psychology* 53 (2002): 279-307.

[8]Jonathan R. Cohen, "Apology and Organizations: Exploring an Example from Medical Practice," *Fordham Urban Law Journal* 2 (2000): 1447-82.

[9]Ibid.

[10]Weiss and Cropanzano, "Affective Events Theory."

[11]Julie J. Exline et al., "Forgiveness and Justice: A Research Agenda for Social and Personality Psychology," *Personality and Social Psychology Review* 7 (2003): 337-48.

[12]R. J. Bies and T. M. Tripp, "A Passion for Justice: The Rationality and Morality of Revenge," in Russell Cropanzano, *Justice in the Workplace: From Theory to Practice,* vol. 2 (Mahwah, N.J.: Lawrence Erlbaum, 2001), pp. 197-226.

[13]Bennett J. Tepper, "Consequences of Abusive Supervision," *Academy of Management Journal* 43 (2000): 178-90.

[14]Russell Cropanzano, Cynthia A. Prehar and Peter Y. Chen, "Using Social Exchange Theory to Distinguish Procedural from Interactional Justice," *Group and Organization Management* 27 (2002): 324-51.

[15]Everett L. Worthington Jr. et al., "Forgiveness and Positive Psychology in Business Ethics and Corporate Social Responsibility," in Robert A. Giacalone, C. Dunn and C. L. Jurkiewicz, *Positive Psychology in Business Ethics and Corporate Social Responsibility* (Greenwich, Conn.: Information Age Publishing, 2005), pp. 265-84.

[16]Michael Oakeshott, *Rationalism in Politics and Other Essays* (Washington, D.C.: Liberty Fund, 1962).

[17]Robert N. Bellah et al., *Habits of the Heart: Individualism and Commitment in American Life* (New York: Harper & Row, 1985).

[18]Stanley Milgram, *Obedience to Authority* (New York: Harper & Row, 1974).

[19]Tom F. D. Farrow et al., "Investigating the Functional Anatomy of Empathy and Forgiveness," *Neuroreport: An International Journal for the Rapid Communication of Research in Neuroscience* 12 (2001): 2433-38.

[20]Oakeshott, *Rationalism in Politics.*

[21]Everett L. Worthington Jr., "Is There a Place for Forgiveness in the Justice System?" *Fordham Urban Law Journal* 27 (2000): 1721-34.

[22]Julie J. Exline et al., "Forgiveness and Justice."

[23]For a thorough account, see Everett L. Worthington Jr., *Forgiving and Reconciling: Bridges to Wholeness and Hope* (Downers Grove, Ill.: InterVarsity Press, 2003).

[24]John J. DiIulio, "America's Ticking Crime Bomb and How to Diffuse It," *Wisconsin Interest* 3, no. 1 (1994), pp. 16-17.

[25]Howard Zehr, *Changing Lenses: A New Focus on Crime and Justice* (Scottdale, Penn.: Herald Press, 1995).

Chapter 9: Just Forgiveness in the World

[1]Bobby Ghosh, "Behind the Sunni-Shi'ite Divide," *Time Magazine,* March 5, 2007.

[2]Robert Sapolsky, *Biology and Human Behavior: The Neurological Origins of Individuality,* 2nd ed., lecture by the author (Chantilly, Va.: Teaching Company, 2005).

[3]Martin Daly and Margo Wilson, *Homicide* (Hawthorne, N.Y.: Aldine de Gruyter, 1988).

[4]Michael E. McCullough, *Beyond Revenge: The Evolution of the Forgiveness Instinct* (San Francisco: Jossey-Bass, 2008).

[5]Steven L. Neuberg and Catherine A. Cottrell, "Managing the Threats and Opportunities Afforded by Human Sociality," *Group Dynamics: Theory, Research and Practice: Special Issue: Evolutionary Approaches to Group Dynamics* 12, no. 1 (March 2008): 63-72.

[6]Sapolsky, *Biology and Human Behavior.*

[7]Ervin Staub, "Constructive Rather than Harmful Forgiveness, Reconciliation, and Ways to Promote Them after Genocide and Mass Killing," in *Handbook of Forgiveness,* ed. Everett L. Worthington Jr. (New York: Brunner-Routledge, 2005), pp. 443-59.

[8]Meic Pearse, *The Gods of War: Is Religion the Primary Cause of Violent Conflict?* (Downers Grove, Ill.: InterVarsity Press, 2007); for a brief summary in more detail, a great readable article is by Ghosh *op.cit.*

[9]Gerald R. Patterson, "A Comparison of Models for Interstate Wars and for Individual Violence," *Perspectives on Psychological Science* 3, no. 3 (2008): 203-23.

[10]Bruce Bueno de Mesquita, *The War Trap* (New Haven, Conn.: Yale University Press, 1981).

[11]Steven Pinker, *The Stuff of Thought* (New York: Viking, 2007).

[12]Patterson, "Comparison of Models."

[13]Mona Sue Weissmark, *Justice Matters: Legacies of the Holocaust and World War II* (New York: Oxford University Press, 2004).

[14]Olga Botcharova, "The Implementation of Track Two Diplomacy: Developing a Model of Forgiveness," in Ray G. Helmick and Rodney L. Petersen, *Forgiveness and Reconciliation: Religion, Public Policy and Conflict Transformation* (Philadelphia: Templeton Foundation Press, 2001), pp. 269-94.

[15]Patterson, "Comparison of Models."

[16]Dave Grossman, *On Killing: The Psychological Cost of Learning to Kill in War and Society* (Boston: Little, Brown, 1995).

[17]Samuel L. A. Marshall, *Men Against Fire* (Gloucester, Mass.: Peter Smith, 1978).

[18]Sapolsky, *Biology and Human Behavior.*

[19]Robert Axelrod, *The Evolution of Cooperation* (New York: Basic Books, 1984).

[20]Botcharova, "Implementation of Track Two Diplomacy"; Joseph Montville, "The Arrow and the Olive Branch: A Case for Track Two Diplomacy," in *The Psychodynamics of International Relationships: Concepts and Theories,* by Demetrios A. Julius and Vamik Volkan, ed. Joseph V. Montville (Lexington, Mass.: Lexington Books, 1990).

[21]Everett L. Worthington Jr., *Forgiving and Reconciling: Bridges to Wholeness and Hope* (Downers Grove, Ill.: InterVarsity Press, 2003).

[22]Audrey R. Chapman, "Truth Commissions as Instruments of Forgiveness and Reconciliation," in Raymond G. Helmick and Rodney L. Petersen, *Forgiveness and Reconciliation: Religion, Public Policy and Conflict Transformation* (Philadelphia: Templeton Foundation Press, 1998), pp. 247-67.

[23]Karen Brounéus, "Reconciliation in the Great Lakes Region: Some Thoughts on Key Topics, Agendas and Challenges" (paper presented at the meeting of the John Templeton Foundation Ad Hoc Task Force on the Possibility of Research in Rwanda, Nassau, Bahamas, June 3, 2008).

[24]Ibid.

Chapter 10: What Can We Do?

[1]*The End of the Spear,* directed by Jim Hanon, written by Bill Ewing, Bart Gavigan and Jim Hanon, Every Tribe Entertainment, 2005, motion picture; based on Steve Saint, *End of the Spear: A True Story* (Carol Stream, Ill.: Tyndale House, 2005).

[2]Edward O. Wilson, *Consilience: The Unity of Knowledge* (New York: Vintage, 1999).

[3]Edward Schillebeeckx, *Church: The Human Story of God* (New York: Crossroad, 1990).

[4]Jürgen Moltmann, *The Crucified God: The Cross of Christ as the Foundation and Criticism of Christian Theology* (Minneapolis: Fortress Press, 1993).

[5]Otis Moss, "Speak Love to Power" (talk given at Chautauqua Institution, Chautauqua, New York, 2005).

Name Index

Subject Index

Scripture Index